Symbolic Stories

. . . there was never a maundering old woman, sitting with others late of a winter's night at the home fireside, making up tales of Hell, the fates, ghosts and the like – much of it pure invention – that she did not feel beneath the surface of her tale, as far as her limited mind allowed, at least some meaning . . .

G. Boccaccio, *De Genealogia Deorum* XIV, 9,
in *Boccaccio on Poetry*, translated by C. G. Osgood

Gorgons, and Hydras, and Chimæras – dire stories of Calæno and the Harpies – may reproduce themselves in the brain of superstition – but they were there before. They are transcripts, types – the archetypes are in us, and eternal. How else should the recital of that, which we know in a waking sense to be false, come to affect us at all? – or

> – Names, whose sense we see not,
> Fray us with things that be not?

Is it that we naturally conceive terror from such objects, considered in their capacity of being able to inflict upon us bodily injury? – O, least of all! These terrors are of older standing. They date beyond body – or, without the body, they would have been the same.

Charles Lamb, 'Witches and other Night-Fears'

> Below the surface-stream, shallow and light,
> Of what we say we feel – below the stream,
> As light, of what we think we feel – there flows
> With noiseless current strong, obscure and deep,
> The central stream of what we feel indeed.

Matthew Arnold

Symbolic Stories

Traditional narratives of the family drama in English literature

DEREK BREWER

Longman
London and New York

Longman Group UK Limited,
Longman House, Burnt Mill, Harlow,
Essex CM20 2JE, England
and Associated Companies throughout the world.

*Published in the United States of America
by Longman Inc., New York*

© D. S. Brewer 1980, 1988

**First published in hardback by D. S. Brewer 1980
Longman paperback edition 1988
Second impression 1989**

British Library Cataloguing in Publication Data

Brewer, Derek
Symbolic stories: traditional narratives
of the family drama in English literature.
1. Family in literature   2. English
literature – History and criticism
3. Tales – History and criticism
I. Title
820.9'355   PR149.F34
ISBN 0-582-01879-X

Library of Congress Cataloging in Publication Data

Brewer, Derek, 1923–
Symbolic stories.

Bibliography: p.
1. English literature – History and criticism.
2. Family in literature.   3. English poetry – Middle
English, 1100–1500 – History and criticism.   4. Tales –
History and criticism.   5. Myth in literature.
I. Title.
PR149.F34B7   1988   820'.9'355   87–22715
ISBN 0–582–01879–X (pbk.)

Set in 10/11 Palatino Roman
Produced by Longman Group (FE) Limited
Printed in Hong Kong

Contents

FOR GUY

Preface

The present book is the product of intermittent specific work over many years, and of general reading scattered over many more. It is in consequence something of a compromise between many different kinds of interest. The essence of it is the attempt to justify and make intellectually, artistically and historically convincing a literal, natural, even 'naive' response to traditional literature as opposed to what seem to me to be naturalistic and literalistic readings that distort the texts in favour of modern prejudices and modern values which are confessedly hostile to those of the past.

The literal level of traditional literature, because it has never aimed at an overall, totally consistent, and plausible, imitation or 'mimesis' of normal life, has always relied on implicit understandings of what goes on 'beneath' the literal surface. The surface events are determined by the sequences of 'inner' or 'deeper' events and meanings. These are real and important for our lives, as our fascination with the stories shows, but they follow laws different from those of material cause and effect which seem on the surface to govern our ordinary lives. Many famous traditional stories, from that of David and Goliath to medieval romances and Shakespeare's comedies, including even many novels, reveal apparent inconsistencies or absurdities if they are assumed to be intended to give plausible representations of normal 'reality'. If this assumption is made about them either the stories are dismissed, or, more usually, since their grasp on our imaginations is powerful, they are misinterpreted and distorted, in either case to our imaginative impoverishment. It is this misinterpretation that I call literalistic, for it often distorts the *literal* meaning (usually by denying its face-value and invoking 'irony', whereby anything can be taken to mean the opposite of what it actually says).

The literal meaning is the face-value of the words, which allows for response to the inner forces which govern the surface text. I believe that readers experienced in reading traditional literature, who accept the traditional values and procedures of long-established societies, or those who have a natural taste for folktale, romance and myth, take for granted and respond unconsciously to the inner structure. They are experienced but have no reason to be analytical, and may be called in the best sense 'naive' readers. I hope that in essential respects I retain this kind of naivety. But it now needs to be justified in the modern world with modern concepts. Hence the notion of 'symbolic' meaning, which is implied by acceptance of the literal text, and hence my rejection of literalistic readings which do not take into account the controlling under-lying symbolic structures. The principles of interpretation involved go far beyond the exemplary texts I have chosen, and concern all those who enjoy and study traditional stories, from Biblical scholars and folklorists to literary critics, even historians.

The introduction sketches some preliminary ideas, but general prin-ciples of interpretation are developed in relation to specific examples. I begin with fairy tales because they are an extreme and relatively clear-cut example of traditional literature which are nowadays at the centre of very many studies especially in Germany and the United States. They are also attractive and interesting to many non-specialist readers. From there I proceed to more elaborate literary works.

It has seemed almost an accident that the same underlying area of subject-matter has forced itself on my attention in so many traditional tales. The general subject of fairy tales is 'growing up', or 'the emergence of the individual', and the intrinsic drama of this lies in the relationships of the central figure with parent-figures and others, or the Other. This subject is literally of universal interest and importance and is the concern of a huge amount of traditional literature, but it is of course not the only subject of traditional story. Its predominance however links together a long tradition of story-telling, and gives some unity of topic to the present study, even though the stories themselves have no direct link with each other.

In justifying a traditional response in modern terms, besides following the usual procedures of the literary historian I also borrow rather eclec-tically from social anthropology and psychoanalysis. I am aware of the dangers of borrowing from other disciplines (and not least, in this case, of repelling the 'naive' reader on the grounds that one murders to dissect) but I have no anthropological or psychoanalytical axe to grind. I follow no school or external theory; only the literary texts themselves. It must be said that some of the stories have surprised me with what I think they show me. They sometimes reverse some generally held ideas. At least the process of following the stories has never been reductive: their variety is great and the intrinsic interest of every story has been enormously in-creased for me, not diminished, as I have found their various inner structures and significances.

For the present book most of the examples have been taken from English, but many other examples, both in English and in other lang-uages and cultures, might have been taken. I cannot suppose that I have always got the meaning quite right in the present instances, but I hope that readers with many different interests, including the famous and elusive 'general reader', will find some problems solved and something here worth discussing.

I am indebted to lecture audiences in Cambridge and in universities in several different countries who have listened to and criticised earlier versions of parts of this book over the last ten years. I have been en-couraged by their forbearance and interest. I also acknowledge with

Preface

gratitude the permission of the editors of *Neuphilologische Mitteilungen*, Helsinki, and Encounter, to use material which appeared in an earlier form in their journals; and to the Delegates of the Clarendon Press, Oxford, to reprint an extract from Jane Austen, *Volume the Third*, ed. R. W. Chapman, London 1951.

I also acknowledge with gratitude the careful criticism of my wife and of Mrs Ruth Smith, which has saved me from innumerable grammatical solecisms, obscurities, and infelicities of expression.

POSTSCRIPT – 1987

The ideas behind *Symbolic Stories* are nowadays more familiar than when the book first appeared, and a reprint in paperback will make it available to a broader range of readers.

I should like to emphasise one general point that has not always been taken. The term 'family drama' which I coined is derived, but is different from, Freud's 'family romance'. By 'family drama' I mean a set of strong but variable emotional bonds that exists between the growing child and the parents. These bonds are made up of both attraction and repulsion. They exist in different strengths and patterns in different cases. The stories which arise from them, though they have fundamental character-istics in common, are also widely different. The family drama is not one story. It is the material for many. To give extreme examples, the story of Oedipus, obviously a product of the family drama, is a tragedy (hence the new view of tragedy briefly argued on p. 58 below), while *Cinderella*, and most romances, have happy endings. Indeed, the true opposite of tragedy is romance, even though there are variants which we must call 'tragic romance'. Shakespeare's later plays, nineteenth- and twentieth-century novels, all play differing variations, though it is helpful to recog-nise the common basis.

The family drama is a part of life for which we need literature to help us live through. One version of it is neatly summed up by George Painter in his splendid life of Proust: 'Ability to love a person of the opposite sex, and of one's own age, is the only valid escape from the prison of the family' (*Marcel Proust*, Penguin, 1983, p. 46). In *Cymbeline* the boy Guider-ius refers to his sequestered life as this 'cell of ignorance' (p. 137). Prisons have warders. Growing children have parents. There are many ways of escaping or not escaping.

Another point which needs to be emphasised is that good stories have several layers of meaning and many possible interactions. To see that a story is based on the tensions of the family drama does not exclude other kinds of interpretation, which the perception may stimulate, guide and protect. Above all, my thesis does not deny the importance of the literal 'face value' of the texts, through which we arrive at less explicit, even subconscious, meanings, though considerations of space in this book have prevented me from pursuing many of the literal significances and even their own symbolic implications.

Introduction

I

Many highly improbable stories offer us deep satisfaction. They can be found in myth, folktale (especially those folktales now called fairy tales), and – in our literary tradition – in medieval romances, Shakespeare's non-historical plays, and even some great novels. Though they are not at all, in one sense, 'like life', they have given many generations of hearers and readers uncorrupted by literary prejudice a deep conviction that they tell us in some way 'what life is like'. Yet they have also since the seventeenth century been frequently attacked and despised, especially by readers with sophisticated literary taste. The words 'myth', 'fairy tale', 'romance' since then have often been used to signify 'lies', especially silly or trivial lies. The very word 'story' or 'tale' (as in 'tale-teller') can be used in the same way. The notion of story-telling has for long been dismissed as the relation of a mere concatenation of events. Although there has been an upsurge of interest especially in the theoretical nature of narrative in recent years most work has been largely limited to formal and technical analyses which are not here my concern. It is still very common to find traditional stories either regarded as trivial or grossly misinterpreted in terms of anachronistic assumptions. My aim in the present book is to recover or re-assert some of the appropriate assumptions for traditional stories, and to show that the apparently improbable series of events is not arbitrary and superficial but reflects and promotes the deeper and often less conscious activities of the mind. I take specific examples and build up principles of interpretation in the course of reading, but it is clear that many different examples could be taken, and the concepts are widely applicable. This introduction (which may be skipped) gives a brief account of the general approach and concepts.

Stories feed our normal human interest in 'what goes on', as popular newspapers in Britain daily illustrate. Their subject-matter is, preferably, both familiar and surprising, and at the surface level of interest that is enough. All stories are, further, in some way symbolic, in that they are examples or illustrations, at a level 'below' the surface, of something of what we feel about human experience. This may be at a very simple level. The story of a motor-car accident may do no more than recommend sobriety. The kind of story that is told and re-told is likely to have a richer, more subtle point, though even this need not be very recondite. Above all, the point need not be consciously or explicitly revealed, and it may be

1

more than any explicit moral. Not every story is a parable, though every story has something of the parable in it. The following chapters try to see what the surface of the story tells us about the deeper movements that it reflects. These deeper movements are often the actual 'driving force', or conditioning factors, that make the sequence of events what it is; the superficial connections between the events are often of secondary importance and give rise to the accusations of implausibility to which traditional stories are often subject. The famous work on mythology by Levi-Strauss and other anthropologists has fully demonstrated how mythic stories of an apparently wildly grotesque nature have at their core a perfectly 'rational' structure. Nor should we exaggerate the twentieth-century novelty of this attempt. From long before the Christian era men were interpreting myths and the stories (for example) of Homer in terms of a fundamental meaning derived from, but expressed differently from, the surface meaning. Parts of the Bible have continuously been interpreted in this way – parts of the Old Testament being thus interpreted from before the birth of Christ. That we now often disagree with such interpretations is no more a condemnation of the attempt than the disagreement of modern scientists from the views of those of a hundred years ago is a discrediting of science. If one cannot be wrong one cannot be right. It is also of the nature of all art in its inter-action with successive generations to call forth new interpretations that correct or supplant the old.

II

Traditional stories which are not sacred myths have received far less attention than myths, but in themselves they are not fundamentally different. Their claim to attention is the simple one of survival; they are told time and time again in many countries of the world. Literary and folklore scholarship has traced the same stories throughout the world, over many hundreds of years.[1] In detail this raises many interesting problems. What is a story? When a similar action occurs in many different stories, what is its status? How similar is similar? We can easily accept that the names of certain characters may be changed, that certain degrees of change in circumstance may not change the fundamental nature of the story, but it may seem that after a certain point of cumulative change the story becomes a different story. These are real and fascinating problems, but I propose a scheme here which will solve them for the purposes of this book. It emerges when one considers a series of stories, but a brief statement now may help the reader.

It is clear in the case of a traditional story that it has an underlying 'shape' or 'pattern' which is held in the mind by the person who received it from a book or from another person. This shape or pattern is largely independent of any particular set of words in which the story may be conveyed, though sometimes a set phrase is of the essence of the story

Introduction

and must be retained. Such will be the case when the story leads up to a witty answer or is the dramatisation of a proverb, but even here only the very core must be verbally maintained. The point of most stories is not verbal in this way, and in such stories every verbal item may be changed and yet the story remain the same. Shakespeare and Chaucer, for example, tell stories which also appear in Boccaccio's *Decameron*. Chaucer's *Reeve's Tale* (cf. *Decameron* Day 9, Story 6) and Shakespeare's *Cymbeline* (cf. *Decameron* Day 2, Story 9) are examples. Anyone can see at a glance that they are the same story, though names, settings, dates, some of the motives, and of course the very language itself, are all different. In the case of Chaucer it is highly unlikely that he knew the *Decameron*, and in any case scholarship has shown that these stories, like others used by all three authors, are widespread. Neither Chaucer nor Shakespeare ever invented a plot, and even if Boccaccio occasionally did so, he put it together out of entirely familiar elements.

III

In the traditional tale we must therefore distinguish between the *verbal realisation* of the story and its pre- or non-verbal existence as 'shape', 'pattern', 'structure' (all such expressions being inevitably metaphorical).[2] Like most literary distinctions this is ragged, not clear-cut. We do not get through to the structure except by the verbal realisation. But the verbal realisation may change with every successive re-telling. It is not identical with the story (even in the case of a novel, for we may tell the story of a novel without using the exact words of the novelist). To the verbal realisation belongs what is changeable in the story. Circumstances, settings, all 'realism', the names of characters, even motives, therefore some considerable degree of characterisation, the narrator's comments, even the moral, or immoral, tone he gives to his version, all these matters belong to the verbal realisation. The distinction I make between them and the pre-verbal intrinsic story, its pattern, etc., is not a value-distinction. The story is prior to the verbal realisation, and governs its general course, but it is not necessarily artistically superior. In the hands of a major poet like Chaucer or Shakespeare the verbal realisation will be vividly expressed, and will bring out certain significant elements of the story, or suppress others, so that the version is a major work of art, while another version, though perfectly adequate, will simply not have the wit, learning, knowledge of human nature, observation, verbal felicity, etc. etc. that constitute the genius of the major poet. In other words, it is possible to tell the same story well or ill to any imaginable degree. In a badly told story we can, if we accept the 'rules' or conventions, see for ourselves by reference to the internal structure, even though it is inadequately conveyed in a faulty version, how the story ought to go. In narrative generally there is no such thing as that old-fashioned cliché of the criticism of

3

poetry, 'the heresy of paraphrase'. Every telling of a traditional tale must be a paraphrase. By the same token, every telling of a traditional story is an implicit interpretation of it. Traditional stories are not sacred myths for which variation is in theory inadmissible. Every teller who knows his art will heighten or suppress, change localisations so as to make them more vivid to the current audience, and so forth.

A dominant element in all tellings of traditional tales is *rationalisation*. That is in itself no more than to say that the teller wishes to make his version as effective as possible. This does not deny the fundamental structure of the tale, which is normally improbable by ordinary standards. If the teller is telling *that* tale, he must abide by that improbability, which is the very heart of the tale. But according to his own talent, his historical circumstances, the demands of his audience, he will introduce or suppress elements in his verbal realisation that will at least superficially account for, will 'rationalise', the events. A favourite device is to sketch in a character-study which seems to the teller to accord with the action. The teller never has perfect freedom, because he has committed himself to telling a particular tale. If the tale concerns an old man and a young wife he cannot change them to a young man and an old wife. But he can make the old man disagreeable and therefore in a popular if not moral sense deserving of his fate of being cuckolded. He can make the girl a charming victim of circumstance, or he can make her a vulgar little piece. He can even switch characterisations so that the elderly husband begins by losing sympathy and ends by gaining it, as in Chaucer's *Merchant's Tale*, a variant of a widespread popular tale which is actually of learned origin.[3] Rationalisations involving characterisation are particularly important to understand because they make the personality of the character subsequent to the deed, whereas the normal theory of the novel makes the deed issue from the personality of the character. The point of view then becomes different. The point of view of the novel is 'within' the character, while the point of view of the traditional story resides in the story-pattern which is focussed on the central figure, the protagonist.

There are other kinds of rationalisation. Shakespeare, in his more extraordinary and folkloric plays, like *Cymbeline*, is fond of putting explanations of, or perhaps rather excuses for, the oddity of the sequence of events into the mouths of characters, and the author of *Sir Gawain and the Green Knight* does the same at the end of the poem. Sometimes the story-teller will himself comment. A favourite device, less logical but very appealing, especially to writers of Arthurian romances, is to preface the account of the hero's deeds by an account of his childhood, his *enfances*. We may be given an account of his parents, and thus sometimes, as in Chrétien's *Cligés*, the story of how *they* fell in love and married. Such preliminaries can do useful things by way of clarifying similarities with and contrasts to the essential story. An early example of it is the birth-narratives of Jesus in the Gospels of Matthew and Luke. This process was carried on in the Middle Ages with further elaborated narratives of the childhood of Christ. St. John's Gospel goes in for a different form of rationalisation, more literary and philosophical. The Gospels give a re-markable model for the nature of traditional narrative (a model I`have discussed elsewhere).[4]

The variations between the four Gospels are only the most striking example among many of the principle that while the same given story may have differing valid verbal realisations, *each version must be regarded as adequate to itself.* The attempt to harmonise the Gospels, to reconcile or eradicate their mutual inconsistencies, though it recognises the funda-mental oneness of their story, is the product of a mistaken literalism. Each version has its own validity, its own character, just as different members of the same family, though sharing similar characteristics, each have their own individuality. Each version must be judged in itself, as well as being an emanation of a general entity. To take a version as being adequate to itself does not oppose the principle that one version may be better than the other, any more than it contradicts the fact that one version may be derived from another which may be better or worse.

IV

I have said so much about the general nature of the verbal realisation because that is our only access to a story and it is vital to understand the part it plays in any version. It constitutes the literal level, but not the only level of the mysterious total experience of reading or hearing a story. To limit ourselves to the literal level without taking into account its re-lationship to other levels and the assumptions which govern it is to commit the literary sin of literalism, denying the obvious further inten-tions of the literal text. The literal level itself may quite properly be isolated if we understand what we are doing, but in none of the stories studied in this book is the literal level itself the object, though we start from specific versions of the stories.

'Within', or 'below', or 'above' the literal level is the series of events by which we recognise the story. Let us say the events begin by the hero's leaving home with a task to perform, and meeting an old man whom he helps (I am thinking of *The Golden Goose*). These events, held in the mind, can be either generalised from in various summaries or propositions, or particularised in the verbal realisation. It will be possible to particularise by giving the hero a name, making him the third son, making him seem stupid or intelligent, making his father a woodcutter or a miller or a university professor. He will leave home because he is oppressed or bored or wishes to help his parents or his father has died or he receives a mysterious summons, etc. The old man may be noble or pathetic or not an old man at all – but here there are constraints; he cannot be an old woman, for old women and old men play different roles. But he might be an animal in a trap. The hero may come to a palace, or it may be a mansion, or just a house, or a hovel, or a glade in the woods. All these variable particular variations of a given event can also be generalised 'upwards' to a more abstract statement of the event, and the perception that many various particular items are all manifestations of the same kind of event which we can think of in even more abstract form is the achievement of V. Propp's now famous study.[5] Basing his observations on the similar shapes of one hundred Russian folktales Propp shows that many different manifestations may be grouped or generalised as realisations of one 'function'. In accepting this we need not follow Propp in his controversial further argument that all fairy tales are selections from a possible maximum thirty-two functions which always follow in the same order. Propp's interest in narrative sequences is not my concern in this book, but his demonstration of the firmness of sequence, and consequently of *relatedness* between functions, is very important. It is one form of evidence – there are others as I shall show – that the apparently arbitrary or absurd sequence of events in an improbable tale is necessary and significant. It does not matter if the sequence does not follow the rules of ordinary everyday cause and effect, which are within the domain of the verbal realisation: the sequence satisfies us because it derives from the inner necessities of the story.

In thinking about stories we can generalise from events to functions; we can also generalise from the sequence of functions. The highest level of generalisation of a story at the literal level may be obvious, and though useful and true, not necessarily interesting. 'This story shows that you mustn't believe all you hear.' But at a different level there are all sorts of interesting generalisations that arise from a story: they need not include every aspect of the story, and certainly not every aspect of a verbal realisation, much of which may be, from the point of view of the story, mere decoration, though it may also be great poetry. In making these generalisations we move away from the sequences of narrative structure and consider the patterns of relationships which the sequence of narrative unfolds and relies on. When the patterns are complete they exist independently of the telling, with its concern for movement, surprise, suspense, etc. The underlying pattern is distinct from the process of revealing it, just as the intrinsic story, held as a whole at one moment in the mind, can be distinguished from the verbal realisation, though progressively revealing it in time; so the slow sequence of an aeroplane's sky-writing differs from the finished word which is now seized at a glance and remembered out of time.

All good traditional stories reveal themselves, as is the case with all good works of art, as a whole series of patterns, configurations of interest, with various appeal, inter-acting with the minds of successive generations. This is one reason why works of art can be continuously re-interpreted throughout the years; because they depend for full life on the contribution of a sympathetic audience which lends something of itself to the story, and receives something of earlier minds. Good interpretations are not arbitrary. They are related to each other and controlled by the story, and have to be continually discovered and formulated anew.

Each story within its configurations of meaning may be said to have an 'inner point' or 'points' of most general import, and then a whole variety of other inner patterns, whose significances become more and more individualised as we descend the scale from general to particular until we come to any given verbal realisation. Such verbal realisation will be one of a whole family of versions with direct and indirect relationships to each other, with cousins and second cousins even unto the thirtieth and fortieth generations.

Manifold patterns are created by a good story. At the literal level of verbal realisation itself they exist on a small scale and may be the subject of valid generalisations. At other levels they exist as 'inner' patterns which are less specific than the details of literal level, yet they actually control the general development of the verbal realisation. These indirectly perceived generalised patterns create the symbolic significance of the stories. Symbolisation is one kind of generalisation. When we perceive the inner or hidden significance which the story symbolises we can compare it with other similar though not identical significances in other stories and in our own lives.

Stories may therefore be regarded as symbolic because they express indirectly some 'hidden,' 'inner' meanings which are related to but not literally manifested in the verbal realisation. The story invites us to register, consciously or unconsciously, these symbolic significances through the literal narration, partly by the very strangeness of the story at a literal level, the way it flouts normal causality. It is the nature of a good story to reveal a series of symbolic meanings, one leading to another. There are many possible symbolic meanings, but it is the aim of this book to concentrate on only one set, very representative and widespread.

V

A very large number of traditional stories, though by no means all, are centred on the basic human experience of growing up. This has always been seen to be of exceptional interest and complexity. It may be said that we never finally complete it. Throughout our lives we find ourselves on particular occasions feeling as if we were children again, and there are probably aspects in all our personalities which never completely mature. Ask any wife if there is not at times something irritatingly or agreeably adolescent about her husband. I have known a man of eighty when ill wish for his mother. Conversely even small children at times display an astonishing maturity of judgement: 'Out of the mouths of babes and sucklings. . . .' We both revert and project in our attitudes throughout life. It is not surprising that in imagination we constantly explore, or re-live, or test alternative versions of, this crucial passage of our lives from childhood to adulthood.

To grow up is not a solitary experience. In particular it involves attitudes to parents. Parents are seen in many different guises, helping and hindering. Parental attitudes, at first needed and desired by the growing child for his or her protection, come to be felt as unduly constrictive. The womb becomes a tomb if it is not left behind. In this universal story the emerging individual, who is each one of us, is the universal protagonist. Each one of us, in growing up, has to cast off the shell which once defended but is now oppressive, and go forth alone, on our own. Either we must find an adequate self-sufficiency, which in the past has usually been achieved through religion, or, more usually, we must find our peer, our equal in status, with whom we can live in terms of freedom yet stable relationship. Traditionally the peer has been the mate, whom the protagonist marries. Having escaped from society in the form of the parental family, the protagonist has to re-enter society and begin to create a family of his or her own. The whole process I call the family drama.

Very many stories, like almost all those examined in this book, deal with the family drama quite openly. But even when they do the transition is so complex and involves so many shifts of attitude, so many contradictory feelings, so many difficulties and inhibitions and transgressions, angers and despairs and joys, that the story is never simple. Does anyone need to be told that growing up is difficult? In consequence the stories often, indeed usually, need to present many aspects of this process in a disguised way. Attitudes which we consciously disapprove of in ourselves, that we think we hate but really like, our schemes and weaknesses and ignoble resentments and cowardice, our hatreds of what we think we like, of our loved parents, our anxiety that perhaps we never shall achieve what others achieve, all these, often and to some extent properly repudiated by our conscious minds, need to find expression, and can in terms of art find richer, subtler expression in indirect ways, rather than in direct and simple communication. There are many things about ourselves that we can hardly know directly but can satisfactorily deal with indirectly. Symbolism is indirect knowledge, often the subtler and fuller, if less precise, for being so.

Symbolic stories of this kind are the subject of this book. They are stories about growing up. Because they are articulated on the basis of powerful patterns to some extent below the level of consciousness they are symbolic. Most of them are traditional and have been laden with significance by many minds, but my instances show how even certain novels, based on apparently quite different assumptions about form and content, can be well understood, indeed better understood, as articulations of the traditional family drama.

VI

The simplest and some of the best examples of traditional tale concerned with the family drama are those folktales now called fairy tales to which I devote my first chapter. Their downgrading at the end of the seventeenth century to children's reading should not blind us to their ancient origins and general acceptability. They are at once the most and the least symbolic of tales dealing with the family drama. The most because they contain obviously impossible events of all kinds; the least because they are so obviously about the protagonist's conflicts with parents and emergence into the world of adults, and so many of the characters are obviously 'repeats' or 'splits' of the main three: stepmothers and aunts and grandmothers all 'repeat', that is, are aspects of, the mother-figure; kings, uncles, ogres, giants, all 'repeat' the father-figure; brothers, sisters, friends 'repeat' the protagonist. The best general account of the fairy tale, which expands this and other points not so central to my purpose here, is that by Professor Max Lüthi.[6]

Within the shared general pattern one must distinguish between a male and a female protagonist. The male protagonist always has to leave home. He goes on a quest, is tested by having to defeat various threatening figures and avoid treachery or seduction by others. He is often helped by inferiors or by magic animals. His ultimate aim, almost always successful, is to marry the princess and succeed to the kingdom. When the protagonist is female the pattern is slightly different. She may well stay at home, sometimes, like Cinderella, ill-treated. Or she may be driven out from her home, like Catskin, but in this case she normally settles in another home, like Catskin, as kitchen-maid, or Snow-White with the seven dwarves. (In all stories siblings of the same sex are usually hostile, of the opposite sex, friendly.) Her oppressions arise from either a wicked stepmother, or her equivalent, or a too-fond father who wants to marry her. Although essentially located at home, she has to arrange to be seen by the prince, who eventually sees her true worth and beauty and marries her.

These events give the basic pattern of the 'canonical' folktale, which is elaborated and variegated in a thousand different ways. At a deep level this pattern is related to such stories as that of Oedipus. The story of Oedipus is explicitly based on the same conflicts between characters that we find in folktale and elsewhere.

The essence of the matter is that the protagonist of the story is a representative of the emerging human adult breaking out from the environment of the home and parents. At the core of the story are the three primary characters, protagonist, father, mother. The story in its nature nevertheless aspires to create a fourth, of opposite sex (usually) to the protagonist, and equal in age and attitude, the peer. To put the matter with crude brevity: what the male protagonist has to do is kill his father, dodge his mother, and win his girl. The female protagonist has to dodge her father, and if not kill at any rate pretty severely neutralise her mother, and make it possible for her man to get her. Achievement of the peer signals success – the breaking out of the family triangle, in which the protagonist is always inferior, into the freedom of adult responsibility and equal stable relationship with another person. Usually reconciliation with parent-figures is also achieved.

Once we understand the procedures it is easy to see the psychic dramas that are vividly portrayed in fairy tales, well expounded, though with primarily psychoanalytical, not literary, interests by Bruno Bettelheim.[7] The basic symbolic concepts are common to both interests. Both literature and psychoanalysis recognise a 'manifest' literal level which conveys the deeper 'latent' or symbolic significance. Different literal manifestations may well refer to the same underlying latent pre-occupation in order to work on it. Repetition is of great importance at the underlying, or indeed manifest level; hence the frequency of 'significant' numbers, especially three. What makes repetition significant is repetition with a difference. We must refer to father- or mother-figures, rather than to 'father' or 'mother' as such, and we soon become aware of how in a story various characters may be different manifestations or 'splits' of the basic father- or mother-image. The 'split' image is a projection by the protagonist, an internal projection turned into an external appearance. A single image may have multiple or ambiguous significance, a phenomenon known to psychoanalysis as condensation. One may also note substitution or 'displacement' of one image by another, associated one, with a somewhat different emotional meaning. Thus one latent character may have several literal manifestations. All characters are significant *only* in relation to the central protagonist, never in relation to each other independently of the protagonist. The protagonist himself may be 'split', as in the world-wide folktales of The Two Brothers type (or Chaucer's *Knight's Tale*). The protagonist himself is also, that is to say, a figure, a projection, of the deep drive of the story, and may be supplemented, or reflected on, by other aspects of himself who appear as 'splits'. The story represents a 'total mind' of which *all* characters are aspects – the evil as much a part as the good. From one point of view it is not unreasonable to consider the whole story as a drama going on in the mind of the protagonist, who sees himself *as* protagonist, and also 'creates', as we do in dreams, the figures who help or oppose him, basing his view of them upon his own experience and hopes of life. As we read, we identify ourselves with the protagonist and by sympathy with him or her 'create' or dismiss the other varied figures, because we all know the same drama in so far as we all inherit the ancient Western and Eastern pattern of the nuclear family. (It is possible that African culture is different.) The earliest version of this story in our tradition is probably not that of Oedipus, but of David in 1 Samuel XVI–XXI, which I discuss more fully in Chapter II. The first part of the story of David is regarded by Biblical scholars as a composite narrative, combining two narrative traditions. But whatever the origins of the duality, the story is perfectly acceptable in traditional literary and psychological terms as a unity. The duality is simply an aspect of the widespread medieval story of 'The Fair Unknown', itself an obvious variant of the canonical fairy tale. It represents the ambivalence we experience towards ourselves when young. The protagonist is lowly and somehow unjustly treated, and at the same time splendidly strong, handsome and gifted. Saul is a father-figure. The killing of Goliath is a fairy tale, where the clever unknown shepherd-boy kills the menacing stupid giant, who is obviously another father-figure. Then the shepherd-boy marries the King's daughter, Michal, though David finds his true peer in Jonathan. The Bible has other examples of the family drama, like the story of Jephtha's daughter (Judges XI). From a symbolic point of view the narrative expresses the resentment against the possessive father. This feeling is also at work in the story of Cinderella, of which the great archetype in our culture is Shakespeare's *King Lear*.

VII

The possible permutations in the play of events deriving from the tensions between the three or four persons of the perennial family drama are almost limitless, and it is for this reason that I refer to the *family drama* as in itself a neutral concept of the multiple play of forces about the emerging adult, which, as the following chapters will show, may take a number of different forms. What is constant is the central focus on the protagonist at that most interesting point of his life, as it is of all our lives, the transition or passage from childhood to adulthood, inferiority to independence, virginity (more important for women) to sexual maturity. In all societies such transitions are marked by stories and ceremonies, *rites de passage*. The obvious Christian *rite de passage* in this context is marriage. The other major transitions are obviously birth and death, with their various attendant rituals in well-structured societies; but because we are conscious in this world on both sides only of the *central* transition, to adulthood, it is of special interest. It is also usually elaborated and extended in various ways. Modern Western civilisation seems to be extraordinarily prolific in inventing minor *rites de passages* (university examinations, for example) while neglecting or abandoning major rites once generally accepted.

The transition (and therefore the *rite de passage*) is also, by definition, usually successful. Students almost always pass; a wedding is rarely abandoned (and when it is, as with Miss Havisham's in *Great Expectations*, it is a disaster); and we undoubtedly are born and die. The *rite de passage*, looked at as a ceremony or as a story, normally has a happy ending, although to give it significance the risk of failure must always be present, usually represented by minor characters in a story. The emerging adult successfully casts off childhood, frees himself or herself from parents, proves his capacity to stand on his own feet, finds his wife, or she her husband, and is then reconciled with parents; in other words, is fully integrated into adult society. Fairy tales and most medieval romances are essentially stories of the successful *rite de passage*.

The failure to survive the *rite de passage*, failure to grow up, that is failure to escape from parents, is usually the basis of tragedy. It is natural for the son to 'kill' the father and evade the mother. It is unnatural for the father to 'kill' the son, or for the mother to continue to dominate him. In some medieval stories of tragic adulterous love the essence of the matter is that the hero is trapped by a mother-image. The superiority of the lady in medieval romantic love involved a dangerously filial element, fortunately usually cured by marriage. The dangers of dominating mother-love are recognised in many folktales and illustrated by the numerous oppressive stepmothers. In the popular mind of Europe as shown in folktale fathers give far less trouble. Giants are always stupid. In this respect Freudian theory appears to over-estimate fathers, and misinterprets the killing of the father, while under-estimating the repellent nature of the fate of marrying the mother.

VIII

The concept of the story as a rich and complex entity has not been accepted by literary intellectuals for several centuries. In consequence the type of interpretation suggested here has been equally unacceptable, and literary criticism has either despised or neglected traditional stories, and rejected symbolic interpretations. Scholars in Classical Antiquity and the Middle Ages analysed both Classical stories such as Homer's *Iliad* and stories in the Bible, normally treating them as allegories, but since this analysis was directed towards the practical utilities of religious and moral instruction, it cannot strictly be called literary criticism. Literary criticism and theory as such began to flourish only in the sixteenth century in Europe as the work of Humanist scholars who re-created what they believed to be the rules governing Classical literature, and whose views may now be called Neoclassical.[8] For England the essence of their views at an early stage is summed up by Sir Philip Sidney's *An Apology for Poetry*. The essence of Neoclassicism is the admiration of idealised naturalism, that is, of a plausible, realistic presentation of possible appearances, which shall also be edifying. Not surprisingly, folktale, fairy tale and medieval romances were all regarded with contempt. The most characteristic product of Neoclassical views of literature is the novel, which makes its appearance at the beginning of the eighteenth century. It is realistic, at least in theory and intention, and usually didactic. In this respect D. H. Lawrence is in intention as Neoclassical as Defoe or Fielding. The story of the novel is normally conceived of as a series of events proceeding by cause and effect from the desires, motives and actions of the characters – the reverse of the situation of the traditional tale. It has to be a convincing 'imitation of nature'. The story cannot therefore have an inner guiding pattern (in theory); it must exist only on the surface. Although the novel as a form has always and rightly been enormously popular, taking its place along with, or even replacing, the traditional tale, the story-telling aspect of novels has always been despised by literary intellectuals. From this point of view Romanticism from the end of the eighteenth century onwards was merely a part of general Neoclassical theory. Thus Shelley:

> A poem is the very image of life expressed in its eternal truth. There is this difference between a story and a poem, that a story is a catalogue of detached facts, which have no other connexion than time, place, circumstance, cause and effect; the other is the creation of actions according to the unchangeable forms of human nature. . . .

A Defence of Poetry

A representative critic, J. S. Mill, considers that ninety per cent of Homer is not poetry but narrative, by definition inferior.[9] E. M. Forster repeated a similar view as late as 1927 in his *Aspects of the Novel*. Shelley's description of *poetry*, however, is quite appropriate to the structure of stories.

There has been no criticism other than that ultimately based on Neoclassical principles until quite recently. Neoclassicism invented literary criticism, and we may consider it to have been the dominant literary theory, for all its internal changes, from the late seventeenth century until the early or middle twentieth century, as I have argued elsewhere.[10] Even now it dies hard. Medieval romances and Shakespeare and traditional literature generally are often criticised according to quite inappropriate Neoclassical assumptions about cause and effect connecting time, place and circumstance, realistic motivation bringing about events which react on other characters and events. Characters are seen as autonomous entities, real people, whose actions may be speculated about even when the writer tells us nothing of them. The classic example is A. C. Bradley's *Shakespearean Tragedy*, which treats Shakespeare's plays as if they were incomplete transcripts from life – or Victorian novels. I show the ludicrous effect of such assumptions at the hands of modern critics when I apply them to the story of Cinderella in my first chapter. Until the twentieth century these assumptions may have deserved the term 'idealised naturalism'. Nowadays *naturalism* describes them best. Whether idealised or not, they imply an imitation of 'ordinary' nature in its materialist working. They also often imply a 'realistic' style, but 'realism' as I use it in this book, and a 'realistic style', describe a more superficial, though highly effective, literary device that may be used, even if intermittently, in telling traditional stories. It is not, like naturalism, basically hostile to them.

At the height of the Neoclassical period in the eighteenth and nineteenth centuries the same dismissive naturalistic attitudes were applied to dreams, those wild stories that we tell ourselves every night. Not all dreams are significant, but no one nowadays can doubt the symbolic significance of dreams, or doubt that in modern times we have at least begun to see something of the way they work. Literary criticism can take some useful concepts from our general understanding of the nature of dreams.[11]

At the beginning of the twentieth century the work of anthropologists

and psychoanalysts, which has continued with much self-correction and
increasing vigour, began to break down the limitations of Neoclassical
thought. Rather, we may say, to give honour where honour is due,
Neoclassical thought itself, a most powerful and valuable instrument,
began to break through into new territory and in so doing to change its
own nature. Within the English-speaking world T. S. Eliot is one key
figure whose perception of large-scale cultural change in the seventeenth
century, and whose concept of 'the logic of the imagination' as different
from ordinary logic, can be paralleled by the work of historians, anthropologists, psychologists, and others. The practice of literature changed.
James Joyce's novel *Ulysses*, let alone his *Finnegan's Wake*, are far from
'idealised naturalism'. The Neoclassical period has come to an end. Its
achievements were very great, but if we unconsciously persist in relying
on its limited assumptions we may find ourselves cut off from some kinds
of high literary achievement, such as that of traditional literature, which
we ought now to be able to enjoy with both an old and a new understanding.

CHAPTER I

Fairy Tales

I

Fairy tales are the most obvious and most typical of symbolic stories. Their symbolism is now also transparent. They are well established in Western culture but have world-wide connections, and some of them have ancient roots. Almost all the fairy tales commonly known exist in many versions, some closely related, others remote, in many languages, in stories not designed specially for children. It would appear from Lüthi's work[1] that the specific qualities that we recognise as those of a fairy tale are found in their characteristic grouping mainly in Europe, and it may be that they are more especially a European genre that developed from the late Middle Ages onwards. Lüthi shows that they are images of deliverance into 'true' existence, representing the total personality, depicting processes of maturation. They are immediately understood as symbolic, presenting internal feelings as external forms of people, animals, monsters, etc.

It is not surprising to find that the first dismissive reference to fairy tale, and perhaps the first time the tales we know are actually called *fairy* tales occurs in 1691 or 1692, in a book actually about fairies,[2] – a reference missed by the Oxford Dictionary, whose earliest reference of any kind (in the *Supplement*) is 1749. It is clear that the term *fairy tale* was from the first normally dismissive. In actual fact the occurrence of fairies is rare in what are now called fairy tales and their appearances are normally eighteenth- and nineteenth-century sentimental intrusions.

Although fairy tales recount extraordinary sequences of events they are not arbitrary and they conform to a recognisable pattern. The most ambitious effort to describe this pattern is that already referred to by V. Propp in *Morphology of Folktale*, based on the study of one hundred Russian folk tales. The outline of the sequence as Propp finds it is that the protagonist must leave home, is given help or advice by someone, undergoes a series of conflicts and tests, and, if male, marries a king's daughter. There are many complications, not least that in which the protagonist returns home apparently successful but is ill-treated by someone (often his brothers), so that he must depart and undergo further tests and conflicts, before returning to enjoy his final achievement.

Here we have at a fairly abstract level the characteristic pattern that is verbally realised in many different ways. But though it gives a good example of an important typical 'shape' it is still neither complete nor

15

general enough to include other examples that will easily spring to mind as typical European fairy tales, especially those whose protagonist is a girl. That the story of Cinderella for example has some relationship to this scheme is clear enough, but it is only a relationship: *Cinderella, Beauty and the Beast, The Frog Prince, Diamonds and Toads, Little Red Riding-Hood*, are not primarily quest-stories and are not easily included in this pattern. Yet they are certainly members of the general group of what we call fairy tales.

I propose therefore to choose examples mainly from a collection of tales which is not selected to suit my own purposes but will empirically decide what are fairy tales. The collection is *The Classic Fairy Tales*, 1974, edited by Iona and Peter Opie, 'the texts of twenty-four of the best-known fairy tales as they were first printed in English, or in their earliest surviving or prepotent text' (Preface, p. 5). The introductions in this selection have the double advantages for my purposes of not only being admirably informative but also categorically rejecting psychological or anthropological interpretation or any elaborate structuralism. The selection and commentary are therefore not skewed in my favour, though even the Opies admit symbolic interpretations at times.

Since the general mass of fairy tales is so great and each tale exists in so many different versions, the texts printed by the Opies give us both the assurance of the centrality of our examples and a given version (sometimes inferior to others) to start with. I adopt the principle that each version is adequate to itself, that is, is comprehensibly worked out in its own terms, though it may be inferior to other versions.

II

Cinderella is by everyone's account the best-known fairy tale in the world. There are many hundreds of versions from many countries from China to Scotland, and the earliest version occurs in a Chinese book written about 850–60 A.D. The earliest English version is Robert Samber's translation (1729) of the version by Charles Perrault in his *Histoires ou Contes du temps passé* published in Paris in 1697. It is the principal or only source of modern versions of the story.

The Perrault-Samber version is realised in a vigorous style with a good deal of local colour and a witty realism, and though it has a number of special features it is a very good representative of the general character of the story. The story has been deeply enjoyed by millions of readers, not only children, since the end of the seventeenth century, and such a cloud of witnesses is primary evidence of its richness of meaning. We can only interpret it literalistically, or symbolically from the literal level. Let us first take it literalistically, in the way that so many modern critics take medieval romance, and the works of Chaucer, the *Gawain*-poet or Shakespeare (cf. above p. 3). The story tells how, Cinderilla's mother being dead and her father re-married, the stepmother (who already has two older daughters) ill-treats Cinderilla by making her do 'the meanest work of the house'. She has to sleep in the attic 'upon a wretched straw bed, while her sisters lay in fine rooms'. The poor girl bears all patiently, and dares not tell her father, who would have 'rattled her off' (i.e. scolded her); for his wife governs him entirely. When she has done her work, she goes into the chimney corner, and sits down upon the cinders! Well, what a perverse child, we may say! Not merely does she have to do the dirty work, but she actually goes and voluntarily sits in the dirtiest and, surely, the most uncomfortable place in the house. After all, she did have a bed, if of straw in the attic. Her beauty and goodness are constantly emphasised, indeed, grossly over-emphasised, throughout the narration. This wanton self-punishment is quite unaccounted for by any comment in this particular version.

Then again, what is the father doing? Cinderilla dare not tell him. He is governed by his wife. The implication of this is that in some way he would do something if he knew, and dared. Yet on the other hand, we are told that he would have scolded Cinderilla had she complained. So he is not utterly dominated. He has voluntarily joined the enemy. How is it that he does not notice his daughter's degradation? The father is a very ambiguous figure. The only thing that seems clear is that whether he cares or not, he is weak.

We are told about the ball, to which the stepsisters depart wearing the finery that Cinderilla has helped them to dress in while she remains at home, and, as the story goes on, 'fell a crying. Her godmother, who saw her all in tears, asked her what was the matter'. There is no explanatory introduction of this new and extraordinary person. Cinderilla explains her plight. Then, we are told, the godmother takes action. 'Her godmother, who was a Fairy . . . etc. etc.' Why does the Fairy godmother not know what is wrong? What has this godmother, who possesses such remarkable powers, been doing up to now? Why did she not improve Cinderilla's position much earlier, or at least tell her father and make him do something? And then why cannot Cinderilla go to the ball as herself, undisguised? Why must she return at midnight?

The glass slipper is superbly implausible as footwear for dancing in. It is hardly more ridiculous, on a naturalistic plane, than a prince choosing a wife according to the size of her foot. Even if we take this latter as a possible, if hardly plausible, method of identifying the beautiful stranger, it is not a very practical way of choosing a wife. It shows, for example, that beautiful as Cinderilla was claimed to be, the Prince could not recognise the face of the girl he had danced with for several hours on three successive evenings and become so enamoured of. And he was certainly not interested in her potential moral qualities as a wife and a mother.

As modern literary critics we can now say confidently that (like so much of Shakespeare) this is a very poor story, not at all well written. However, we proceed in our self-appointed task of showing how bad most famous literature is, in the hope of discovering a few shreds of merit. Let us turn to the examination of character, which is a very usual procedure in literary criticism, though I am afraid we shall find that, like Othello, Cinderilla is not at all the noble creature that so many generations of readers have taken her to be. We are told *ad nauseam* how good, kind, forgiving, beautiful, she is. Yet we are also told that she goes and sits upon the cinders. True, we are never told that she is intelligent, so we may conclude that she is simply stupid, as so many good and beautiful girls are. It seems that the Prince finds her conversation entertaining, but her beauty and good-nature might account for that, and she might be a very good listener. Moreover, we are never told that the Prince is intelligent either, and to judge from the way he chooses a wife, or rather, lets his gentleman do the actual work, he is more than a bit of an idiot. So we have this very stupid pair. However, there seems to be more to Cinderilla's character than this, in sitting upon the cinders. There is a certain wanton dirtiness about her, even a kind of spitefulness towards herself, which is partly towards her stepmother. This may lead us to think that the Narrator of the fairy tale, in his emphasis on her goodness and beauty, is perhaps being ironical. The idea of the Narrator is a very powerful one in modern criticism, and indeed for a truly modernistic interpretation of a traditional story or poem is a device we can hardly do without. The concept of the Narrator is of *someone who is different from the author* telling the actual story, and telling it badly, even not understanding it. He *must* be different from the author, who is the real teller, or otherwise there is no point in imagining him. If he is different, he is saying something different from what the author *really* means. If the Narrator says that Cinderilla is good, then the author must really mean that she is bad. The whole narration must be ironical. This is what almost all modern critics say about the stories by Chaucer and the *Gawain*-poet. It is a wonderfully useful device. Thus if we look at the story of Cinderilla in a modernistic way we shall naturally come to the conclusion that she is not by any means really so good and beautiful as we are told she is. We have already been able to deduce on good literalistic evidence that she is stupid. She must be spiteful and ugly as well, really. This may lead us to reconsider the character of the stepmother. The Narrator tells us that she was 'the proudest and most haughty woman that ever was known'. But we have already found reason to suppose that we are not meant to take the Narrator's word at its face-value. Dozens of studies of Chaucer's poems and of *Sir Gawain and the Green Knight* and of other traditional literature have shown that these stories are told by a stupid Narrator and that when the text praises a person (such as Gawain or Troilus) the poet intends to convey the opposite meaning. So we should reconsider the character of the stepmother. We shall soon realise that her treatment of Cinderilla is entirely justified. There is this stupid girl, with her positive love of dirt. Her father may well have good reason for scolding her. How do we *know* that the sisters never help with the housework? Even the Narrator, who is so prejudiced in favour of that slut Cinderilla, never actually tells us that they do not. It may well be that the sisters helped and that the stepmother, unfairly labelled by the prejudice that popularly attaches to all stepmothers, did no more than make Cinderilla do her fair share of the housework, which she then exaggerated. We may conclude that the stepmother is an unfairly maligned woman, whose scrupulous desire for cleanliness at home, and for dividing the housework fairly, is evidence of a strong-minded sensible decent character not inclined to stand much nonsense. As to the godmother, one can see that the invention of this unconvincing character is a device (since we know that magic does not really exist) for ironically concealing the fact that Cinderilla, highly competitive in spirit as she was, had access to some hidden wealth (perhaps her dead mother's) which ought to have gone to her father, but which she somehow retained to give her an unfair advantage over her sisters by dressing in expensive clothes to catch a husband. The glass slipper is obviously a mistake in the French original of *verre* (glass) for *vair* (fur). Her slippers would really have had those lovely furry tops you often see nowadays. That there was something tricky about the slipper is shown by the fact that the cunning Cinderilla retained its companion, part of her 'magical' outfit, when the rest of her clothing, her coach, etc., were supposedly turned back into rags, pumpkin and so forth. In fact she must have retained her whole outfit, though she only revealed the slipper in order to catch the Prince. We can see that this must be so, since it can be the only true explanation of the absurd fantasy about the godmother coming back and touching her rags to make them into fine clothes at the end of the Perrault-Samber version. This must mean she quickly changed into her finery. Cinderilla was not only a stupid slut, she was cunning and deceitful too. The whole story is ironical, designed to show that however sluttish and deceitful you are, you can succeed if you play your cards properly. A characteristically modern reading shows that far from being the heroine of the story, Cinderilla is the villainess. On the same criteria, far from being the hero of the story of *Sir Gawain and the Green Knight*, Sir Gawain is the fool. On the same criteria, Patient Griselda, in Chaucer's *Clerk's Tale*, is a proud and foolish woman who ought to have put up more of a fight for the liberation of women and the safety of her children. She too is not a kind of saint, as traditionally maintained, but a villainess. King Lear is a tiresome old man, and there is much to be said for those long-suffering, unfairly condemned daughters, Goneril and Regan.

It is all nonsense, or almost all nonsense. The grain of truth in this mass of error is that it is always possible for there to be a vein of naturalism, hostile to the essential nature of a story, and therefore inevitably mocking and ironic, in any given verbal realisation. A story-teller is not under oath. He can do what he likes, and what he thinks his audience will like. The nature of a traditional story, a pre-verbal cluster of actions, which is verbally realised according to the genius of many different tellers, encourages the teller to use any device he wishes to make it acceptable. Any telling of a traditional story is an interpretation and a rationalisation. There are many different kinds of rationalisation. I have used one myself in suggesting a telling of Cinderilla's story that reveals her as not heroine but villainess. (Like so much criticism it is more of a re-creation, with the status of fiction, than an analysis – extending one set of symbols in terms of another set, though not for that reason necessarily in error.) It is easy to imagine a re-telling that might use a marginal mockery or criticism while allowing the main movement to carry us on. Chaucer himself to some extent invites modernistic criticism by the ambivalence with which he seems to regard, and with which he therefore verbally realises, some of his traditional stories. Perrault himself in his minor way resembles Chaucer in this. There is a vein of irony in Perrault's version, not un-common in adults who tell tales ostensibly to children but always with a consciousness of the parental reader. Such tellers as it were give a patronising wink to the adult-accomplice, so as to assure them that no one, in the real world, actually takes this nonsense seriously. Perrault gives such a wink when he has lizards as footmen for Cinderilla's coach, playing on the French expression 'lazy as a lizard', and on contemporary jokes about the laziness of footmen.

Perrault's ambivalence towards his own story, taken up by it yet mocking it, would be most natural at the end of the seventeenth century, when Neoclassical literary criteria were well established, especially in France, and when in consequence the value previously accorded to romance and fantasy was rapidly declining. To provide fantasy for children was a way of evading that decline yet accommodating it, allow-ing, as is surely the case with fairy tales today, a legitimate gateway (the needs of children) for the entry of subconscious potencies that even adults cannot do without.

It is not only a case of cultural period. Every healthy mind at every period has a need to register what it feels to be real, and equally a need to accommodate stories, our fundamental imaginative activity, to that per-ceived reality. At all periods there are temperaments exceedingly aware of the demands of analytical thought, of ordinary material cause and effect, of the ordinary world, and of the apparent clash between the ordinary world and narrative fantasy. Yet even such sceptics respond to fantasy. In some periods more people respond more easily to fantasy. In a period favouring fantasy in literature, the fourteenth century in England, Chaucer was a major artist who was exceptionally aware of the material ordinary world and of the clash between fantasy and realism. Thus his telling of the story of Patient Griselda, though supremely beautiful, is extraordinarily tense in the strain between the powerful strange fantasy and the extreme realism of the telling. I do not find such strains in the *Gawain*-poet, realistic as he is in detail.

It is now evident that a *naturalistic* interpretation of even Perrault's version is so opposed to any *natural* reading of it, a literalistic reading is in this case so far from the literal meaning of the text, that we must invoke different criteria if we wish to make conscious to ourselves the story's unquestionable compelling power. The first point to be made is that the reader strongly identifies himself – perhaps even more *herself* (but the sex of the reader is unimportant) – with Cinderilla, with the protagonist. This is more than to say that she is the central character. The central character could in a novel be presented with detached dislike. Our identification with Cinderella – as with Hamlet, or Gawain – goes beyond liking or disliking, beyond moral judgement even, though the Perrault-Samber version (which I refer to as Perrault's) crams moral judgements down our throats. We see through Cinderilla's eyes, and no one else's. We sympathise with the way she feels. We know now (unless we are too old, in which case we certainly have known, and remember it), that we are, each individual of us, central to the universe, or at any rate, to that part of it which we know, the home; we know that we have many good qualities, and that they are not recognised. We know that we are downtrodden and neglected by the grown-ups, specifically, by our parents. Perrault invokes a further twist of the knife; the well-recognised fact that we have equally a strong sense, as children, that our parents love us, and that they would help us in our dire need, if they could, and if they knew of it. But they do not know, and *we cannot tell them*. The absolute incapacity of a child to tell beloved parents how he or she is for example persecuted at school is one of the astonishing discoveries of adulthood, out of both one's own experience, and that of one's eventually grown-up children. Perrault thus hits off, in a few sentences, a profoundly human characteristic concerning the relationships, and the distances, between a child and the parents. The gulf is a fundamental *donnée* of the whole *Cinderella* complex, because it is also inevitable in the process of growing up. Perrault thus symbolises a vital stage of individual growth, the break with the parents.

We see the parents through Cinderilla's eyes. The father-image is, as already noted, ambivalent. We feel he both would and would not help us; he loves us yet scolds us. As is usual in fairy tales, though good he is remote, and being weak is at the service of the mother. The force of feeling concentrates on the mother-image, or rather, mother-images. At the literal level Cinderilla's mother is dead. But who are these others, the stepmother and the godmother? It is no violent jump, in this tale, to take them as versions of the mother. Here is a virtually incontrovertible example of a process which takes place less obviously in many more exalted and complicated works of literature. It is the process recognisable in some dreams, when the dreamer's sense of hostility to someone who apparently should not attract hostility results in a 'projection' of the hostile aspect of that person in the form of another person. This is the 'splitting' of characters, whereby one person may be 'split' into several. The stepmother and the godmother are 'splits' of the composite mother-image towards which is felt such fierce and often socially or morally unacceptable ambiguity. The stepmother is an image which represents all that is resented in the mother, the one who, at the simplest level, reproaches us for our dirtiness, makes us clean up our room, or the house, the one from whose jurisdiction the process of growing up makes us wish in the nature of things to escape. The Fairy godmother, on the other hand, represents that aspect of the mother which provides all that we want, and which, as we feel when young, is all-powerful. Bettelheim in *The Uses of Enchantment* points out that Perrault's version of *Cinderella*, in contrast with other versions, is mainly located in the areas of feeling of a very young child. Thus it is the godmother, rather than, as in other versions, Cinderilla herself, who provides coach-and-horses, though Cinderilla enters into the fun of the thing and brings the rats. This makes Perrault's version literally more childish, less mature, than other versions, unconsciously flattering the parent, and indulging the child in a certain self-pitying feebleness in such a way as to encourage the popularity of the version by lessening the story's power.

The intrinsic power of the story is by no means lost by Perrault. Particularly strong is the evocation of sibling rivalry between Cinderilla and her stepsisters. Rivalry with those of similar age and status when of the same sex is a feeling so common that even children without brothers or sisters know it, since they respond intensely to the incursion of other children of similar age from outside the family. We may take the step-sisters as psychic images a little further. They are strongly associated in the early part of the tale with the stepmother, and to that extent they represent and re-inforce the sense of the protagonist's hatred and jealousy of the mother. The stepsisters' fine clothes and demands for assistance are therefore an aspect of the mother-figure's painful super-iority and tyranny. By contrast, at the end of the story – stepmother and godmother left out of account, as such characters usually are in fairy tales, their only validity lying in their relationship with the protagonist, who has so to speak now outgrown them – the sisters are more closely asso-ciated in Perrault with Cinderilla, who forgives them, 'desired them always to love her', and has them married the same day as herself to two great lords of court. At this stage the siblings are seen rather as projections of the protagonist than as projections of the mother-figure. This may prompt us to consider them also as in part aspects of the protagonist earlier on. If taken as aspects of the protagonist but allied with the mother-figure they show the protagonist's unconscious contempt for herself, partly perphaps as compensation for the inordinately high degree of virtue also attributed to her by the version. In no other version of the tale is there such a degree of sibling rivalry combined with such insistence on the protagonist's own virtue. The two are complementary. A strong sense of self-righteousness arouses self-admiration, *and* guilt, which must be projected on to externalised figures, who thus express it towards the protagonist.

Cinderilla's forgiveness of the unkind stepsisters is from this point of view forgiveness of herself, now that she has been recognised as she truly is. She can accept and love all the aspects of herself and also has no need to choose to go and sit among the cinders, a sulky child, which again is unique to Perrault's version.

The stepsisters, at first associated mainly with the hostile mother-figure, then more closely associated with the protagonist at the end, however improbably and even unjustly forgiven in Perrault's version (unlike other versions in this) make manifest a development found in so many fairy tales as to constitute part of the usual development. In the most general terms this is the transference of feelings from parent-figure to peer, one of the main objects of the 'passage' from childhood to adulthood. The feeling toward the sisters is switched from 'vertical' to 'lateral'. This crucial transference is normally centred on the love-relationship between the sexes, less emphasised in Perrault's version, though its main exemplar is still of course the love for the Prince. The attitude to the sisters nevertheless reflects the neutralisation of the ambivalent mother-figure, the removal therefore of dangerous dependence (verticality) and the substitution for it of equal relationship (laterality) once the rival siblings are shown to be Cinderilla's equals or even inferiors. (It seems to be a rule of fairy tales that we are not afraid of our inferiors.) Cinderilla neither forgives her stepmother nor thanks her godmother. As already noted, they simply disappear from the story; but forgiveness and gratitude are not omitted from the story as a whole, in this version.

The switch of the stepsisters from allies of the mother-figure to allies of the protagonists illustrates the fluidity of images in the fairy tale, controlled as they are by the needs of the pattern. No character, with the possible partial exception of the protagonist, has an autonomous inner life, a self-motivated independent existence of his or her own. This is an exceedingly important point, the corollary of the fundamental principle that the whole story is told from the point of view of the protagonist. A realistic verbal realisation may give us some appearance of a character's independent self-motivated existence, but it is always superficial, and does not prevent totally improbable shifts of character and motivation within the person represented according to the over-riding needs of the story. This is where the essential nature of fairy tale (and of folktale and romance) comes into head-on conflict with the nature of the novel and why to the degree that autonomous characters concern our interests, as in many novels, the actual structure, and especially the inner structure, of the novel's narrative is the less important. The novelist whose characters are most at the mercy of the story-pattern is probably Dickens, whose characters, like Pickwick, or Micawber in *David Copperfield*, or Boffin in *Our Mutual Friend*, undergo the most improbable transformations, but are nevertheless extremely effective as agents within the pattern of the story.

In the fairy tale characters are simple even to the point of having a single characteristic. At most they are ambiguous, like the weak and good/bad father of Perrault's version. They may be said, from this point of view, to be all of them projections of the protagonist. They are his or her father- or mother-images, sibling-images, peer-images.

By the same reasoning the protagonist *within the story* must be regarded as himself or herself a projection, an image, of the actual 'full' protagonist. Once again dreams offer the most appropriate analogy. We all know the kind of dream in which we ourselves take part in an action but as a person different from what we are in 'real' life (though dreams are after all as real as our other experiences, and a lot more vivid than most). Similarly, it is a common experience in dreams (or at any rate in my dreams) to be more than one person, to be both hunter and hunted, etc. In a fairy tale, therefore, while the protagonist is the central, leading figure, to whom all other figures must be related, these other figures are aspects of the protagonist, so that the totality of all the characters and actions adds up to as it were a total protagonist, the whole mind of the tale, just as, in a dream, everyone in it is part of the whole mind of the dreamer even if they represent real persons in waking life. It is most convenient to think of this totality as another level of action, of greater generality. At one level we have the protagonist and other characters inter-acting in some ways like separate characters in life, and to that extent self-contained: at this other more general level the characters, including the protagonist, are all aspects of one enveloping mind, its contradictory desires, internal conflicts and attempts to solve them. This enveloping mind is not particular to any one individual or story-teller: it is a partial model of the human mind itself expressed in the terms of the given culture. Thus the crowd of unrecognised, latent, fears and desires that make up so much of our inner life is expressed by the other characters of the tale, by the father- and mother-images, in all their variants, just as reasonable hopes, expectations and psychic preparation are expressed by the figure of the beloved. The progress of the tale, therefore, at this level, may be regarded as the process by which the consciousness brings itself to recognise, overcome, accept, often forgive, other elements of the total personality, and prepare to absorb further realities from the outside world. This is why it is useless to speculate about the motives and personality-structure of the characters in these stories, as I did in my parodic interpretation. They do not exist as autonomous characters as they would in a novel.

The fairy tale, and those literary works, especially romances, which share its nature, do not study the particular psychology of individual characters as it might be deduced or represented from individuals in everyday experience, but they are nevertheless intrinsically 'psychological'. The psychology is in the structure of the *whole* tale, representing the experiencing mind in such a way that the reader, whatever his own particularity, can find his own mind and experience of the world indirectly reflected in the story.

This may make the fairy tale seem solipsistic, restricted to its own world of debilitating wish-fulfilment. It is sometimes argued that the mere movements of the mind are never as significant as the usually disagreeable confrontation with materially based, external 'objective reality'. This is the basis of the Neoclassical view, which is essentially materialist, and the basis of the often expressed view that tragedy is the true final model of human existence, since everyone must die. The alternative, archaic, and medieval view is by contrast 'mentalist'. It asserts that the mind is the dominant factor in human experience. (Ideas *cannot* move matter, said the materialist, impatiently jumping up from his seat.)

The understanding of fairy tales implies a mentalist view of life and literature. Fairy tales (and most traditional literature) are not a direct imitation of a specific slice of life, but an activation of known forces, a model, a meditation on what has happened, a preliminary run-through of what will or should happen. They are like games, whose autonomy and generality make them able to represent the life-situations of many different kinds of people. The forces of life themselves, the ambivalent attitudes felt by everyone to parents and to the self, the hopes and fears all of us experience about personal relationships, are perfectly real. Though they are personal and mental they do nevertheless exist independently of our own personal preferences. There is an intrinsic human need to have them represented to ourselves, and to share the representation with other people, in order more fully to grasp, to comprehend, our lives. Out of this need arises art, and much of religion. Even Neoclassical theory demanded of literature that it should not only imitate nature but please and instruct the reader. There is no doubt that the subject-matter that fairy tales presents is present in life, and equally no doubt that it is often painful. It is also true, though less fashionable to believe, that life is full of success stories in that most of us grow up. Hence the passage from childhood to adulthood may become both in precept and accomplished fact a story with a happy ending, the successful integration of the protagonist into society, with mature relationships with those of his own age and freedom from undue domination by his parents.

III

Perrault's *Cinderilla* is a version of this perennially interesting achievement, but it is only one version of that particular cluster of themes and motifs, the Cinderella story in general, which is itself only one set among many of the possible versions of this almost infinitely rich process. We can learn more of these matters by comparing some aspects of other versions.

In her late-Victorian study of 345 Cinderella-type stories Marion Roalfe Cox proposed three major groups.[3] The first group is identified by two basic distinguishing characteristics: the heroine ill-treated by her mother and her recognition by the Prince by means of some identifying object. There is an essential bridge-passage between these two, whereby the heroine is wooed by the Prince or King. Although this bridge-passage does not isolate the Cinderella story from other stories, since it is common to the nature of fairy tale, it must not be overlooked, for it is integral to the structure of the tale.

The second large group contains an important addition. The heroine's Cinderella-state is brought about by her flight from her father, who wishes to marry her. The third group is identified not by the father's desire to marry his daughter but by a weakened variation of this – King Lear's. The father demands that his daughter express extreme love for him. She cannot express herself as warmly as he wishes, and she is banished, this bringing her to the Cinderella-state. This King Lear version is of course extraordinarily interesting when we consider Shakespeare.

Underlying the three groups is the general subject of the family drama. The protagonist is the child, whose relationships with the parents are in a state of tension. The action, at its most general, is escape from the parents and re-alignment with a beloved from outside the family group and of the child's own age. More specifically, the child is a girl, which determines the course of events. The objections to the parents are that father loves too much, but is weak and gives no support, while mother loves too little, and is domineering. While this pattern is specific to daughters, all readers of either sex easily sympathise with it. We all share male and female characteristics. We can easily generalise the situation to represent that ambivalent paradoxical sense of both tyranny and neglect by parents that is caused by the necessities of childish wilfulness and ignorance and also by the process of growing up and so growing out of, in uneasy stages, the need for parental control and guidance. We can generalise the situation further, to apply to all our superiors, for whom we are liable to feel both respect and dislike, and in relation to whom we may easily experience (sometimes profitably, sometimes not) that sense of 'injur'd Merit' which Milton's Satan (a very spoilt child) feels, or 'the scorns that patient merit of the unworthy takes' which Hamlet notes. Whether Father loves too much or Mother too little they both make unfair demands, as the heroine feels. The heroine's desire is to get rid of them both and set up with someone of her own age who loves her for herself, dirty as she appears to be because of her unfair treatment. He must penetrate through appearance (dirt) to reality (beauty).

Another way of looking at this at another level is to recognise that the drama as presented is the heroine's psychological projections upon her parents. A process of reversal is involved here. The father-image's desire for her is her fantasy of her desire for him, her desire to associate herself as closely as possible with him, to dominate and monopolise him. But this is only one desire on the part of the heroine. Only very little girls want to marry their fathers. The dynamic, growing, increasingly conscious female self does not want to. She wants a young husband. As few daughters wish to marry their fathers as sons their mothers. But we are nothing if not ambivalent. If the daughter in one part of herself desires her father it is not surprising that also in one part of herself she finds the mother to be a hated rival. Thus the mother is presented in the image of a tyrannous stepmother. Here is a very powerful source of the hated mother-images which are so prominent in fairy tales. If we were looking for the seed of the general cluster of stories that make up the general Cinderella version of the family drama it might well be found in the heroine's desire to monopolise her father. Hence her hatred for her mother. Hence too her rejection of her father, because the growing impulses of the young are away from the familiar constricting ageing nest, away from home and parents and the single self, towards young people not old, towards the outer world. The typical movement of the action in the fairy tale is the very opposite of solipsistic.

Much as she dislikes her mother-rival, the protagonist has also been fostered by her and continues to feel her guiding care. Hence the god-mother in Perrault's version, who is a displaced and therefore favourable mother-image. In the earliest, Chinese, version the daughter is as usual ill-treated by a stepmother, but in this case she has a tame fish who consoles her. The stepmother discovers this and kills it, but a man descends from the sky and tells her that if she collects the fish's bones and keeps them in her room she can pray to them and they will grant her whatever she wishes. These would seem to be displaced and therefore favourable mother- and father-images. In the earliest European version of the Cinderella story, 'La Gatta Cenerentola' ('The Hearth-cat') by Basile in the Italian *Pentamerone* (Day 1, Tale 6), first published in 1634, the heroine is given by her father a tree which she plants and which almost immediately grows to the size of a woman. This tree either is, or is the abode of, a fairy, who similarly gives the heroine everything she asks. The earliest reference to the Cinderella story in the British Isles is to a Scottish version mentioned in the sixteenth century, though Andrew Lang's nineteenth-century version is the earliest actually recorded. Here the heroine, so ill-treated as to have to wear a coat of rushes, hence called Rashin Coatie, has been given by her mother before she died a little red calf which now brings Rashin Coatie everything she wants. The step-mother, as in the Chinese tale, discovers this and kills the calf. The calf itself, though dead, tells her to gather up its bones and bury them under a stone, which done, the bones, like those of the fish in the Chinese tale, provide whatever Rashin Coatie asks. The Grimm brothers found a similar group of tales in Hesse in early nineteenth-century Germany and produced a composite called 'Aschen-puttel' (Ash-fool). In this the her-oine, ill-treated by her stepmother, is offered a gift by her father when he shall return from a journey, and instead of the fine clothes and jewels asked for by her stepsisters, asks for the first twig that pushes off her father's hat on his return from his journey. She plants it, prays to it, waters it with her tears, and a white bird comes to sit in it. This bird gives her all she asks for. The Opies remark that in most of the seven-hundred-odd Cinderella tales that have now been collected 'A friendly animal or a bird, rather than a fairy, is the creature who succours the orphan; and it becomes clear that this creature is the spirit or re-incarnation of her mother'. But the helper is never presented as spirit or re-incarnation at the literal level. One may divine the relationship: it is not expressed: it is a psychological symbol, not a literalistic proposition.

When the father, neglectful of his daughter as he is, provides the magic twig, or when, as in the Chinese version, it is a man descended from the sky who advises the heroine what to do with the fish bones, we may also see a variant father-image, working in conjunction with the variant mother-image, to provide help for the protagonist. Once again this is an important point. Both other people and helpful animals, magic trees, etc., are 'splits' of parent-figures and thus aid in the working out of the set of tensions set up in the family drama in an entirely convincing yet completely non-naturalistic way. The 'absurdity' of the story in terms of ordinary experience, like the 'absurdity' of games, from those so seriously engaged in by 'muddied oafs and flannelled fools' down to those of tiny children playing at 'mothers and fathers', enables real experience to be modelled and grasped at least as profoundly as by literalistic imitation – and more entertainingly.

The profoundly poetic images of sleeping, or at least sitting, on the ashes, and of identification by the slipper, are very good examples of how images of ordinary fully humanised artefacts, as opposed to the world of nature (animals, plants), can also act as reservoirs of significance, to be tapped by various tellings of the tale. The ashes appear to come in with European variants, though not as early as Basile's first, Italian account. We can see here how a story may 'grow' through the versions of various tellers, as what is implicit in the pre-verbal *données* is made more explicit and more powerful by the insight and artistic skill of some unknown teller. His developments in turn become incorporated in the story if the hearers are of sufficient intelligence to appreciate the new growth and to reproduce it. The fundamental *donnée* of the Cinderella story is not only that it starts at home, like every fairy tale, but that it concentrates very specially on the home both as the place of oppression and as the place of rescue, thus differing from the quest type of fairy tale, which is more suitable to a masculine protagonist. The heroine is oppressed at home, and though she goes out, in many versions, to the ball, she must in the later version be sought at home by the Prince who loves her. This is only implicit in the Chinese version. There is literally sharper *focus* (the Latin for 'hearth') in the Italian version, which as already noted bears the title 'The Heart-cat'. (Cats, for so long familiar domesticated creatures, responding to and expressing affection, yet egotistically seeking the cosiest place in the house, and equally egotistically retaining an untamable uncanny independence, are potent images in the folktale.) The Italian heroine is firmly relegated to the kitchen, the central place in the traditional house, for the heart of the house, the hearth-fire, is there. This restriction is an oppression. But the kitchen is, or at any rate traditionally was, a more natural place for a girl, and the oppression has something ambivalent about it. The ashes may signify death, but the hearth is also an image of the female role, of life, of central warmth, cooking, generative and regenerative powers. The heroine is not denatured by the oppression she endures, and the efficiency with which she performs her lowly duties in some versions is a mark of her virtue, and consequently of her worthiness of promotion.

But her plight is mainly a debasement. As the Opies point out, it is of the essence of the story that the heroine is *really* a princess, either literally in the story, or at least metaphorically, someone particularly good and beautiful who marries a prince. The metaphor of royalty with its profound psychological power is as powerful today, in a mainly republican West, as in archaic times. The power of parents over a child as easily represents royalty, as the child's own sense of inner worth is represented as being a prince or princess. In the case of Cinderella it is equally important, in the most effective realisations of the story, that the heroine should be accepted by the prince in her dirty, workaday clothes. There is a double truth to life here. First, inner worth is represented as independent of outward appearance. One of the fundamental rules of traditional tales of this type is that for most of the time appearance does *not* coincide with reality, and we have to work to make them come together, to constitute the happy ending, involving the full integration of conscious and un-conscious, successful maturation as an adult, and successful union with the beloved in the social (not merely personal) bond of marriage. Second, the acceptance by the Prince of the heroine in her apparent dirtiness gives the further truth that beauty is to some extent in the eye of the loving beholder. This is not in any neurotic possessive sense; unselfish love sees the true inner beauty, that is really there, in the beloved, though it is obscured by the misfortunes of life.

It is possible to see further symbolic power in the image of the hearth, as Bettelheim does. There is a sense in which the image of the hearth is also an image of the mother. In those versions which represent the father as wishing to marry the heroine (which can be taken as a reversed image of the heroine's unsuccessful attempt to capture the father), the hearth may symbolise a return to the mother, yet a mother who is inevitably, as time has passed, an unsatisfactory, even repellent, place of refuge, an image whose essential comforting power is no longer a support to the develop-ing protagonist, but a humiliation, as is the female role in general.

Even further significance may be traced (as by Bettelheim) in this potent image of the hearth, but the point has been made. The slipper is equally rich. The underlying element in the story is the need for an identification device. In some versions it is a ring, but a slipper is rather more individualising. The essential characteristics are its small size and the impossibility of stretching it. (This latter characteristic in the German version leads the stepsisters to perform gruesome amputations on their feet, revealed by bloodstains.) It should also be splendid. Thus in one version the slipper is of gold, which however small the heroine's feet would surely be almost as impractical as glass. The glass slipper is first found in Perrault's version and may be his invention. The argument that he mistook French *vair* for *verre* is an irrelevance which reveals a desire for naturalism totally inappropriate to the story. A fur slipper might be more comfortable to dance in but would be less appropriate as a recognition symbol for a paradoxically naturalistic reason; it would stretch. Perrault's *glass* slipper is a stroke of genius. A rich, strange material for what is after all an item of dress procured by magic; rigidly unstretchable; and trans-parent – no good cutting off your toes or heel to make it fit. The use of the slipper in the story to identify the heroine as bride to the bridegroom would prove that it is an effective sexual erotic image here, were there no other references elsewhere to the symbolic use of shoes in such contexts. In fact there is even nowadays a range of 'folkloric' uses of or reference to shoes, which can be seen to be sexual or erotic symbols, from people throwing old shoes at the departure of a newly married couple to the fantasy (as surely it must be?) of drinking champagne out of actresses' shoes at wild theatrical parties. An interesting folktale analogue is noted by Bettelheim. An Egyptian tale two thousand years old tells how an eagle snatched up the sandal of the beautiful courtesan Rhodope and dropped it on the Pharaoh. He was so attracted that he had the whole of Egypt searched for the owner, so that he could marry her. When the Prince in the Cinderella story obtains her slipper, he symbolically obtains her, but only potentially. He has to hand her back to herself before she can give herself up to him. Her loss of the slipper may be said to symbolise her willingness to give herself to him, though the loss is accidental. It is once again important to note that this is a girl's story, and though in many versions she makes strongly positive efforts to go to the ball she cannot, in her traditional female role, directly seek out her man. She has to put herself in the way of being sought.

It would be possible to follow through the implications of symbolic meaning of the shoe in much greater detail. This has been done in Freudian detail by Bettelheim, elaborating the significance of the slipper as symbolic of both female and male sexual organs, and symbolic of the allaying of sexual anxieties in the loving relationship between heroine and her beloved as they come to maturity. Bettelheim's interpretation is interesting and may be valid, though the problem always with such elaboration is to know how it could be proved not to be so; how testable it is, even if found detestable. Leaving such details aside, the main point about the symbolic nature of the story, and what it symbolises, must be beyond debate. A story like that of Cinderella is not easily exhausted in its significances and I make no attempt to discuss them all. It is equally plain that the methods of interpretation of such a story must take into account its non-mimetic qualities and proceed accordingly.

IV

A very similar story, or version of a group of similar stories, is usually translated as *Catskin*, and comprises Cox's second main group. In this story a beautiful Queen dies and on her deathbed asks the King only to marry again one as beautiful as herself, and with golden hair like hers. The King can find no one as beautiful as his own daughter. She and his courtiers are shocked at his proposal to marry her. In order to make it seem possible she demands three dresses before she shall be married, one of gold like the sun, one of silver like the moon, one sparkling as the stars; and she also wants a cloak of a thousand different furs. When the King provides them she flees secretly by night, taking some jewels and the dresses, wrapped in the cloak, and smearing her hands and face with soot as a disguise. Very soon discovered by another King, she becomes his kitchen-maid and lives a miserable life. He then holds three feasts. As the reader will easily guess (for we all know the rules of these stories) the disguised kitchen-maid contrives both to cook him delicious soups and mysteriously to appear at the feasts successively in the sun, moon and star dresses. In the soups she has each time thrown one of her jewels, which has puzzled the King very much. At the third feast she has been late in secretly departing and has had no time to take off her dress and dirty herself properly before answering the King's usual enquiry about the superb quality of the soup and the splendour of the jewel. She has had time only to throw over her dress the fur cloak (= the cat-skin, in the translation). She has inadvertently left one of her fingers white and clean. Thus she is recognised, and marries the King.

The story is not so popular as *Cinderella*, as Wilson notes.[4] In her view the story is not sufficiently 'disguised'; the heroine's suppressed wish to marry her father presented by the familiar process of reversal (attributing to the other the unacceptable desire that one feels oneself) is too plain, too clearly symbolises her (and our) mixed feelings for, and ambivalent valuation of, the self. This is perhaps to take too psychoanalytical a criterion. From the literary point of view we may say that though the story has some fine images and an interesting story, it is certainly not as rich as the main *Cinderella* group. The image of the dresses, uniting natural imagery with human artefact, expressing profound inter-relationships of humanity and nature, is one of the finest things, though not so intimately related to the essential schema of the story as Cinderella's ashes. More intrinsic to the story is the splendour of the dresses as related to her dirtiness, which clearly symbolises her, and our, mixed feelings for, and ambivalent valuation of, the self. That she acts more positively than Cinderella, both in escaping from the home and in winning a husband, shows how a basic theme (transition, obtaining a mate) can be validly varied. Perhaps the heroine is more modern, less archetypal because she is so positive. But the story is less strong than the main *Cinderella* group chiefly because though the transference from father to equal, vertical to lateral relationship, is clearly made, the actual conduct of the story is too simple, too much like wish-fulfilment. There is no range of varying parent-figures. The ambivalence of the father-image is not recognised, and the complete absence of mother-figures, good and bad, also reduces the dramatic play. Not enough of the potential variety and complexities of the family drama is deployed. The story is too self-centred. Although attractive and within limits inventive, it is an interesting example of a relatively weaker artistic achievement as a *story*. Whether we regard it at the level of the verbal realisation, or at some pre-verbal level of story-structure, it is not, though very good in some ways, in itself a sufficiently rich and complex pattern to do full justice to the complexity of the inherent situation. We see from this that the story-structure in itself, hard to formulate as it is, existing at several different levels, is an imaginative artefact in theory distinguishable from the basic underlying life-situation. This is why an examination of story-structures in themselves and as they relate to the underlying situation is not reductive, but a valid act of a general literary criticism.

V

The story now so well known as *Snow-White and the Seven Dwarves* through Disney's film is one of a cluster of stories also analogous, though in a remoter way, with *Cinderella*. The modern version descends from the Grimm collection, but some interesting similarities occur in a version in the *Pentamerone* (Day 2, Tale 8) of 1634. In the *Pentamerone* the heroine dies, aged seven, through having a comb stuck in her head. She is placed in a crystal coffin, but continues to grow normally, as fortunately does the coffin (an interesting example of 'rationalisation' which takes the child's age into account when considering her marriage). She is discovered by her aunt, who hates her on the supposition that she is having an affair with her uncle. An aunt is as good a mother-image as a stepmother, and an uncle, as Hamlet knows, is always liable to be an uncle-father in this numerically small world of the family drama. So we have here an example of only slightly displaced mother-image hostility related to jealousy of the father by the mother-image.

The first English version of the story of Snow-White is *Snow-Drop* of 1823. Once again the heroine's mother is dead, the King her father marries again, and thus a wicked stepmother appears. She is wildly jealous of Snow-Drop's beauty – a motif not explored in the *Cinderella* or *Catskin* stories. As so often in traditional tales the servant deputed to murder the child cannot bring himself to do so but abandons her in the forest (another deep image of our early sense of abandonment by a not necessarily unkind parent, a feeling all too often repeated, *mutatis mutandis*, throughout our lives, when we are thrown back on our own resources, left to carry out the quest on our own).

As everyone knows, Snow-Drop finds the house of seven dwarves who dig for gold in the mountains. They foster her, and she does the housekeeping. No question about the female role here! Once again the centrality of the image of the home in these stories is apparent. The protagonist is driven out of or wants to leave home, for very good reason, and that is a fundamental *donnée*. It symbolises the need to grow up and the play of forces around the need. But the protagonist in these stories – more obviously when a girl – also has to stay at home, because there (though we do not believe it when young) is where the action is. In our end is our beginning, and we travel in order to find our starting place.

The Queen renews her assaults on Snow-Drop (this is *home*, after all), and at the third (of course) attempt appears to succeed by tricking her into eating a poisoned apple. Snow-Drop, found apparently dead, is laid in a glass coffin. Then a Prince appears who falls in love with her although she is dead. He wishes to take away her body in its coffin. The piece of poisoned apple falls out of her mouth with the movement, she recovers, and the Prince marries her.

The 'Snow-Drop' version makes no mention of the father-image at all, and to that extent the drama is less complex. We are left with the Queen's jealousy of Snow-Drop's beauty, but that is sufficient index of more complex emotions. There is no compensating good mother-image, either, but the seven dwarves represent sibling solidarity against the parent, which all children in large families (and all children who meet others of their own age) recognise as easily as they recognise sibling rivalry. Sibling solidarity is the basis of much comradeship in life generally. The rule in fairy tales is that siblings are friendly when of the opposite sex, hostile when of the same sex (a rule which is rather different in the related set of stories found in ballads, where we have jealous brothers; the only exceptions in fairy tales seem to be 'split' protagonists mentioned later). The dwarves, perhaps because they are obviously older than Snow-Drop, protect her, and presumably dislike housework, may also be taken, within the battle-ground of home, as representatives, much displaced, of the father-figure. They dig for gold – that is, they work for money, to keep things going (this being taken for granted to be the way with fathers), while young princes by their nature do not have to work. Perhaps also the dwarves represent something of the good mother-image, but their helplessness at housework and in succouring Snow-Drop is more like that of fathers. Good mother-images are usually positively helpful, as in *Cinderella*.

The dwarves cannot wake Snow-Drop. Only the Prince, equal in age, and of the opposite sex, who loves her, not as the dwarves do, but (as they said in the Middle Ages) with love *paramour*, with love that *is* love, i.e. sexual love, can awaken her. The story thus is about the awakening of the protagonist to adult life and marriage which the hostile mother-image has been trying to prevent. The 'mother' would like to keep her little girl always a little girl, out of the way. But the dynamics of growth are irresistible. The mother-image is usually abandoned without a thought at the end of a tale, whether good or bad, as in *Cinderella*. The German version of *Snow-White* has a vein of characteristic violence in making her more savage during the story and in exacting a correspondingly cruel punishment. Slippers of iron are heated until red hot and the Queen is made to put them on and dance until she dies. No doubt the lives of eighteenth-century German peasants were harsh enough to make them envisage savage pains; and the whole German artistic tradition has a marked vein of outstanding brutality from the Middle Ages onwards: but the extravagance of the punishment preserves it from too literalistic an effect. It reveals the passionate hatred of the mother-figure conjured up in this story, and in view of the symbolism of slippers invoked in the story of Cinderella we may feel in the imagery of dancing in red-hot iron shoes something of the powerful sexual feelings which lie beneath the story of Snow-White. The Queen's punishment grotesquely represents, perhaps, the pains of frustrating natural sexual growth. Looking at the story as a whole from a completely internalised point of view as an image of the whole mind we may also say that the tensions in it also partly represent (in so far as the Queen's hostility represents the protagonist's own attitude to self) a reluctance to grow up, a desire to stay as a child. But the dominant wish ultimately is to grow up.

VI

A similar set of motifs is found in the story of Sleeping Beauty, a fairy tale which actually has a fairy in it, though almost certainly she is an invention of Perrault's. The essential motif is again an ancient one. The heroine is put into an apparently unending sleep by a parent-figure (the ill-tempered Fairy at the christening) and surrounded by an apparently impenetrable barrier. Yet a hero will come, known to be the hero by the fact that he penetrates the barrier. He loves, frees and marries the heroine. The focus is on the awakening to adult life from what has become the stultification of the home, though the motifs of father's possessiveness and mother's jealousy are either suppressed or considerably displaced. One of the earliest and most powerful versions is the story of Brunhilda in the ancient Germanic Volsunga Saga, which has had various re-handlings down to Wagner. The story also occurs in the fourteenth-century French romance *Perceforest* and in Basile's *Pentamerone* (Day 5, Tale 5) of 1634. Perrault in his turn must have selected those elements he wished to use from a popular tale, and Perrault's version translated by Samber was the first to be recorded in English. The disgruntled old Fairy whose 'gift' was that the newly born Princess should pierce her finger on a spindle and die, and the young Fairy, whose gift was to mitigate death to a hundred years' sleep, must be a rationalising device of Perrault. His genius here is quite in keeping with the general type of narration and rationalisation that characterise these stories, despite his veneer of whimsical Neoclassical naturalism. It is a version of an ancient motif. In *Perceforest* a disgruntled goddess, Themis, casts the spell, though its force is not known by the characters. In the *Pentamerone* the heroine's father is warned at her birth that peril will come to his daughter from a splinter in some flax, so that she is kept from knowledge of spinning (traditionally a fundamental female activity). When she is grown up an old woman, whose motive is not accounted for, passing by, shows her how to spin; a splinter of flax pierces her finger, and she dies. These three versions are an excellent example of the predominance of event in this kind of story. The individual circumstance and the actual person who brings about the event are secondary to the event itself, which is crucial to the story. The event, like the story, exists at a pre-verbal stage. The verbal realisation will localise the story according to the taste and fancy of individual teller and audience. Though the event already exists in the story, a particular teller may devise a character in quite realistic terms with quite realistic motives in order to activate the necessary event. Separate tellers may devise a number of different types of character and motive to suit the event, which itself may be varied provided it keeps its inherent character in relation to the total action. Perrault invents a whole rigmarole about the gifts of the fairies, the accidental omission of an invitation to the touchy old Fairy, her malice, the young Fairy's hiding behind the curtains to overhear the old Fairy's curse, and her generous mitigation. He puts the whole business into the domestic family setting of a quarrel in a large upper-class family in seventeenth-century France, as far as surface narration goes, and does it very well. We can all still recognise querulous old ladies at family gatherings. Perrault's verbal realisation with its realism is exactly the same kind of process that Chaucer and Shakespeare follow when they re-handle traditional tales, and with exactly the same implications for our understanding of motives and characters in action. Event precedes character. Motives etc. are *post facto* rationalisations. Characters do not (as in the theory of the modern novel) generate actions. From the point of view of the story, events generate characters. That is to say, the essence of the event and its place in the story is given, while the teller may vary the 'accidentals' of incident, activating character, and setting.

The achievement of Perrault (and of other successful writers) comes in the marriage of characters to the given event, and in making sure that it is reasonably in keeping, though the potential range of invented character is always very wide. In this particular instance it is plain that the goddess, or old woman, or disgruntled Fairy, is a symbol for a hostile mother-figure. She has perhaps evolved (doubtless through many re-tellings) from earlier versions in which, as in the Volsunga Saga, it is the father who has put his daughter as it were into cold storage – an ambivalent act, both jealous and preservative. From the point of view of the protagonist the age-long sleep must be seen as the parental desire to stop her growing up.

Perrault rationalises the big sleep in ways that need not detain us, but the effect is the same: a great barrier of the wild wood grows up around the sleeping beauty, which only the Prince can pass through, which in Perrault's version he easily does, thus causing the Princess to wake. They immediately fall in love with each other. In *Perceforest* and the *Pentamerone*, when the visiting Prince or King discovers the sleeping girl, being unable to waken her, he nevertheless has sexual intercourse with her – this is an earlier, rougher, more aristocratic world! Yet it would seem to be wrong to use for this the Opies' phrase, 'rapes her', since that would imply a violence on his part, and a reluctance on hers, for neither of which does there seem to be any evidence.

In Perrault's version, translated by Samber as *The Sleeping Beauty in the Wood* (1729), the Prince immediately marries the Princess and they go to bed together the same night. He does not proclaim their marriage but continues to visit her and after two years they have two children. In Basile's *Pentamerone* version the King who has not awakened the protagonist does not re-visit her because he is married already and she bears twins in her sleep. Eventually one of these awakes her by sucking her finger and drawing the splinter.

The fundamental image here, so differently realised and rationalised by Perrault and Basile, seems to be concerned with the inadequacy on the part of the heroine to respond positively to sexuality. The heroine is emotionally passive, and perhaps a reason is that so far there has been an inadequate transference of feeling from father to lover. But it is also because the hostile mother-figure has not so far been sufficiently neutralised.

An unusual feature of this story is the birth of children to the protagonist. It associates the story with such tales as those of Patient Griselda (Chaucer's *Clerk's Tale*) and of Constance (Chaucer's *Man of Law's Tale*), where children are similarly aspects of the heroine's vulnerability, extensions of her, whereby a hostile mother- or father-figure can further persecute her; or to put it the other way round, whereby the protagonist can further represent both her innocence and determination to be a woman, and further blacken the image of the mother.

In Perrault's version the Prince eventually succeeds to the throne and as King brings in his bride as Queen, together with their two children. This could be the end of the tale, and indeed the remarkable image of the magic sleep and wood which has dominated it so far has now been fully deployed. There is however a second stage or movement whereby a further variation of the same family drama is played out and brought to a more definite conclusion. The variation here interestingly has effectively nothing to do with the husband-image. It is a straightforward battle with the mother-image, in the form of the King's mother, the heroine's mother-in-law. It turns out that she is an ogress. Mothers-in-law in traditional stories have as bad an image as stepmothers. And though we are here dealing with the displacements, 'splits', projections, reversals, etc., of psychological patterns, that does not by any means preclude, rather it *includes*, the easily observed facts of ordinary life, that stepmothers often are harsh, or are felt to be, and that mothers-in-law and daughters-in-law do, for obvious reasons, often find it difficult to get on together. Stepfathers to a much less degree (though we remember David Copperfield's) and fathers-in-law hardly ever achieve the same bad eminence, perhaps because being normally older men, their chief ground of action is outside the home. While men may dominate the household in their prime, they have nothing to do in the house and the advent of younger men traditionally displaces them without more ado. Women are (or were) more important to the home, and older women are made of sterner stuff than older men. (Thus time brings in his revenges.) In traditional societies the older the woman the more dominant she is.

Sleeping Beauty's mother-in-law has outlived her husband, like so many women, and in her son's absence proposes to eat first her two grandchildren and then Sleeping Beauty herself. The grandmother is but an extension of the mother-image, and the doubling of the image here re-inforces the image of fierce possessiveness, itself given special power as cannibalism. Once again all are saved by a kindly servant, that minor 'split' representing a basic confidence in the real kindness and goodness of the mother or, in other stories, of the tyrannous husband. When the King returns the ogress-mother-in-law is so enraged that she hurls herself into the tub of horrible creatures into which she had proposed to throw her just-discovered daughter-in-law and grandchildren. Evil destroys itself.

The grandmother is an obvious mother-image, just as the grandfather may be an extension of the father. Grandmothers need not always be bad, though the strongly ambivalent association of grandmother/wolf in *Little Red Riding-Hood* shows that they should be treated with caution. In the version in the *Pentamerone* the persecuting lady who wishes to kill the heroine's children is motivated by being the King's wife, the heroine being his mistress. No doubt we have here plenty of echoes direct from ordinary life in sixteenth-century Italian courts. But the fact that she has the children turned into a rich stew for the King to eat shows that we are primarily in the passionate world of the family drama to which also the Classical Greek myth of the Thyestean feast belongs. Unlike that characteristically gruesome Classical tale, the *Pentamerone* has also a kind-hearted servant who substitutes animals for the children, but we can be fairly certain here too that in the person of the excessively indignant wife we have a displaced mother-image. The rivalry between mother and daughter for the King is thus expressed, but we may well feel in this version that the transference of heroine's feeling from father to lover, though effective enough in the end, is somewhat clumsily managed in the pattern of the story. Effective as is the image of eating up the children, whereby both love and hate are expressed with symbolic richness and economy, it needs more elaborate artistic formulation to be fully effective; but it is a motif which will crop up again.

VII

In the tales so far discussed the protagonist has been relatively passive. Three other tales show a more positive heroine and illustrate different aspects of the central complex. I do not offer anything approaching full analyses. *The Frog Prince* has been known in the British Isles from the sixteenth century. It involves a girl going to a well and being either helped or hindered by a frog (an interesting example of how the given event may be varied). In payment for a safe return she promises to marry the monster. To her consternation he turns up in the evening and insists on going to bed with her. It is plain in the earlier versions that they have sexual intercourse. The frog then instructs the girl to chop off his head, and he turns out to be a handsome Prince. The earliest full text in English is adapted from the Grimms' collection, and somewhat prettified. It is however a thoroughly charming version, and there is a further change of the event of the original meeting which is not unsuccessful. Instead of going to the well for the mundane necessity of fetching water (woman's role) the heroine is a young Princess who loses her golden ball in the well. A richer, more leisured milieu than a peasant life is envisaged. And the gold ball may well symbolise *joie-de-vivre*, lost as the child matures, she does not know how or why. The frog returns it to her. The story is obviously about love and especially sex. The relationship with the frog symbolises the fear of sex, slimy, monstrous, nasty. It has to be redeemed by love, and love is shown by doing what the lover wants, even to metaphorically chopping off his head. When loved the ugly one becomes beautiful. The juxtaposition of sexual intercourse and chopping off the head of the male partner is found elsewhere. (Not least, in an interesting variant, in *Sir Gawain and the Green Knight*. Sexual intercourse for a man is 'like' having his head chopped off.) The comparison and symbolism seem obvious, and not without wit or even delicacy. The context determines whether it is a happy or unhappy image. In this tale it is obviously happy. This may be because the tale is told from the point of view of a female protagonist. The acceptance of love, and the giving of love, is a way of taming male sexual aggression, though admittedly a notably female-pacifist solution – let it happen, don't resent it, love him who does it, and all will be well. It could not be a traditional masculine attitude. From an internalised point of view the frog represents those sexual desires in oneself that seem nasty and aggressive. Accepted and loved they became manageable. In this tale there is a complete lack of father- and mother-images, with a consequent lack of complexity and power, but it still validly concentrates on the essential moment of passage from childhood to adult sexual experience of a responsible kind. The heroine has to take positive and repellent actions, in both accepting and apparently murdering the lover. The ambivalence here is directed towards the partner. If one wishes to insist that some sort of parent-image cannot be escaped, one would have to argue that the frog, who is a crucial helper of the pro-tagonist, represents either Mother (as helpful animal) or, more likely, Father (as protective animal and supplier of necessities). Then the heroine has to kill the parent-image in order to transfer her feelings to the lover. But this does not 'feel' right, even though it does not distort the essential pattern. Nor is it needed to solve any problems in the story. There simply are situations where parental relationships are not a complication, in folktale as in literature or life.

VIII

Beauty and the Beast is described by the Opies as 'The most symbolic of the fairy tales after Cinderella and the most intellectually satisfying' (p. 137). It is an example of the 'beast-marriage' or 'animal groom' story which is found all over the world, and is elaborately analysed by Bettelheim. Among its notable analogues is *Cupid and Psyche*. I follow the version of

1811 printed by the Opies. There are many traditional motifs. There is, for example, a variant of the tyrannous or lecherous father, though in this version he is neither. He has fallen into the hands of Beast, who owns a magic castle where the father has been by accident benighted. The father takes a rose which is all his modest youngest daughter has asked him to bring back. For this Beast threatens to kill him, unless he will give up his youngest daughter to him. This is analogous to the ancient and popular motif of Jephtha's daughter, when a father, in order to save his own life, promises to sacrifice the first living being to greet him on his return home, thinking it will be a dog, but being tragically met by his loving daughter. The rose is analogous to the twig in a version of the Cinderella story. In a dream of Beauty's a lady comes to comfort her, who later turns up again as a good Fairy, and may be interpreted as a 'split' of the mother-image. The father's sorrow is well emphasised, but Beauty is determined to do her duty and go to Beast. She also is well supplied with envious and spiteful sisters, and genial brothers, the usual sibling-pattern. The story tells how she comes in the end to love Beast, and when she marries him he turns out to be a lovely Prince, not only rich but extremely good-natured and intelligent.

This is a charming story, though not very powerfully if vividly realised in English. The poetic images are in no complex relation to each other. The theme deserves notice as underlying a good many popular novels and stories; there are strong touches of Beast in both Mr. Darcy in *Pride and Prejudice* and Mr. Rochester in *Jane Eyre*. The story illustrates the willingness of the heroine to go out and get her man, once given an opportunity, as do the heroines of *Pride and Prejudice* and *Jane Eyre*. Such tensions of the family drama as may activate the story are very deeply entrenched.

IX

One fairy tale with a female protagonist deserves mention because of its powerful but baffling structure. This is *Bluebeard*. In summary the heroine in Samber's 1729 translation of Perrault marries a dubious gentleman, Bluebeard, who goes away leaving her several keys to all his riches and the key to a little room which she is absolutely forbidden to open. She naturally opens it. The breaking of legitimate prohibitions, leading to suffering but eventually a fuller life, is one of the most frequent and potent elements of fairy tales. (*Felix culpa!*) The heroine discovers the room to be full of blood and the corpses of previous wives. She drops the key, and the blood upon it is impossible to clean. On his return her husband for this reason discovers that she has opened the room and prepares to kill her. She manages however to spin out the moments before death until her brothers turn up and kill Bluebeard. She inherits his estate and with his wealth marries a very honest gentleman.

I quote this because the power of the separate images seems greater than that of the story as such. It is a cluster of traditional elements, but what is the whole story about? The analogue in the Grimms' collection makes the husband a wizard who tests (and murders) successive wives until the third daughter of a poor man successfully resists him and thus gains power over him. Other analogues are similar to the story known as 'The Robber Bridegroom' which is widespread. In this a bride-to-be discovers the crimes of her bridegroom and recites them at the wedding feast to the repeated formulas of denial by the groom, until his eventual unmasking and death. These stories must be borne in mind beside those of the emerging adult, of the successful passage, and its happy ending of love and marriage. They have happy endings indeed, but the happiness consists in *rejecting* marriage as the central theme. Perhaps they are rejections of marriage when it is without love. They have little to do with parent-figures, and there seems no reason to suppose that the rejected bridegroom or husband is in any way a father-figure. They are stories of triumph over the would-be mate.

They are stories of escape from death, rather than, it would seem, stories about sex. Although in this imaginative world sex and death are closely allied, the major theme of the triumph over death, prime subject of religious myth as well as folktale, would need a book different from this one. In *Bluebeard* the heroine's marriage seems to symbolise the knowledge of death. All previous wives have opened the door to the little room. Women's curiosity is traditional. The heroine is meant to die. To that extent the story is about the recognition of death. Death is the horrible little room behind all images of wealth and splendour. Death itself is so to speak an absolute prohibition that we have to break. We all have to open the door of the little room, where our predecessors have gone. Why then should the heroine *not* die, as her predecessors did? She undergoes no resurrection like Snow-White and others. She survives because she keeps her wits about her and the family (her brothers) save her. In this rather minor respect, far from wishing to escape from the family she is rescued by it. This is not very strong at the story level, not up to the horrifying yet irresistible disclosure. The story survives on this one image, and perhaps on the astonishing name of the villain – but why *Blue*-beard?

X

After this reminder that not all fairy tales are single-minded about the central issues of our developing lives, it is time to turn to other variants which present other aspects. In the symbolic world of the fairy tale female protagonists are able to exert as potent a spell as male, although they live in a traditionally masculine-dominated society, because fairy tales operate at a level less dominated by the conscious masculine intellect. Heroines more obviously sort out their problems at home. Heroes have a greater need to get away from home, in appearance, while at the same time dealing with the problems which actually arise in the home. The story of *Hans and the Cat* illustrates this. The version I shall use as it happens came to me through oral delivery, if not tradition, and is not among *The Classic Fairy Tales*. I had a small class of undergraduates with whom I conducted some experiments in oral tradition. One was to repeat, from week to week, the same story, without relying on anything but memory, so that we could trace (by the use of a tape-recorder) the kind of changes that tend to take place. The situation was artificial, for it was not a 'natural' group as determined by relationship or long acquaintance and common place of origin, and the dreary class-room setting was imaginatively less stimulating than an evening relaxing with friends with stories for entertainment, after a day of hard physical work. Nevertheless we learnt something about the narrative process. Not least interesting, having regard to the age of the group, was the story chosen, admittedly from traditional tales, but not determined by me. The undergraduates, men and women, responded equally to the story, though their analytical intelligence and memories were too good for major narrative variants to emerge.

The story, which I abbreviate, is of an old miller who has no wife or children but three apprentices. He wishes to retire and tells his apprentices that he will give the mill to the one who brings him back the best horse, and who will look after him for the rest of his life. Hans, the youngest, is stupid and the two elder ones treat him with contempt. All three set off together, and at nightfall find a cave where they sleep. In the morning the two elder ones leave Hans sleeping and go off on their own. Hans wakes up and wanders about rather worried in a forest. He meets a tabby cat who promises him the best horse he has seen if he will serve her for seven years. She takes him to her castle, where all the people are cats. They feast him, then send him off to bed, with servant cats to light the candle for him, undress him etc., and in the morning to dress him, wash his face (and a cat to dry it with her tail) etc. He serves for seven years, chopping wood with a silver axe and silver saw, reaping with a silver scythe and golden whet-stone. After this time, which seems no more than six months to him, it occurs to him that he should get his horse and go. The tabby cat asks him as a favour to build a little house for her, which when finished he finds contains twelve splendid horses, one of which is to be his.

All this time he has had no change of clothes, so when he returns to the miller in dirty clothes which are far too small for him, the two other apprentices who have already returned laugh at him, though each has brought back a very poor horse. Hans is made to eat outside and sleep in the goose-house. But next morning a beautiful Princess turns up; she is the tabby cat transformed. She provides Hans with fine clothes, and a beautiful horse for the miller, but Hans will not be left to look after the mill, for the Princess carries him off and marries him, and they live in the little house Hans had built, now turned into a beautiful palace.

The minor variants of the re-telling of this story to some extent illustrated how the verbal realisation may vary, and may sometimes explore the potentialities of the pre-verbal story-structure. For example in one realisation the miller became a tailor. This made the horse less satisfactory because a tailor has presumably less use for a horse than a miller. On the other hand it allowed for a witty piece of rationalisation when Hans turned up in his old clothes, for he was not recognised, on the grounds that a tailor's apprentice could not be so ragged. With all the variants the story remained essentially unchanged.

It is obviously a story about growing up. Apprentices are slightly displaced versions of sons. The central character is as usual the third and youngest son. The story is seen entirely through his eyes. The elder apprentices for example (as it were siblings of the same sex and consequently rivals) disappear and appear entirely on the time-scale of Hans. Numbers are conventional – three boys, seven years, twelve horses. The self-consciousness about clothes is familiar when we are young, and the sense of smallness of clothes is apposite to the growing child. (The image is turned to powerfully pathetic use by Dickens with Smike in *Nicholas Nickleby*.) The hero has to, and wants to, leave home and prove himself. But the enchanted castle of the tabby cat is clearly a displaced image of home and the authoritative though genial tabby cat is equally clearly a mother-image. The way Hans is looked after on arrival at her castle is particularly revealing. The story is partly an image of the developing youth, who must work and provide for himself and get his own house, away from the parental home which is so firmly rejected at the end of the story; and partly an image that reveals an infantile stage without development, in that the protagonist is set up and looked after at home with no one else but his transformed Mummy. The transformation is sufficient for the ideal not to be boring (living with the same old woman the rest of his life), and to show that the protagonist knows what he really wants, but is inadequate in that the story-structure has not articulated any devices whereby the protagonist *really* reaches outside the family-structure to find a genuinely new person as mate, though he has indeed responded to the need for hard work in the adult world.

Although there can be no doubt that this story centres on the nuclear family-structure it is delightfully free from generational conflict. The father- and mother-images are not oppressive but helpful, and even the siblings are not particularly obstructive. On the other hand the notable lack of tensions may be complementary to the absence of desire really to get away. Suppose the tabby cat had had a rival!

XI

The most famous cat, and helpful animal, in all folktales, let alone fairy tales, is Puss in Boots. In Europe the story is recorded as early as the

Italian Straparola's *Piacevoli notti*, 1553, though the splendid and significant detail of the *booted* cat appears to have been Perrault's invention – when we remember Cinderella's glass slipper we may feel that he was strong on footwear. But it is a story with world-wide analogues, and has even been collected in our day in oral form.[5] It is worth noticing that a number of oral versions have a heroine as protagonist, which illustrates the general human appeal of so much folktale and fairy tale, and the fact that we can usually identify equally with a male or female protagonist. Other versions have a different helpful animal, or a grateful dead man. In others the cat is killed at the end, which has interesting implications. These variants do not affect the basic structure.

In Perrault's witty version, translated by Samber in 1729, a miller has died and has left his third and youngest son only his cat, while the two elder sons are better provided for. Never mind, says the cat, 'you have nothing else to do, but to give me a bag and get a pair of boots made for me, that I may scamper through the dirt and brambles . . . '. This is a nice detail of rationalisation for the cat's boots, but is of course entirely superficial, while no attempt is made (rightly) to account for the apparently hitherto unnoticed fact that the cat can speak.

Puss, once booted, catches a series of tasty animals which he sends to the King in the name of 'the Marquis of Carabas'. I omit with regret the repetitions which are so important a part of the telling of a traditional tale. At last the cat takes the 'Marquis' to bathe and as the King passes by shouts that his master is drowning. When he is rescued, Puss claims that thieves have run off with his master's clothes. The King clothes him splendidly. By another famous trick the cat convinces the King that the Marquis owns vast properties. The Marquis and cat then come to a castle owned by an ogre who can change his shape but is not remarkable for his intelligence, it being a rule of folktale that ogres are stupid, as fathers may care to note. The ogre changes to a lion and frightens the cat on to the roof, where his boots cause him much difficulty (another delightfully witty rationalisation, with important if unconscious symbolic effect). Puss then taunts the ogre, challenging him to become a mouse. The stupid ogre boastfully asserts his power by changing into a mouse, upon which the cat pounces on him and eats him, which is a variant of a well-known folktale motif. The King arrives and since the Marquis claims he owns the castle, is sufficiently pleased for him to marry his daughter.

This traditional story, an amusing and interesting variant on a by now obvious theme, using traditional and familiar motifs and methods, has since the nineteenth century increasingly come to be regarded as immoral because of the deceitful tricks employed by the cat to promote his master's welfare. Whereas it is quite sensible, though denied by Neoclassical theory, to recognise that good literature may be thoroughly immoral, the absence of the realistic naturalism and of the didacticism required by Neoclassical theory of literature makes the immorality of a folktale more a wryly comic observation about what people are like than a lesson to be learnt and followed. Literature, when it is self-evidently an 'absurd'

43

fiction, allows us to act out in displaced fantasy what we certainly would not allow ourselves to do in fact. We can accept in ourselves something of our own evil, or at any rate, anti-social, impulses, without (in a decent society and with a well-ordered personal constitution) approving them. The nature of fairy tales is that they are little concerned with objective social conditions in the adult world, except in so far as such conditions are an implicit fact of life. They are concerned with working out dramatic models, not naturalistic imitations, 'plays' in both senses of the word, by which the protagonist as emergent individual can sort out the psychic conflicts which are the product of his internal drives and responses to his objective experience.

The story as usual images a successful passage into established adult life with home and wife. The protagonist is on the brink of maturity, free of parents in an independence that is sought after but nevertheless brings anxiety. Father is dead, or at any rate, is no help, and is not wanted, and the protagonist has the usual touch of resentment at parents who do what he really wants them to do, that is, leave him alone. The story has several father-figures. Besides the miller, there are the King and the ogre. We recognise them as father-figures because they are older, bigger, more powerful than the hero, and though he is in opposition to them, it is their function to clothe him and provide him with money and property. The father-figure must not only provide for the protagonist; he must also be neutralised, tricked and eventually in his threatening aspect killed, which he can now be because he is shown to be both stupid and 'really' small. He is found to be not nearly so lion-like, or ogre-like, as he appears, but after all only a mouse, traditional image of timidity.

The cat is best interpreted as a mother-image, even though masculine, since cats have an ineradicably domestic association. Sons accept help from mothers much more easily than from their rival-fathers. Mothers also tend to exert less natural authority over sons. It is a normal rule of fairy tales that only daughters, not sons, have *cruel* mother-figures. The mother-image's characteristic threat to the male protagonist is of excessive tenderness if she is a superior figure, while if helpful she is an animal. (Another rule is that *male* protagonists do not have good Fairy god-mothers.) At another level the cat can be seen to be an aspect of the protagonist himself – his cunning, unscrupulous, ambitious determination to succeed against all the odds. He rightly deplores the unscrupulous means he takes, but his 'true' self is not really unscrupulous, it is only the 'cat', ambitious mother-image, ambitious alternative-self-image, who does all these dubious things. Why booted? The boots emphasise not only the fantastic and absurd element of the story, amusing and silly enough to open a gateway through our serious moralistic literalism; they also denote the fundamentally 'human' quality of the cat. What real cat needs boots to go through the bramble and dirt? What real cat ever found difficulty in passing over the roofs, traditional habitat of cats – but the only place where the ever-resourceful Puss in Boots finds himself in a difficulty. The literal comedy of this touch adds to its symbolic effectiveness. Perhaps one might also feel that the boots, normally a male characteristic, and the masculine sex attributed to Puss in Boots in Perrault's version and the title The Master Cat, allow him also to share something of the aura of a father-figure, deploying the helpful not oppressive aspects of the father-image.

In some analogues the cat is killed. In Straparola's version he only pretends to die, and is then so incensed to overhear expressed the unregretful ingratitude of the hero that he rushes away never to be seen again. This is as suitable a dismissal as any for a parent-figure, and also a symbolic rejection of trickery. In Perrault's version the cat becomes a great lord, but no gratitude (or ingratitude) is explicit, and the tale ends there. In other versions the cat's head is cut off and he returns to his original form as a Prince. The cat may then be seen to express not only the protagonist's own resourcefulness but also his sense of his own true splendour. But this last variant looks like the employment of a well-recognised motif rather inappropriate to the inherent structure of the tale.

Some complexity of attitude towards parent-figures is developed in this amusing story, which also has a refreshingly ingenious ambivalence towards the strivings of the self. A still richer evocation of more aspects of the great inner complex is provided by *Jack and the Beanstalk*.

XII

Jack and the Beanstalk is one of a well-known group of tales[6] with many common motifs, though the magic beanstalk as an introductory episode appears to be an English invention still found only in British and American versions. There are some close analogues and some puzzles about the historical evolution of the tale, but in the present literary study we may for the moment remain with the principle that a version is adequate to itself and begin with the first full appearance of the tale in prose in English, published in 1807 and edited, curiously enough, by the rationalist philosopher William Godwin. Its publication is perhaps an example not only of the poverty of that good man, but of his unconscious recognition of worlds of imagination undreamt of in his philosophy. Since there are elements in his version often ignored in later re-tellings a fairly full summary will be necessary, though one still loses much of the individual flavour of what I will call Godwin's version, though we do not in fact know if it was actually he who wrote it.

Jack is the spoilt idle child of a poor widow. The widow is forced by poverty to sell her cow, a sale which Jack offers to arrange. Meeting a deceitful butcher he exchanges the cow for a few beans, much to his mother's anger. She throws them away, and they go supperless to bed. In the morning Jack discovers that the beans have sprouted to the sky. He climbs the intertwined stalks, finds himself in a barren country and feels very disconsolate. Then he meets a tattered old woman, who after asking him how he got there asks him, rather oddly, if he remembers his father. He does not, but says that his mother has always been distressed if he has asked about his father. The old woman then declares that she is a Fairy, and will tell him about his father on condition he promises to do everything she tells him to do, which of course Jack agrees to.

Jack's father had been a remarkably rich, kind, much loved man. But a neighbouring Giant, being poor and envious, had insinuated himself and his wife into Jack's father's house where they had been most generously treated. One day, Jack's father's servants all being out, the Giant had murdered his father and would have murdered his mother and him, a three-month-old baby, but she escaped by promising never to tell what had happened, and wandered in poverty far away. The Giant and his wife had carried off Jack's father's treasure and burnt the house down.

The old woman was Jack's father's guardian, but she had transgressed fairy law (we are not told how) and her punishment had been a total suspension of her power (unfortunate in that Jack's innocent father seems to have been the only one to suffer!). The day on which Jack had met the butcher her power had been restored and it had been she who prompted him to take the beans and who had caused them to grow. Jack is now in the Giant's country. It is his duty to revenge his father and punish the Giant, or Jack will always be miserable. Any damage he does to the Giant will be justified, for all his wealth is really Jack's.

This long explanation is an interesting example of the traditional device of rationalisation, supplying motives or causes or circumstances to account for a given event, or series of events, in a known, i.e. traditional, story. Almost all story-tellers use it to some extent and many instances have already been given of Perrault's rationalisations. But the temptation to rationalise is particularly strong when a writer imbued with the naturalism of Neoclassical literary theory tries to account for the non-naturalistic events of traditional stories. The problem essentially is that these later literary rationalisations tend to operate in terms of material cause and effect rather than, or without much regard for, the general underlying pattern which operates in terms of juxtapositions, associations, similarities or dissimilarities whether displaced or direct. The aim is also often different. Godwin's literary rationalisation here attempts to create a liberalistic imitation of the morality of the normal everyday world, whereas the story is concerned with psychic confrontations of a different kind, though the story's imagery is selected from the everyday world before being placed in fantasising juxtapositions. Thus Godwin's anxiety to make an honest boy of Jack here by inventing a motif of just revenge misses the true point of the story. Moreover, by attempting a literalistic and analytical mimetic extension of a non-literalistic symbolic pattern, and yet attempting, as it must, to operate with the same symbols, his rationalisation creates the kind of absurdities it seeks to remove, because the rationalisation is itself an uncomfortable mixture of analytical and symbolic modes. An example of how out of tune it is with the nature of fairy tales, and thus of how it breaks the rules, is given by the presentation of a good Fairy in relationship to a male protagonist, Jack (or by extension, Jack's father). In genuine fairy (that is, folk) tales, male protagonists do not have kind old ladies, that is, displaced but kind human mother-figures, to help them. Even so, the logic of the genre has its own strength, for though the Fairy is presented as kind and of good-will, a guardian, *in actual fact* she has betrayed her trust and shown herself not merely ineffectual but the cause of disaster to Jack's father. To this minor extent, without the apparent intention of the teller of this particular version, she approaches the authentic status of a symbolic mother-figure when presented as human and superior to the protagonist, that is, hostile. The general awkwardness of this rationalisation must be felt by any practised reader of fairy tales and it is often omitted from later versions, though it is not without a certain inappropriate charm.

After this attractively absurd attempt to justify the ungrateful and immoral pillaging of other people's property which we know very well Jack is about to indulge in, the story proceeds. Jack finds a mansion with 'a plain-looking woman' and asks for food and lodging. Though she is the Giant's wife she is compassionate and takes him in, but she points out that the Giant eats only human flesh, and Jack hears the groans of victims reserved for that purpose in the dungeons. However, the Giant's wife takes Jack to where else but the kitchen, where he makes himself very comfortable. Now the Giant appears and hastily his wife hides Jack in the oven. After a vast meal the Giant plays with a hen that lays golden eggs, then falls asleep. At day-break Jack breaks out, steals the hen, and returns home, where for a while he and his mother live happily.

But Jack 'being very desirous of travelling', and, adds an editorial note, remembering the Fairy's commands, goes off again, though against his mother's will. The same sort of events at the Giant's mansion take place, though the Giant also ill-treats his wife for her previous kindness to a strange boy, and Jack is this time hidden in a little lumber-room. He carries off two large bags of silver and gold. On his return he finds that his mother is apparently dying because of his absence, but the sight of the money revives her, and they live happily together for three more years. Jack's restlessness then becomes insuperable and he once again makes the journey, following the same sequence of events, this time being hidden in the 'copper'. This is a large copper tub with a fire under it used, as in my boyhood, for boiling clothes in, with a thick round wooden removable lid across the top, though it is also inadvertently and wrongly referred to a sentence or two later as the oven. It is big enough for a small boy to get into and easy to get out of. Jack can peep up from under the lid to watch the Giant playing with his magic automatic harp. When the Giant falls asleep Jack gets out and runs off with the harp. Unluckily it calls out 'Master! Master!' and the Giant wakes and chases him, but is too drunk to catch him. Jack thus gets down the beanstalk first. The Gaint follows but Jack speedily hacks down the beanstalk and the fall kills the Giant. Jack's mother is delighted when she sees the beanstalk destroyed. The last of a series of editorial footnotes in the 1807 edition brings the

Fairy in to explain Jack's behaviour and clear him in the opinion of his mother. The text continues that he apologises to her for the trouble he has caused her, 'promising to be very dutiful and obedient to her for the future. He proved as good as his word, and was a pattern of affectionate behaviour and attention to parents. His mother and he lived together a great many years, and continued to be always very happy.'

This is a very rich set of images and events, and different tellings may emphasise different aspects. All tellings cannot but emphasise the centrality of the hero. Time is only his. Other people relate only to him. No one else apparently knows about or tries to climb the beanstalk though we are told that the mother has neighbours. It is a story about growing up. There are essentially only three characters: the protagonist, his father and his mother. People in the story are a series of father- and mother-figures, whose relationships to him express the protagonist's views about them.

To take the father-images first: they are Jack's 'true father' and the Giant. The 'true' father is dead, and in the logic of this kind of imagination is 'therefore' good. We have the usual rule of fairy tale that good father-figures are weak, or, as an extension of weakness, they are helpless, being dead. (Thus Hamlet's father.) The live father-image is the wicked, oppressive, but inevitably stupid Giant. He is to be outwitted and pillaged. Or one may say that the protagonist has already killed off his father once (symbolised by his death at the hands of the Giant) and that now, though a bit ashamed of himself (an idle boy etc.) he justifies his continuous need to kill him by representing him this time as the disagreeable Giant. The mother-images are first the 'true' mother, regarded a little ambivalently even in this notably mother-venerating realisation by Godwin, for she is often cross, and the degree to which the protagonist is idle and useless is to some extent witness of internalisation of the unfavourable, and therefore disagreeable, comments by the mother. Moreover, the second mother-image, the Fairy, is shown (as already noted) not fully to have done her duty, having 'transgressed' to the detriment of the protagonist's father, and thus of his own right to his father's wealth. The third mother-image is the Giant's wife, also at fault from the inner point of view in so far as she *is* the Giant's wife, and deservedly beaten. She is kind in so far as she is not superior to the protagonist. She gets no thanks for her repeated foolish kindness to what from an external point of view might be called an ungrateful and deceitful little thief and murderer (but an external view would be as inappropriate here as in *Hamlet* or *King Lear*).

Relationships between characters have significance only in so far as they appear to the protagonist (again as in *Hamlet* and *King Lear*). The Giant and his wife may speak to each other and be loving or hostile to each other, but the importance of these attitudes lies in the way they affect the protagonist, not in their representation of gigantesque marital harmony or disharmony. We are never told, for example, how big is the Giant's wife. From lack of comment when she is first introduced we might suppose her to be of normal size. (Similarly it appears that Jack's 'true' father can entertain the Giant and his wife perfectly well in his own home without having to raise the ceilings.)

Jack and the Beanstalk is about growing up. Bettelheim makes an extensive Freudian analysis of it in relation to other 'Jack' stories, which I need not repeat, nor entirely agree with, to find often helpful. The initiative of selling the cow may well symbolically represent the need of the protagonist, both with and against his will, to leave the cosy world of milky maternal sustenance – the cow being another, rather further displaced, mother-image. (This image is by no means so far displaced as to be extravagant; many a woman and mother has been called, in vituperative slang, 'an old cow'. When about forty years ago in my late 'teens innocent of all knowledge of Freud I was playing the 'associative' word-game with some undergraduate friends, one of them, rich in psychological imagery, immediately, and to his own deep embarrassment, produced the word 'cow' as a response to the stimulus-word 'mother'!) Another set of mother-related images is employed when Jack is hidden in the oven, lumber-room (less vivid), and copper. All these are obvious images for mother's protective care, associated with the kitchen, heart of the home. When Father is angry Mother protects. There is a lot about eating and drinking in this tale and Bettelheim attributes it to the earlier oral stage of infantile development rather than to the oedipal. Those who do not like schematic Freudian interpretations may wish to reject this without giving up the symbolical significance of the images of home, of food, of maternal care. One may also note in this version a certain regressive element. It is true that Jack ardently wants to get out of the home, does actually get the beans, and insists on climbing the beanstalk into what is symbolically in part the outer world, though still mainly a displaced image of home. But as soon as he is threatened he dashes back to Mummy, even if he does get rid of Father.

The beans, or seeds, have inevitably been seen as symbolic of developing masculine sexuality, and the beanstalk as a phallic image. Bettelheim, more subtly, takes it as symbolic of boyish sexual fantasising, and the destruction of the beanstalk as symbolic of a more mature rejection of such fantasy. Restricting ourselves to the particular version I have used, and remembering the emphasis on obedience to mother and the regressive elements already noted, it seems more satisfactory, while noting the phallic undertones, to regard the beanstalk as symbolic of the protagonist's developing sense of his own growing masculine power, his need to challenge and defeat the father. Chopping down the beanstalk then symbolises a certain self-destructive, regressive urge. Father is killed by being brought down out of his upper outer world, where he enjoys food, wealth and culture (the latter represented by the harp; culture being on Father's side). The protagonist in the end rejects the upper outer world, cuts down the beanstalk, stays with Mother and makes no attempt to find a mate. To this extent *Jack and the Beanstalk* is unusual in not in the end breaking out of the bounds of the nuclear family.

It may be that Godwin's version is truncated, and reduced to an earlier stage of the child's psychic development from the original. The Opies note that the earliest reference in English to the tale is a parody, occurring in a chapter entitled 'Enchantment demonstrated in the Story of Jack Spriggins and the Enchanted Bean' inserted in the second edition in 1734 of *Round about our Coal-Fire: or Christmas Entertainments*, first published in 1730. In this parodic version Jack, on his way up the beanstalk, calls at an inn (maintaining the insistence on food and drink in this tale-complex), and soon the innkeeper turns into a beautiful lady whom Jack marries. There was also a version of the story in verse published in the same year, 1807, as the version by Godwin. Among other differences the Giant's wife has become a girl servant, whom Jack marries.

The predominance of a given version is no necessary index of its superior artistic merit, as the Perrault version of the Cinderella story shows. Yet when a version is genuinely popular, especially in this type of story-telling which cannot by definition be highly specialised or idiosyncratic, we may assume it does some things specially well. The Godwin version articulates the various interests and stresses of some aspects of the family drama with vigorous and poetically rich images. No story can do everything, and this version concentrates on that period which precedes the protagonist's final breakaway. Its imagery can be seen to have a social dimension unusual in the fairy tale. The Giant may easily be seen, up there with his wealth and culture, to represent a superior social class which lower-class Jack may legitimately pillage. As this form of the story seems to have evolved in the second half of the eighteenth century we may reasonably think of the virulence of class antagonism of the time, most evident in the French Revolution but noticeable in England also. Godwin himself was the revolutionary philosopher from whom Shelley learnt much of his radicalism. (I do not suggest that Godwin consciously saw any revolutionary radicalism in the tale. On the contrary he seems to have gone out of his way to emphasise the moral duties of filial obedience and of hard work.) The social aspect of the tale may be peculiarly English since Jack, as a representative of the English lower classes, appears to have no interest at all in the Giant's culture (his harp). This is an English characteristic in strong contrast with the lower classes of the Celtic fringe, Scotland, Ireland and Wales, where there seems never to have been a similar lack of interest in 'high culture', or at least where class distinctions (sharp enough, especially in Scotland) do not appear to have operated in quite the same way in cultural matters. The Celtic fringe never experienced so fully the rigours of Neoclassical high culture which from the seventeenth century in England strongly associated what was 'low' in literature with what was 'low' in class. All this must here remain no more than a note in the margin. It is worth making in order to suggest the poetic richness of meaning that can be generated by the images and sequences of a story that most literary criticism ordinarily despises. One might add, in this connection generally, that notwithstanding the veneer of instructively moral observations in the English eighteenth- and nineteenth-century verbal realisations of fairy tales, the fairy tale, and folktale in general, are, like most children, not much impressed by the socially dynamic middle-class notions of bettering oneself by hard work, honest dealing and moral integrity. Much more significant to the fairy tale and folklore are: being the right person in the right place at the right time; kindness to others; absence of conceit (rather than positive humility); persistence; the self-confidence to take a chance and a 'reasonable' risk; ability to make people laugh; and above all, 'luck', a secular equivalent of religious grace. Fairy tales are entirely secular; they envisage good things in this world. They come from a lower substratum in the mind (and by historical accident in England since the seventeenth century from a lower social substratum) than that which produces high-powered scientific, theological or literary culture, or which is distinguished by a self-sacrificing determination to achieve a single objective.

XIII

Examples have been given of female and male protagonists. There are also instances in folktales of dual protagonists, either two brothers, or brother and sister. There is a story with three sisters as 'protagonist', *Finette Cendron*, referred to by the Opies (p. 236), first published in French in 1698. *Little Poucet*, or *Hop o'My Thumb*, printed by the Opies, has no less than seven brothers, though they are effectively subsumed in the youngest and most enterprising after whom the tale is named. It is perhaps significant that the tales with a multiple 'protagonist' are analogous to each other, and to *Hansel and Gretel*, in their main point, which is the shortage of food, and the abandonment of the children by their parents. From an expository point of view, since the multiple protagonists act as one, without rivalry, they are best described as 'splits' of the single protagonist, deploying a slightly more complex presentation of the protagonist's quality and less concern with ultimate development even if the protagonist-figures achieve their appropriate mates. The stories often illustrate a strong fear of the parent-figures and are focussed more on the oral stage of psychic development and the earlier pre-sexual aspects of the family drama. Lüthi comments that it is unusual to have children as opposed to adolescents as protagonists of such stories. They are resourceful and successful but they seek to return home rather than go out into the world (pp. 65–6). *Hansel and Gretel* is crammed with potent images of a familiar kind but is referred to here mainly as an example of the dual protagonist, in the undated nineteenth-century version printed by the Opies.

Hansel and Gretel are the children, son and daughter, of a very poor woodcutter whose wife has died. The stepmother persuades the father (good but weak) much against his will to lose the children in the forest. But Hansel secretly drops pebbles by which the children find their way back. A second time he drops crumbs which are eaten by the birds, so the children wander a long time starving and lost in the forest. On the third day they come to a cottage made of bread, cakes and sugar, which they eat from, but it belongs to a witch who imprisons Hans in a cage in order to eat him. Gretel is to be put in the heated oven. But Gretel tricks the witch into putting her own head into the oven, and Gretel pushes her in and bolts the door. She burns to death. The children take her wealth and return home, where they all, parents and children, live together in great happiness.

The dual protagonist allows for an interesting articulation and slightly greater complexity of action, since the love of the children for each other adds pathos and there is a variety of action. The dominance of wicked mother-images suggests that the fundamental protagonist is female, and the decisive action in getting rid of the witch is indeed Gretel's, though Hans is the main executive in the earlier part of the tale. The dominance of the female protagonist is also suggested by the return home. Hostility to and anxiety about the parents, but especially relating to the mother, are dominant in the tale, and the tale advances by triumphing over, indeed one might say absorbing, the hostile aspects of the mother, a necessary achievement in psychic development. The womb-like oven, it is perhaps not too extravagant to suggest, is seen as a trap. The womb will be a tomb if the growing individual is forced back into it. It can however be taken as an ally, too, of the protagonist, who by its help can swallow up the enemy, render her ineffective. When the protagonist has done this, by pushing the maleficent mother-figure into the oven, the main mother-figure is forgiven. The aesthetic of fairy tale is well demonstrated by this happy ending. How, in ordinary realistic characterisation, could a family live happily with a wife and mother of such proven criminal tendencies? But I hope that by now such a reflection will be seen to be obviously irrelevant to the inner pattern of the tale.

XIV

We are far from exhausting the riches of fairy tales. We have been concentrating on one principal aspect to the exclusion of many others. Although fairy tales as we have them may be mainly a European late-medieval and early modern genre, they are perhaps for that very reason an admirable representative of traditional stories. Their roots certainly spread wide in East and West, and in the depths of time, yet they are still much read by many people with no specific literary interests. Although some versions have been sophisticated they are still absolutely intractable to Neoclassical and novelistic criteria – as crude and cynical modern parodies occasionally demonstrate. They present a model of traditional narrative and because of a certain simplicity in their power they demonstrate the need for particular assumptions and for the recognition of certain rules and conventions more clearly than do more literary works in more complex verbal realisations. Taking this model we now proceed to apply the lessons learnt to more complex literary works.

CHAPTER II

The stories of David, Judas and some medieval romances

I

The earliest examples of both manifest and latent treatment of the family drama in our culture are Biblical, with the verbal realisation not much elaborated beyond the basic pattern of the story. The story of Joseph shows us the favoured younger son subject to the hostility of siblings of the same sex. The 'emergence' of Joseph differs from that of the protagonist of later folktale and romance, but he has to leave his primary home. In his ultimate triumph over his siblings we note the association of food and famine with stories containing many siblings. As this is an archaic story Joseph's marriage is not as significant as his relationship with the Pharaoh. His temptation by Potiphar's wife (Genesis XL), who is in a superior station to him, with its equally difficult alternatives (either be seduced or be condemned for attempted rape) is a motif which echoes through later literature. From the psychological point of view it may be seen at the latent level as a version of the seductive mother whom the protagonist must resist, the 'mother' element being deduced from her social superiority to the hero. We are not told her age. (This episode surely cannot have been quite out of the *Gawain*-poet's mind, knowing the Bible as well as he did.) The birth and early history of Moses is shown by Otto Rank[1] to share many elements of the usual pattern of the birth of the hero, and is therefore another version of one aspect of the family drama, with the Egyptian Princess as a displaced mother-image. The story of Jephtha's daughter (Judges XI), caught in his vow to sacrifice whatever first comes to meet him from home if he should have victory, gives another aspect of the family drama. It is significant that the daughter asks for two months' grace in which to go into the mountains with her companions 'and bewail my virginity'. That she remains a virgin, and that it should be so emphasised, and lamented, is a powerful realisation of the jealous father's possessiveness of his daughter, even though no suitor has appeared. The outstanding Biblical version of the family drama, remarkably close to many medieval and later versions, is the story of the origins of David. The story begins in I Samuel. Samuel is told by God to find a king for Israel from the sons of Jesse, notwithstanding the hostility of Saul, the reigning king, who is rejected by God.

Jesse has eight sons, the eldest of whom seems very suitable to Samuel, but neither he nor any of the first seven is pleasing to God. Then the unregarded one, David, who has not been presented to Samuel by Jesse but has been left in the fields keeping the sheep, is called for, found to be 'ruddy, and withal of a beautiful countenance, and goodly to look upon'. Strange grounds for choosing the king of an embattled people, but this is he (I. Sam. XVI, 12, Revised Version). At verse 14 another story abruptly begins of how Saul was troubled by an evil spirit. His servants recommend a harp player to cure his moodiness. One of them knows the very man, a son of Jesse 'that is cunning in playing, and a mighty man of valour, and a man of war, and prudent in speech, and a comely person, and the Lord is with him' (v. 18). David arrives and is loved by Saul and becomes his armour-bearer. This talented, skilful, experienced, prudent man is very different from the unregarded shepherd-boy we have just been told of. When the story of Goliath is told in the following chapter we revert to David the shepherd-boy. Scholars have in consequence seen the juxtaposition of the two accounts in Chapter XVI as a combination of two different historical traditions, and they may be right. But from the point of view of the hearer or reader of traditional stories there is no problem. We can easily accept juxtaposed and inconsistent accounts, and constantly do, in the Bible and elsewhere, because we do not seek a naturalistic account. We respond to an underlying pattern, and supply connections vaguely in the mind if we need to rationalise the account. The essence of the matter here is that we are conscious of two aspects of David; first, that he is young and disregarded, second, that he is in fact splendidly talented. The historical truth of what was the actual situation about three thousand years ago is now irrecoverable. The psychological and spiritual truth of the origins of one who when young was both obscure and splendid remains incontrovertible. It arises out of, and reflects upon, a profound insight about humanity, just as, *mutatis mutandis*, the Cinderella story does. It is 'psychologically' true of the emerging hero, because this is what everyone feels about his or her childhood and youth. To see it in this way is an essential preliminary to understanding how the Jewish genius for a combined historical and spiritual insight sets the story in a specific context which, as it progresses, eventually becomes uniquely historical. Goliath the Philistine is a huge man who wears grotesquely large and heavy armour, and when he challenges the army of the Israelites to a representative single combat which shall decide the fate of all (an archaic challenge which was still put forward by medieval English kings in person) no one can be found brave enough to confront him. David is introduced as the shepherd-boy again, not himself serving in the army which Saul is leading (though he was said earlier to be his armour-bearer) but bringing up food for his elder brothers, who are. David hears the challenge of Goliath. The men of Israel tell him concerning Goliath 'that the man who killeth him, the king will enrich him with great riches, and will give him his daughter, and make his father's house free in Israel' (XVII, 25). This is straightforward folktale and medieval romance; and one may say that without denigrating its historical and religious significance, for such significances are necessarily conducted through symbolic narratives.

When David refers indignantly to Goliath he is slapped down by his eldest brother in typical folktale same-sex sibling style. David goes to Saul who now apparently knows only that he is a raw youth, in contrast with the experienced soldier Goliath. Nevertheless David gets permission to fight Goliath, is armed with Saul's armour, rejects it as too cumbersome, takes his sling and 'five smooth stones out of the brook', and confronts Goliath, who disdains him as a beautiful boy. When David has killed Goliath he decapitates him with his own sword. He is brought to Saul who now has no notion at all who he is. The story continues a good deal further with David as a servant to Saul and no mention of his being chosen as king to replace Saul.

So far the story has had a very characteristic development which hardly needs emphasis. Leaving aside any discussion of the superb verbal re-alisation, we can see that at one level we have the traditional story of the obscure but highly gifted youth who kills the major inhibiting father-image (who is in this case also weighed down with an old-fashioned technology). The protagonist then goes on to marry the king's daughter and eventually inherit the kingdom. This is exactly what David does, but there are minor variations in the realisation. Leaving aside a minor variant about the daughter, David does indeed marry Saul's daughter Michal whom he loves. But before this happens the essential break-out from the emotional bonds of the family and the establishment of a soul-satisfying rapport with an equal has taken place through David's passionate and reciprocated friendship with Jonathan. The significant personal relation-ships in a primitive peasant and warrior society are those between persons of the same sex. A very similar situation appears to have obtained in the peasant society of the early-fourteenth-century French Pyrenean village of Montaillou. It seems absurd to attribute such masculine friend-ships to homosexuality in any ordinary understanding of the word as perverted sexuality, unless any friendship between persons of the same sex is to be called homosexual. What we have here is a sentiment of male friendship practically unrecognised in the modern Western world of recent years, and entirely lost to a modern literature interested almost exclusively in illicit or perverted sex. The latest instance of innocent but deep male friendship in literature that I know is Conan Doyle's 'The Case of the Blanched Soldier' in *The Case-Book of Sherlock Holmes*, where an ex-soldier stockbroker's explicit and unembarrassedly expressed love for his 'pal' during the Boer War is a motive for action that calls for no query. The relation between Holmes and Watson itself is another instance, normally implicit, but given vivid brief expression when Watson is wounded ('The Adventure of the Three Garridebs' in *The Casebook*). Friendship of such depth between men arises most naturally in a warrior-society where men have shared danger together and perhaps owe each other their lives, and though it depends mainly on such circumstances, on segregation of the sexes and exclusion of one sex from some activities of the other, it seems unlikely that such a fundamental human sentiment will ever be completely lost, even if neglected by the conscious structures of society and dominant trends in literature. In modern literature if it occurred it would probably be denigrated or celebrated as a homosexual perversion. While no doubt it could be and sometimes was accompanied by homosexual practices, these have traditionally in our era been regarded with disgust or contempt even in Italy. The essence of masculine friendship as an historical sentiment has always been that it is an equal relationship between grown men, as homosexuality has not usually been. It may rival but is not at all of the same kind as the marital relationship. Male friendship is an important, nowadays sometimes misunderstood, or neglected, factor in medieval and later social life, in some romances, such as *Amis and Amiloun*, and (implicitly) in Chaucer's *Knight's Tale* and the relation between Troilus and Pandarus.

Returning to the story of David we may see how Saul continues to be a difficult father-figure even after the main image has been defeated, but the folktale basis merges into a somewhat different objective 'historical' narrative. The narrative becomes more complex and 'analytic' after the tragic deaths of Jonathan and Saul, when it recounts the many subsequent events of David's life, given in the so-called 'Court History of David', of surpassing literary greatness, sadly neglected today. The interests of the 'Court History of David' go beyond the emergence of the protagonist as David, and the whole cultural background is different, but the opening account of David provides a striking example of the family drama from a very early date. The only major element lacking here is the complex mother-image, a lack perhaps due to polygamy and to that very strong masculine emphasis in ancient Jewish culture which went so far as to claim that women were in origin born of men (Eve from Adam, Genesis II, 22).

II

Classical mythology is so remarkably rich in treating so many aspects of the family drama that it deserves a book written by an expert. The best-known story of all is that of Oedipus, who killed his father and married his mother, now irrevocably associated with the name and theories of Freud. Other notable Classical stories of the tensions of the family drama are those of Hippolytus, Adonis and Orestes. Only the briefest suggestions can be made here, disregarding the further significances in the story-patterns and in the rich verbal realisations especially of Euripides and Ovid.

Hippolytus is killed because he resists the passionate desire of his father's wife, Phaedra, for him. Phaedra is not his mother, Theseus having had several wives in succession ('withouten other company in youth', as the Wife of Bath says of herself). Nevertheless the latent pattern is clear, and much the same may be said of the story of Venus and Adonis. Each hero is symbolically torn to death by animal passions, not necessarily or only external, arising out of relationship with a mother-figure who wishes to seduce him. (They are variants of Sir Gawain, as will be later seen.)

Orestes has to kill his mother for murdering his father and is tormented by female furies, but is in the end forgiven and achieves his own survival.

When we group these stories together with that of Oedipus and other Classical stories, comparing them in turn with medieval romances, we notice an important fact about tragedy which Freud and Propp do not see. *Tragedy only arises within the family drama when the parent-figures kill the protagonist; not when the protagonist kills the parent.* This will become more fully apparent as we consider medieval romances. From this point of view it is romance which is the true opposite of tragedy, since it is of the essence of romance that it issues in a happy ending.[2] In order to achieve the happy ending in medieval romances the hero has to kill one or more father-images, which is usually not too difficult, and he has to resist and escape from mother-figures, which may well be much more troublesome. He feels more equivocal towards them. If the protagonist is female she may have to 'kill' the mother-figure, who comes to a symbolically bad end. To sum up, albeit crudely, it is all right, indeed it is necessary, for children to kill parents. It is tragic if parents kill children, or if children *fail* to kill parents. The reason is that the protagonist is thus crushed by the family, he does not escape. The story of Oedipus by Sophocles is a tragedy not because Oedipus kills his father but because he is trapped by fate into marrying his mother and so never gets away. The implications of this for psychology, anthropology and literary criticism are widespread, and a wholesale re-valuation is called for. Thus *Hamlet* is a tragedy because Hamlet's uncle-father Claudius, an obvious father-figure, kills the protagonist. Cordelia is trapped by her father after being first excessively loved then excessively hated. (The tragedy is more complicated here.) In the medieval stories of tragic adulterous love the latent pattern is recognisably similar. The hero, Lancelot or Tristan, lover of a lady married to his feudal lord, is trapped into love of a mother-figure, who is possessive in the extreme, as is seen from her anger when the hero appears to take up with a lady of his own age or status, an Elaine or a second Yseult. But the hero is not able to love his equal. As already noted, the element of 'worship', of asserting the superiority of ladies in love, in so-called courtly love, has a dangerously filial element. It is sound psychological sense, as well as observed social fact, that after marriage, which is the normal aim of romantic love in medieval romances, the lady becomes an equal or an inferior.

The statement that the protagonist has to 'kill' his father and escape from his mother must naturally be understood symbolically. It will be shown that a very important aspect in some medieval romances is *reconciliation within the family*, of the protagonist with his parents, which may well be more warmly portrayed than his achievement of his beloved. We must then understand the ambivalence of the human mind and the way stories can activate that ambivalence, can recognise and finally reconcile inherent tensions within both the individual and his group. It should hardly be necessary to re-iterate that at a literal level the murder of a parent was regarded as an extreme sin and crime. Many stories make clear how odious this was considered to be at the natural or literal level.

An example of direct confrontation with the crime of the murder of parents is provided by the story of Julian the Hospitaller, well known even today, having been re-told with vivid naturalistic detail by Flaubert. Julian, a knight, returns from hunting to find his wife, as he thinks, in bed with another man. In his rage he immediately kills them both, only to discover that they were his parents who had visited him unexpectedly and been put in his bed by his wife. The basic story has sufficient power combined with implausibility to prompt speculation about the displacement of images. Is there a latent sense which proposes that the protagonist, so jealous of his wife, has failed to disengage her from the mother-image? At all events he murders his parents in jealous rage and spends the rest of his life expiating this heavy sin. In so far as he becomes a saint it may be thought to be a *felix culpa*, a fortunate transgression, which leads him to a higher life, but the price is heavy.

In another remarkable story there is no question whatsoever of a *felix culpa*. To kill your father is shown to be the blackest of deeds which could be committed only by the worst of men. Since the story is not widely known in its astonishing medieval form, though studied extensively many years ago, I quote it from its improbable main source, *The Golden Legend*. This compilation of Saints' Legends developed over several centuries in the manner of traditional stories, so that the latest version, translated by Caxton into English in 1483, is the fullest. In it is gathered up the harvest of medieval hagiography.

Although the work of clerks and written for edification, these legends share most of the characteristics of medieval folktale narration. They have a close relationship to folktale and romance, pious as they are. The fundamental interest is in pattern not causality, and they are consequently highly implausible. Yet they are also subject to rationalisations of various kinds. They have a particularly ambiguous relationship to the natural material world. In one sense, since their ultimate aim is to teach, and they deal with a world of pious aspiration, they have no more need to represent a plausible, possible, natural, material world than any romance, or even any consciously fantastic folktale. The development of the meaning of *legend* from 'that which should be read' (originally by and for monks at meals, etc.) to 'an improbable story in the past' shows how most people came to regard them. They occupied that indeterminate area where events are not tested but accepted; an area which is now occupied by conscious fictions, but is still much more extensive for most people than is often realised. On the other hand, Saints' Legends should by their very purpose have a closer connection with 'what actually happened' than have conscious fictions or fantasies, just because they are meant to convey both miracles and edification. Who wants to go to the stake for a fiction? And this was indeed the choice for many earnest men and women under Queen Mary in sixteenth-century England. Protestantism, like Humanism, owed much of its power to its demand for literal truth. The Reformation killed Saints' Legends in England, as it did the inventive meditations of devotional poetry.

Even earlier there was some doubt felt by learned men about miraculous narratives, while there was always a stout vein of commonsensical secular scepticism in medieval popular literature generally. Thus it is that the story about to be presented is a rationalisation in at least two senses. It is rationalisation in that it 'accounts', by pattern as much as by causality, for the wickedness of the worst traitor known to medieval men; but the story is also in itself so fantastic that it is carefully described as 'not authentic'. The worst of men is Judas. The story, in its bare bones, is that of Oedipus. We are given the life of Judas. How, it may be asked, does the life of Judas, worst of men, placed next to Satan himself in Dante's vision of Hell, come to figure in the Legends of saints? It is the product of further rationalisation, and appears as the prelude to the Life of Saint Matthew. Saint Matthew was elected an Apostle by the remaining eleven after the defection of Judas. Judas's fate has to be told to account for his absence. His life is narrated in order to account for his behaviour. In this respect it is the formal equivalent of the *enfances*, or account of the childhood, which was often added to pre-existent Arthurian romances of the adventures of a famous hero, such as Tristan or Lancelot. As will be seen, Christ knew of Judas's life and had forgiven him. Heinous as had been his misdeed, no sin is too bad to be forgiven. The narration itself is matter-of-fact in tone.

We are told that on the night that Judas was conceived his mother had a dream that he would destroy all their people and she convinced her at first sceptical husband that it was 'a revelacion and none illusion'.

Whan the chyld was born the fader and moder were in grete doubte and thoughte what was beste to doo, for they durst not slee the chyld for thorrour that they shold haue therein, neyther they wyst not how they myght nourysshe one that shold destroye theyr lygnage. Thenne they put hym to a lytyl fyscelle or baskette wel pytched, and sette it in the see, and abandonned hym to dryue whyther it wold. And anon the floodes and waues of the see brought and made hym aryue in an ylonde named Scaryoth, and of thys name was he callyd Judas Scaryoth. ¶ Now it happed that the quene of this contree wente for to playe on the ryuage of the see, & byheld thys lytyl nacelle and the chyld therin, whyche was fayr, and thenne she syghed and sayd ¶ O lord god how shold I be eased yf I had suche a chyld, thenne atte leste shold not my royame be wythoute heyre. Thenne comanded she that the chyld shold be taken up and be nourysshid, and she fayned her self to be grete with chyld, and after publysshyd that she had born a fayr sone. Whan her husbond herd saye herof he had grete joye, & all the peple of the contre made grete feste. The kynge & quene dyde do norysshe and kepe thys chylde lyke the sone of a kynge. ¶ Anon after it happed that the quene conceyued a sone, and whan it was born and growen, Judas bete ofte that chylde, for he wende that he had ben hys broder, & ofte he was chastysed therfore, but allewaye he made hym to wepe so longe, that the quene weyche knewe wel that Judas was not her sone, and atte laste she sayd the trouthe, and tolde how that Judas was founden in the see. ¶ And er this yet was knowen, Judas slewe the chylde that he had supposed to be hys brother and was sone to the kynge, and in eschewyng the sentence of deth he fledde anon and cam in to Jherusalem, and entred in to the court of pylate whyche tho was prouoste. And he so plesid hym that he was grete with hym, and had in grete chyerete, and nothyng was doon wythout hym.

Now it happed on a day that pylate wente for to dysporte hym by a gardyn bylongyng to the fader of Judas, & was so desirous to ete of the fruyt of thappelles that he myght not forbere them. And the fader of Judas knewe not Judas hys sone, for he had supposed that he had be drowned in the see longe to fore, ne the sone knewe not the fader. Whan pylate had told to Judas of hys desyre, he sprange in to the gardyn of hys fader, and gadred of the fruyt for to bere to hys maystre, but the fader of Judas deffended hym, and ther bygan bytwene them moche stryf and debate, fyrst by wordes, and after wyth fyghtyng, so moche that Judas smote hys fader wyth a stone on the heed that he slewe hym, and after brought thapples vnto pylate, and tolde to hym how that he had slayn hym that ought the gardyn. ¶ Thenne sente pylate to sease all the good that the fader of Judas had, and after gaf hys wyf to Judas in mariage, and thus Judas wedded hys owen moder.

Now it happed on a day that the lady wepte and sighed moche strongly and said, alas how vnhappy that I am, I haue lost my sone and my husbond. My sone was leyd on the see and I suppose that he be drowned, and my husbond is dede sodeynly, & yet it is more greuous to me that pylate hath remaryed me ayenst my wyll. Thenne demaunded Judas of thys child, & she told hym how he was sette in the see, and Judas tolde to her how he had be founden in the see, in suche wise that she wist that she was his moder, and that he had slayn hys fader and wedded hys moder, wherfor thenne he wente to Jhesu cryst which dyde so many myracles, and prayd hym of mercy and forgifnes of his synnes. ¶ Thus fer it is red in thistorye which is not autentike.

(W. Caxton, *The Golden Legend*, ed. F. S. Ellis,
Kelmscott Press, 1892, pp. 406–7.)

The story as told lacks the horror, as it lacks the self-awareness, of Oedipus in the Sophoclean version, and is entirely bereft of Sophocles's artistry. It is very much a question whether or not this story has some remote connection with the many versions in Antiquity attached to the name of Oedipus.[3] It has been reduced to little more than an anecdote of pious but shocking folktale. Obvious motifs taken from the Bible, but found elsewhere, are the setting adrift of the baby; his discovery by the Queen, exemplifying the fantasy that we have 'royal' parents (cf. Moses); and the killing of the brother (cf. Cain and Abel). The abandonment of the mother by the narrative, so that we do not know what happened to her, is another folktale characteristic which actually destroys the impact of the story. All is centred on the protagonist, and it is crucial to know about his final relationship with his mother. The essential point of the story is lost. The failure here makes the family drama meaningless, and illustrates how important the central point of the story is, and what it is. From the point of view of the story the reconciliation scene, which should come after the working out of ambivalent and mutually incompatible wishes and desires, has come too soon, and is too extraneous, being brought about by a figure outside the story. Because of this failure of pattern, and because we are unable to identify ourselves with the protagonist, or even with the parents, the story, though a clear example of the basis of the family drama, and interesting as a measure of the attitude to the literally conceived situation, is neither tragedy nor romance. Its external and simplified point of view presents the protagonist simply as a villain, with no mixture of good and bad, no moral struggle either in himself or in the total mind of the story as represented by a variety of good and bad characters, no progress towards self-knowledge or reconciliation. From our point of view it remains an important datum and an artistic failure.

III

The legendary life of Judas lies in the background of several medieval centuries. We may now select some differing examples of English romances from those centuries. Most of these romances have been neglected or despised because the nature of their symbolic stories has not been recognised, and because the style of the particular verbal realisations varies from no more than vigorous and witty through ordinarily competent to occasionally pathetic, without achieving major artistic merit in the class of Chaucer or *Sir Gawain and the Green Knight*. But some of these romances can give us pleasure and real insight, though like ninety-nine point nine per cent of the literary productions of any age they are not the products of major genius.

Since they are self-evidently literary fictions, unconstrained even by the hope or pretence of historical authenticity of the Saints' Legends, they can freely deploy non-naturalistic fantasy. Their fictional nature allows the underlying conflicts of the family drama to be symbolically represented in several different ways, to be explored and worked through.

I take as representative examples, not in chronological order, a minor late-fifteenth-century Scottish romance, *Eger and Grime*, which is close to folktale; *King Horn*, one of the earliest of the English romances, written in the thirteenth century, which particularly well illustrates the importance of repetition with variation in traditional narrative; and finally, the fourteenth-century romance *Sire Degarre*, a briskly moving tale which may have been known to Chaucer, and which particularly well illustrates the theme of reconciliation with parent-images which is so important in medieval English romance.[4] All these tales are part of that great flow of European traditional story, fed by tributaries from as far as ancient India and Classical Greece, which also developed in itself especially in the story-loving Middle Ages. They were broken up and re-combined, told in various versions, with different interests in mind, at all social levels, from court to cottage, a truly popular possession. On this oral base were built, in more elaborate but intrinsically similar narrative forms, the manuscript versions which begin to appear from the twelfth century onwards and which, with comparison with oral forms still current on the edges of Europe, in Africa and elsewhere, constitute the evidence of our study. With all the changes involved in changing times and societies, in the shifts from oral narrative to script to print, they still illustrate under their variety continuing common human preoccupations.

IV

The relatively naive Northern romance of the late fifteenth century, *Eger and Grime*, connects two very widely spread motifs, 'the Twin Brothers' and 'the Fairy Mistress'. The brothers Eger and Grime make up a 'split' protagonist. They defeat a series of kings (variously repeated father-figures) to achieve fame, which is the manifestation of the latent process of growing up, and they fall in love with two ladies. Eger is at first the leading figure. It is hardly necessary to add that he is the younger, and landless, son. After killing his enemies he is accepted by the Fairy Princess. In characteristically folkloric manner he does not remain with her but immediately sets out for the Forbidden Country, though warned not to do so. We see here the usual attempt to establish a firm relationship with a woman, and the usual latent sense of insecurity, indeed of sexual anxiety, at the first apparent success in doing so. We are not surprised when he is soon attacked by a monster-knight and falls down in a swoon, during which the little finger of his right hand is cut off. I omit many other adventures, for what is significant here, from the point of view of the protagonist, is that his brother Grime then takes over, does not lose his little finger or anything else, and helps Eger finally to win his lady, while also winning his own. In one of the two main versions of the romance Grime then dies and Eger confesses to his lady that he won her by Grime's help. She promptly leaves him so Eger then marries Grime's widow. Thus a final uncertainty about genuinely acquiring a wife outside the family has been solved, and the 'split' hero (and heroine) brought back again to unity. (*The Knight's Tale* similarly 'simplifies' a 'split' protagonist by killing off one of his manifestations.)

There is a group of three Scottish folktales which may be remote analogues of *Eger and Grime*. The protagonist is a rough fellow doing menial jobs, but is served by friendly beasts. The King's daughter is to be sacrificed to a great monster in the loch. When she is on the shore the protagonist comes along and tells the Princess to let him lay his head in her lap – in one version she is invited to perform that traditionally female friendly act (men never do it) of picking vermin out of his hair. He sleeps. She is to wake him when the monster arrives by cutting off the top joint from his little finger. In fact the three-headed monster makes three attacks, and for the first and second he is wakened by losing less significant portions of his anatomy (hair and point of his ear). Then he kills the monster and, like a true hero, departs.

In one version the King's daughter after his departure says she will only marry the man whose finger fits the joint which she has cut off, and which she keeps in her pocket, and this would seem the most significant version. Thus the protagonist is found.

It is obviously a story about initiation into sex. The central issue for the story seems to be about the need to tame the cruel, selfish, depredatory aspects of sexuality, represented by the monster, but the top joint of the little finger is obviously a phallic symbol as well as an identifying item; or we may say that identity and controlled faithful sexuality are seen as two sides of the same coin. The combined emphasis on identity, sex, love and marriage, as principal aspects of the family drama, is very common in medieval romance.

V

The thirteenth-century English romance *King Horn* is a very good example of a direct sharp narrative style and a series of absurdly implausible adventures which combine to give the modern reader a quite mistaken notion of the naivety of the tale. It is in fact told with zest and robust enjoyment of the fantasy, while the fantasy itself is purposively patterned to great effect. There are some memorable scenes, especially that of the traditionally last-minute return of the hero Horn to save his beloved from marriage to a villain. The poem has been well discussed by Wilson.[5]

Horn, the protagonist, is driven from his home (where his mother remains) by pirates who kill his father the King. He remains anonymous in Westnesse, across the sea, where he lands with two friends. This compulsive anonymity is of course not rational and can be understood only at the latent level. The King's daughter Rymenild falls in love with him but he claims that he is too lowly, even though in fact he is the son of a King. He then undertakes to prove himself. He kills numerous Saracen pirates, but soon the King, wrongly believing that Horn has seduced his daughter, exiles him. In other words, the protagonist still feels hostile towards father-figures and is unable to reach out to his peer. Again he goes over sea. This time he kills the gigantic Saracen who had killed his father – a nicely ambivalent way of dealing with yet another father-figure. Horn is greatly successful and is offered another King's daughter but politely declines. He is called back to Westnesse where Rymenild is to be married to another King. He arrives not only anonymous but as a beggar. Nevertheless he makes himself known by riddling signs, kills the King who intends to marry Rymenild, and is acknowledged by her father. But he does not stay. He immediately goes off again to win back his kingdom.

In his absence his faithless friend attempts to marry Rymenild but Horn returns again in disguise, kills him, and now at last marries and settles down. I leave aside the faithful and faithless friends ('splits' of the protagonist's character), and other interesting variations. The protagonist has a touch of the 'male Cinderella', but being male continually leaves the primary home, though it is in order to defeat oppressive father-figures even while associating himself with his dead, therefore good, father. He is trying himself out, proving his own identity in various ways. The postponements of his marriage to Rymenild and his refusal of the other princess reveal both his desire for the love of his peer and his sense that the image of the beloved is not yet disengaged from the oppressive father-figure, nor yet sufficiently distinguished from the mother-image. Although the mother-image is little emphasised in this poem, it is only when he has restored his mother to her kingdom, which he then leaves, and has killed his faithless friend, that he finally marries.

Such a bare analytic outline of the latent drives does no justice to the vigorous and witty verbal realisation at the manifest literal level. This particular story makes particularly effective use of a notable major device of traditional story, that of repetition, which needs more extended comment.

Repetition is a fundamental characteristic of traditional literature. At its base it relates to the fundamental re-iterations in which our lives consist, of heart-beat and walking, eating, sleeping, eating again, night following day following night following day. Simply to live is to repeat oneself. Rhythms establish themselves, recognised or only experienced, and one of the major functions of art is to re-create, at imaginative levels, so that they can be doubly experienced and more deeply recognised, the rhythms of life. The fundamental issues of life, the passages and problems of passing from one stage to the next, common to us all, repeat in themselves something of each other. At every becoming, with its new life, something of us has died. Every birth issues from a death; ripening is growth but also rotting; every death has a promise of new life. We live most vividly at moments of transition from one stage to another, when for a brief while we can juxtapose the two stages with a more vivid sense of what each is, for example to be both child and adult, and thus more exquisitely to experience what is, and what one is. Each transition is so multiple in aspect, so complex in internal structure, that no single statement or proposition can exhaust it. Each moment has its special relation to other moments and to the flow of other lives that surround it, with their similar but not identical patternings. What more natural than that, in the imaginative contemplations of what is, what may be, what could be, what was or might have been, we come back again and again to the central issues? In an individual work of art which operates through time, like music, or in a story, we are particularly able to return to the central motif, whether it be a series of sounds of some deep non-rational significance, or a pregnant situation. One might say with only a little exaggeration that all music, all stories, are a theme with variations – the bigger the work of art, the richer and more complex theme and themes, and their changes and relationships. Even an exact repetition in art can never be precisely the same imaginative experience, because we ourselves change. The second or the hundredth hearing of a symphony or a story differs from the preceding hearing because that hearing itself took place and affects our expectations, which energise and control our understandings, and other things have happened to us as well. We *bring* understanding to our experience, especially our experience of art, before we can take it away. Knowledge precedes perception. So when the object perceived is that complex, suggestive, obscure set of movements and tensions that constitutes a major development or acquisition, it is not surprising that we come back again and again, to the same object even in the same work of art, because repetition is always variation as well. Even a modest story, as it returns to the same issue, models it slightly differently, gives yet another possible version, extends our capacity to absorb, understand, as it were digest.

Certainly there may be poor art, as there may be poor food, with too little variation, too little nourishment, compared with what is available elsewhere. Repetition itself however is not at fault.

Traditional literature of a high quality makes use of repetition in many ways. The psalms, some of the greatest poetry in our tradition, make single repetition their chief structural principle. In much native English verse, rhyming couplets have a similar though not so essential effect. In story-patterns such as that of *King Horn* and many fairy tales we are conscious of the importance of repeated event in order to achieve the desired end. 'If you first don't succeed, try, try, try again', chants the old saying, making use of triple iteration and suggesting the life-quality, the mode and the imaginative satisfaction, of effort, progress and achievement.

Traditional literature, both within the structure of individual works and in the familiar motifs shared between many tales yet differently presented, illustrates the importance of repetition. The risk in analysis is of over-emphasising the basic similarities, which may make them seem elementary, or of over-emphasising the variety of individual realisations, which may denature them by digging them out of their natural context. Only the very greatest works of art, like *Sir Gawain and the Green Knight* and Chaucer's poems, can long survive such uprooting.

VI

Sire Degarre is a delightful poem written in the earlier part of the fourteenth century. One of the half-dozen surviving texts is written in the Auchinlech Manuscript of about 1340, which Chaucer may have known. It must be said that if he did he shows it only by the parody of *Sir Thopas*;

and *Sire Degarre* is not at all his kind of thing. The story tells us of a King of 'Little Britain', who is so strong that no one can defeat him in tournament. His Queen has died in childbirth but has left a beautiful daughter whom the King now dotes upon. Although the daughter is of age, no one can marry her unless he can defeat the King in tournament. Many try and all fail. Here we clearly have the possessive father. Every year the King commemorates the death of his wife with a solemn feast at an abbey in a forest. One year, when the daughter is grown up, as they are going to the abbey, she has to detach herself from the main party in the forest for the simplest and most pressing of human needs. She fails to catch up and is lost on her own in the forest. A young knight, noble, lively and hand-some, wearing a scarlet robe, approaches her. He is, he says, a Fairy knight, his nature being to wear armour and ride about with shield and spear. But he tells her not to be afraid for now he is carrying only a sword, and as he has loved her many a year, she must be his beloved. Upon which he rapes her, notwithstanding that she weeps and screams and tries to run away. Then he stands up and tells her that she will bear his son, to whom he will leave his sword. When grown up the son must seek his father. He will recognise his father because his father has broken the point off the sword in a giant's head and retains the point in his pouch. The knight concludes, 'have good day, I must go hence'.

The lady eventually finds her way back to court and is able to give birth secretly to a son who is immediately well wrapped up, laid in a cradle with four pounds of gold and ten pounds of silver and a pair of gloves sent to the lady by her Fairy lover. The child is also provided with a letter saying that he is of noble birth and that when he is grown up he must love no woman unless the gloves fit her, for certainly they will fit no woman but his mother. This interesting parcel is placed on a cold, clear, moonlit winter's night at the door of a holy hermit. When he discovers the child, the hermit rather surprisingly gives thanks and christens the child Degarre, 'the lost one'. He is the only person in the story to bear a name, and that is specifically symbolic. The hermit causes the boy to be fostered until ten years old by his sister, who is the wife of a rich merchant in the city. The following ten years the boy spends with the hermit learning 'clerk's lore' with the surprising result that he becomes very stalwart. At twenty, his mysterious origins are revealed to him, and having thanked the hermit and made satisfactory financial arrangements with his foster parents he sets out to find his true parents, carrying with him a good oak sapling. With this he kills a dragon for an earl who then offers him rents and treasures. Degarre tries the glove test on all available women, but none fitting, he departs, having been given horse, armour and a man-servant and been dubbed knight by the grateful earl. After riding many a day, Degarre meets a crowd of earls and barons come from parliament in a city where the King has proclaimed that if any man can defeat him in tournament he may marry the King's daughter and inherit the kingdom, for the King has no other heir. Many have tried and all have failed. Degarre's attempt, however, is welcomed by the King. A long jousting takes place, vividly described, and eventually Degarre throws the King from his saddle, as the poet says, 'tail over top'. Everybody cheers except the daughter, who does not relish being married to a man she does not know. The King bears no grudge and they are married, and, says the poet, very dangerous it is to marry without knowing a person's family, because Sir Degarre has there married his own mother. (He has, of course, defeated the father-image in the person of his grandfather.) But God will prevent sin. They should go to bed immediately, but it suddenly occurs to Degarre to try the glove test. The gloves, of course, fit. The lady falls down with emotion and thanks God that she has found her son. And he, too, is delighted to find his mother, whom he clasps and kisses many a time. He immediately asks where his father is. He then receives the sword and vows to find his father.

He rides far to the West until he reaches the forest where he was begotten. He comes to a castle. He walks in over the lower drawbridge through the open gate and stables his horse, but no one is to be seen. He sits by a fire in the empty hall. Girls come in and go out. They will not speak to him. Then a lady of great honour comes forth with ten maidens and begins to feast, but none will speak to him. However, Degarre sits down before the lady herself and as he looks at her he falls in love. After the meal all depart and Degarre follows the lady to her chamber where he and she sit on her bed and he enjoys the music of a damsel playing the harp. This is so sweet that he falls fast asleep until morning. The lady wraps him up, puts a pillow under his head and sleeps in the same bed. In the morning she mocks him for having slept like a beast all night and paid no attention to the maidens. He asks pardon, and asks who she is and why there are so many women without men. She tells him that she is the only daughter of a rich baron who has died, and whose possessions she has inherited. But a neighbouring fierce knight wishes to marry her or ravish her, and he has killed all her men. Degarre immediately promises he will help and the enemy immediately appears. Degarre splits his helm and head down to the chest. As soon as he returns, the lady welcomes him enthusiastically and repeats her offer of her land and herself. Degarre thanks her courteously but says he must go off to seek adventure for twelve months and then he will return. They both weep bitterly at his departure. But he gives no proper reason. Degarre rides west again a long time until a fierce knight meets him. They fight. So the battle begins, as the poet tells us, without seeking suspense, of father against son. But soon the father sees the pointless sword. They realise who they are, and each swoons away. When they come to, the son asks his father pardon for his misdeeds and his father asks him to come and live with him in his castle. Degarre says he cannot, but they should both go and seek his mother, for she is in great mourning. So father and son go to England. The lady immediately recognises the knight and says 'My dear son, you have brought your father with you.' The King, her father, thanks God. He now knows who Sir Degarre's father is; while the lady swoons yet again. The marriage between her and her son is immediately dissolved, because they are too nigh of kin, as the poet says, and Degarre goes and marries the lady he has won.

This charmingly ridiculous story is told strongly and simply with agreeably realistic touches. The author never makes any attempt at fundamental plausibility. It is impossible to imagine that he or any fourteenth-century audience ever took it any more literally than any modern adult takes literally the story of King Lear or of Oedipus or of Cinderella.

The story is highly representative, with many analogues in many European languages. Yet no one can ever have taken it as a serious imitation of life. It is a series of fantasies based on our innermost experiences, though not in any solemn way. The latent arena is, of course, the home, and it is very clear that the chief contestants are protagonist, father and mother. The story is ingeniously complicated by the introductory passage about Degarre's mother where the protagonist at first seems to be the lady herself, who is embarrassed by her father in a way that reminds one of the Cinderella versions. In this episode, the Fairy knight is a rather rough Prince Charming. At the latent level, we may say he rescues her from her father. But the rapidity and violence of the rape make the transfer of the protagonist's feelings from the father to the peer very inadequately articulated. The introductory passage however turns out to be no more than an introduction, not the main theme, and only important as explaining the mysterious birth of the hero, and providing him with a more magnificent true parent than those who actually bring him up – an aspect of the family 'romance' in its narrow form. The main theme of the whole poem is that of the emerging male protagonist. Degarre is the lost child, common in traditional literature, but universal in appeal. The dragon fight is an extremely common motif, and is often accepted as an image of latent sexual fears and inhibitions which have to be overcome. The dragon fight signifies the protagonist's coming of age, at any rate physically. What is more unusual in this poem is the specifically open theme of seeking his mother. Generally speaking, the dominating mother-image is a repellent one, even for male protagonists, and some writers go so far as to say that the mother is never sought in fairy tale. She is, at least in romance.

Another strong theme related to the need to identify the mother is that of the anonymity of the protagonist. Presumably everybody feels anonymous when very young. Anonymity is associated with the protagonist's search for his own identity, for which the identity of the mother may be important evidence.

A peculiarity of this particular story lies in the ambivalence of the image of the gloves, which fulfils in part a function like that of Cinderella's slipper, of identifying the beloved as such. But then the beloved is identified in order to show that she is unavailable. The story is about the way the growing youth rightly loves his mother, but must switch his affections away from her to someone of his own age. A mother is first loved, then identified as unavailable. As all mothers know, most little boys at a very early age have said 'I will marry you, Mummy, when I grow up.' They never do. The identification of the mother as true mother at the manifest literal level forces the protagonist to recognise reality and find another beloved. The protagonist always risks seeking the mother-image again, rather than a true peer. At first that is what Degarre does. His being put to sleep and tucked up in bed by the lady of the castle is a marvellous image of maternal fondness which paralyses him sexually. But he then defeats another father-figure rival, that is to say the knight who oppresses the lady of the castle, and is thus paradoxically able to think of the lady of the castle less in terms of a mother-image. So he wins her. Like so many other romance and folktale heroes, he insists on not staying to enjoy his winnings. On the face of it there is no reason why he should not, so it seems reasonable to look for some underlying psychological force or power here. That underlying power is surely some unworked-out fear of sex or of the lady, or indeed of the rival father-image. There is a sense that even now he is not quite 'ripe', not all inhibitions have been shed, the mother has not been finally cast off, the father, and therefore the self, not yet finally identified. Ultimately, there is a mysterious latent feeling of 'work' so far not done, of destiny to be achieved, of identity to be fixed, before the protagonist can settle with a wife. We should also not neglect the fact that his departure may be no more – and no less – than the last kick of male restlessness before being tied down to domesticity and what Hemingway in *A Farewell to Arms* calls 'the biological trap'. (Did Hemingway's imagination ever really grow up?) For many reasons, then, the hero goes out to seek more adventures. He beats down yet one more father-figure and actually identifies him as the real father. This is most satisfactory to all, not least, be it noted, to the father. Most fathers want to be outdone by their sons.

The story itself offers the notion that it is important to identify oneself, to find one's father, to be accepted by him as fully grown, before one can settle down with a wife. This is a version of the family drama that we hardly encounter in fairy tales, especially when, as nowadays, they are narrowed down and directed to children. The story of Degarre seems most interested in the relationship of the protagonist to the parents. It provides an image of how when we recognise the goodness and indeed the nobility of our parents we can recognise ourselves as the same kind of people; we can associate ourselves with them.

In the symbolic internal world represented by *Sire Degarre*, the father's sword is significant of the father. It is presumably a phallic emblem. The hero inherits it, but it is still incomplete. It lacks its tip. The hero has to prove that he can use it, as he does in the battle with his father, and then make the sword complete. His masculine character is now fully integrated. He can identify himself by identifying his father. He can also identify himself *with* his father, but also with differentiation. He is both friendly and superior. He is, and is not, his father. In so far as he is not his father he can save himself from his mother by ensuring that Father and Mother are re-united. Both of them now safely tied up, he can go off and

marry his girl-friend. But he can only do this after the essential recon-
ciliations with Mother and Father. We can come to the conclusion that this
remarkable story is the very opposite of Sophocles's version of Oedipus.
It is romance, not tragedy. The common traditional mind of Europe, fed
from other parts of the world, meditated for many centuries on these
patterns. Nowadays we live at a time when a literary nihilism is fashionable, when traditional virtues are despised and happy endings denied.
Modern literature often practises a literal grossness. The goodness of
imagination and the imagination of goodness are treated with equal
scorn. In consequence, medieval romance, like fairy tale, is often regarded as silly and escapist. But there are both truth and optimism in the
fantasies of fairy tale and romance. These fantasies are certainly not those
of the modern novel, but they do show that love and reconciliation, like
truth, can make us whole.

CHAPTER III

Sir Gawain and the Green Knight

'If father didn't mean anything,' blubbered the injured Grinder [a young boy], 'why did he go and say anything to mother? Nobody thinks half so bad of me as my own father does. What a unnatural thing! I wish somebody'd take and chop my head off. Father wouldn't mind doing it, I believe, and I'd much rather he did than t'other.'

(*Dombey and Son*, 1848,
Chapter XXXVIII, p. 381)

I

Sir Gawain and the Green Knight,[1] greatest of English medieval romances, is most typical and most idiosyncratic. It is focussed on the family drama, whose latent drives control the story, which is brilliantly realised with the most vivid detail at the manifest literal level. The manifest images are Arthurian adventures which have little ostensibly to do with the family drama, but there is no sign of strain between the various levels. The explicit story is clearly about the establishment of the hero's independence and maturity, but does not rely on creating a heroine to whom the protagonist transfers his feelings for his mother. It is as if the highest form of mature self-realisation for a man is seen by this great poet and story-teller as complete independence, though not in isolation from society.

The prologue emphasises what extraordinary events have taken place in the past here in Britain, and promises that the poet will now tell an outstandingly remarkable example of one. The story begins with the festivities at King Arthur's court at Camelot at Christmas time. There are the most famous knights under Christ, the loveliest ladies, the comeliest King. It is the most fortunate company under heaven, and all are 'in their first age' (54), that is they are all young. This is all expressed in the terms of hyperbolical idealisation characteristic of the favoured images of medieval romance and indeed of traditional literature generally. It is by definition not a plausible picture of ordinary normal everyday life, at court or elsewhere:

Hit were now gret nye to neven
So hardy a here on hille

(58–9)

(It would be very hard nowadays to name such a brave company any-where.)

This takes place in the past, 'once upon a time', and as the introductory stanzas emphasised, we are to hear a wonder, not something normal and commonplace, but deeply interesting because of its unusual nature. The hyperbole of description is thus protected and justified. The emphasis on strangeness is itself a rationalisation of the non-rational which is very characteristic of this poet and is the opposite of Chaucer's practice, where realistic rationalisation contrasts with and strains the non-rational to the limits. The *Gawain*-poet has a very powerful vein of literal realism at the service of, not as a test of, the latent pattern of the story. His realism is very rarely ironic. In his description here of Arthur's court in its Christmas festivity there is no hint, signal or suggestion anywhere in his words of a double meaning. We must therefore take his enthusiastic presentation of the joyous splendour of Arthur's courtly festival absolutely at face-value, indeed quite literally, for the argument here, as elsewhere in this book, is not to deny the obvious literal face-value of the words of the text, but to show that the words also have wide associations and symbolic implications. In most traditional literature (Chaucer may be a partial exception) the latent re-inforces while extending the literal meaning.

We have here a natural, not naturalistic, description of the ideal Christmas party, with youth and jest and jollity, at Arthur's ideal court. I emphasise its natural acceptability in a way that may seem unnecessarily obvious to any ordinarily experienced reader of romance, folktale or fairy tale, because so many modern critics see this and other descriptions of the delights of Arthur's court as an ironically sarcastic criticism of its childishness and irresponsibility. Presumably they feel that Arthur should be at his desk getting on with governing the country, not giving such a deplorable example of the conspicuous consumption of the *dolce vita* when so many people are starving, the peasants oppressed, the woodwoses and other monsters not yet restricted to National Parks, and the Wirral itself an unreclaimed wilderness, still without benefit from the industrial spread of Liverpool and Port Sunlight. Thus inappropriate assumptions lead to inappropriate responses. The assumption that literature is always, or should always be, a naturalistic, mimetic and literal account of 'real', i.e. ordinary, appearances, paradoxically leads to a distorted reading which actually denies the natural literal meaning. The *Gawain*-poet needs to be read with genuine literal acceptance because he is fully aware of the demands of rationality.

We see this a few lines later, when he describes how on New Year's Day Arthur, who was youthfully gay and somewhat boyish, *childgered* (86), stirred by his young blood and restless brain (89), could not sit and eat until some marvel had occurred, or strange story told, or someone had come to claim a joust. Arthur's habit of thus refusing to eat at a feast until some marvel occurred is a well-established convention of Arthurian romances. The poet need not and does not comment on it. But to some extent he does rationalise it by emphatic references to Arthur's youth.

Once again, there is no hint of criticism, unless we believe that to be young is in itself culpable. It is an *explanation*, a rationalisation. The emphasis on youth also serves the poem's deeper purposes well, because, like most romances, even Malory's, it is a story about being young, and growing up.

At this wonderful party, when they are eagerly waiting in expectation of both a marvel and their dinner, there rushes in at the door a terrible 'master' (*aghlich mayster*, 136), enormously big, almost a giant, though on the other hand extremely handsome. An ambivalent visitor! And the most extraordinary thing about him is that he is bright green all over. His rich clothing is described. It begins to emerge that he is also on horseback, with equally splendid saddle and trappings, and the mighty horse itself is also green. Vivid as the realistic description is, it does not follow any naturalistic model of perception, as Benson points out.[2] The most obvious detail, the greenness, is postponed to the very end of the description, with fine literary effect.

The Green Knight, who carries a holly branch as a sign of peace, but also a huge axe (more ambivalence), is insolent. 'Who is in charge here?' he says in effect, as if he does not recognise who is the King. Arthur encounters him both boldly and courteously, and the upshot is the proposal of the beheading game – you cut off mine, then I'll cut off yours – which, though the youthful Arthur is not afraid, is taken up by Gawain, in a speech of wonderful courtesy, analysed by Spearing in a classic piece of literal verbal criticism.[3] The Green Knight emphasises the youthfulness of the court. They are none but beardless children (280) he sneers hyperbolically. Gawain will behead the Green Knight, and in twelve months' time, if he can, the Green Knight will return the blow. So Gawain emerges as the protagonist, champion of the court. But where do you live? asks Gawain. The Green Knight will tell him after the blow. The visitor when decapitated is as vigorous as when in one piece, notwithstanding the fountain of blood that follows the blow. He tells Gawain to keep his promise and seek him at the Green Chapel, which he can easily find if he asks, and gallops out.

The year passes and Gawain sets out. The elaborate arming, another commonplace of traditional literature remarkably well handled by the poet, without any irony,[4] marks him as the hero about to undertake his first great battle. His shield explicitly symbolises his virtues: his strength, religion, purity, bravery, courtesy, liberality, compassion. On the inner side he has a picture of the Virgin Mary. Gawain is free from every imperfection, adorned with all the virtues. None of this can be ironical. None of it implies that such perfection is impossible. Why should we not accept the description of Gawain at its face-value and take this perfect young knight as our hero? Because no man is perfect? But no one should suppose that we are reading a transcript of ordinary existence. Does not the Bible positively command us 'Be ye perfect' (Matt. V, 48)? Plenty of romance heroes are as ideal as Gawain. We ourselves live in a period of literary culture which is normally (at best) bored with goodness, as if

74

there were so much of it in the world; and cynical devaluations of the motives and actions of the best men are *à la mode*. There is a truth in that, no doubt, but traditional literature organises its presentation of inadequacy and evil differently, and we are not given here or elsewhere a naturalistic characterisation of a possible young man called Gawain, acne and all.

Gawain wanders off, eventually passing through the wilderness of the Wirral, never questioning that he must keep his fatal promise. He suffers in the winter weather, sleeping out in barren countryside, in human terms entirely on his own, 'no man but God to talk to'. On Christmas Eve he finds himself in a wild forest among the high hills, and miserably prays to the Virgin Mary. Hardly has he made the sign of the cross three times after his prayer and religious repentance than he sees the most beautiful castle. Thanking Jesus and Saint Julian he hastens to it and is courteously welcomed by the porter and others, his horse stabled, himself brought to the hall, where a great fire burns and the lord of the castle greets him. The lord is a huge man of full age (*hyghe eldee*, 844) with a broad beaver-coloured beard, very stalwart, a face as fierce as fire, noble of speech, altogether a man fit for command. Leaving aside many details even more fascinating than usual, we may note that the welcome by the people of the castle emphasises Gawain's name and his reputation for courtesy and for courtly conversation about love. No problem about his identity here.

At evensong in the chapel he meets the lord again, who welcomes him by name. With the lord are the two ladies of the house, though during the service men and women are as usual in the medieval church service separated. (The literalism of some critics takes the brief remark that the lord took Gawain by the gown to lead him to his place (936–40) as indicating that Gawain had to be held back from rushing at the ladies, like a randy stallion off to the mares in the fen!) Men and women do not meet till after they have soberly sat through the service. The younger of the two ladies, who is never named, is more beautiful than Guinevere, and we assume, though it is not explicit till later (1098), that she is the lord's wife. A much older lady accompanies her, ugly to look at. Gawain respectfully greets her and kisses the younger, as was the courteous custom of those times.

The time passes in Christmas merriment, from Christmas day till the 28th December, when the other guests depart and Gawain says he must go too, to seek the Green Chapel, not apparently having worried about it over Christmas. But his (and our) inner confidence is justified, for the lord says that the Green Chapel is not two miles away. Gawain can remain till the very morning of New Year's Day, chatting during the day to the lord's wife, while the lord goes hunting. The lord moreover proposes a sort of folk-game with profound archaic associations, the Exchange of Winnings, whereby Gawain and he will each give to the other in the evening what he has won during the day – a complex image of relationships and contest between the two. To give a gift is to assert superiority and a claim over the recipient, which can only be resolved by returning an agreed equivalent of the gift.[5] The lord goes hunting early in the morning, and meanwhile the lord's wife comes, as everybody knows, to Gawain's bed to tempt him sexually, though in the most courteous way. It is her courtesy, and his, which allow Gawain to fend her off. There are several reasons why he should. First, chastity is for him a supreme virtue, and was generally taken as such in the culture of the time, even for men. The great examples of the importance of male chastity in Arthurian literature are the romances about Galahad and Percival. Lancelot failed to achieve the Grail because of his unchastity with Guinevere. In the present poem Gawain's chastity is his most significant virtue and to lose it would be both to commit a great sin and to lose his heroic quality. Second, a married woman's faithfulness to her husband concerns not only her honour but also his, and Gawain is under an obligation to his host for hospitality and friendship. He therefore does not want to dishonour the lord, to be a 'traitor' to him, for though that would not affect Gawain's own honour in relation to the lady, it would break his 'truth' to the lord of the castle. The basic situation is more explicit in the episode with Sir Persant's daughter in Malory's *Gareth of Orkney*, discussed more fully in Chapter V (p. 105). In the present poem everything is said politely and indirectly, if occasionally with *double entendre* (e.g. 1237), in accordance with the fully accepted convention that courtesy, most especially for this poet, is an essentially Christian quality.[6] The idea that the medieval virtue of courtesy was purely secular and consequently anti-Christian is an historical and critical error, though it is true that courtesy is not the same virtue as chastity. At the end of the first temptation scene the lady kisses Gawain when she goes. In the evening Gawain 'gives' this kiss to the lord, who 'gives' him (equally symbolically) the dead deer. The second day it is two kisses to a boar. On the third day the lady is particularly seductive. Gawain awakes miserable because of his approaching death, but is much cheered by her joyful and pleasing behaviour. It is here that courtesy threatens to become a trap, because the lady almost abandons her own courtesy and all but directly confesses her own love for him and blames him for not making love to her on the bed there (1779–81). A blunt refusal of a lady's request would be discourteous. It is explicit in the poem that courtesy is a virtue which the knight is obliged to practise, which it would be sinful not to practise. So here courtesy is at odds with chastity, and with Gawain's obligation to his host. It is an exquisite problem when virtue is assaulted, not by vice, but by another virtue. The lady however is shown to make a tactical error. She asks if perhaps Gawain has a beloved whom he prefers to the one who of all women loves him, meaning herself. This allows Gawain to reply that he loves no lady, and intends to love none, at present; so that he is able to deny her without making it seem particular. The wit of this exchange is delightful, but the surface realism also relates to the latent force of the poem.

The lady then tries him with a love-gift also courteously declined, and at last, as if it were an afterthought, offers him her belt, a green 'lace', or girdle, which she claims has the virtue of preserving its wearer from being slain by any manner of means. A gift so *à propos* Gawain cannot refuse, and he agrees furthermore to her request to conceal the gift from her lord. The acceptance of a gift has to some extent put him in her power, though as the gift is of little material worth it is the less serious.

The next stanza shows Gawain at confession and the poet says he was as completely absolved as if the Day of Judgement were to come in the morning. No mention of the belt. It has been argued by Professor Burrow in his notable book,[7] and accepted by many critics, that this is therefore a false or at least inadequate confession. If that is so then the poet's words must be ironical. Yet there is no verbal hint of irony, and I believe that we are meant to take the words at face-value. At the most literal level Gawain has committed no sin concerning the belt. He intends, it is true, to conceal the gift from the lord, but a sinful intention is not a sin and cannot be confessed. At the literal level, too, the Exchange of Winnings is apparently only a trivial game. The matter will appear differently later, it is true, but not in relation to a false confession; rather, in relation to the deeper latent guiding forces of the poem. At the Exchange of Winnings Gawain 'gives' the three kisses the lady has also given him, but not the belt, and 'receives' the fox's skin the lord has won.

The next day Gawain must go to his sad tryst. He takes his leave and arms himself, not forgetting the green belt, with its polished pendants and glittering gold, called by the poet a 'drurye', love-token (2033), which he wears outside upon his red surcoat. On the way his guide gives him a grisly description of the Knight of the Green Chapel and suggests that he should flee, the guide promising never to tell. Gawain refuses. This is perhaps the last temptation, to save his life. But is it really a temptation? Should we not say that now that Gawain has his magic belt he is quite safe and may readily meet any enemy? Has he not effectively already failed? Can he any longer retain our admiration, since he would seem to be no longer running into any kind of danger?

If Gawain has thus already failed, and needs no bravery now to carry out his promise, the poet would seem to have managed these culminating episodes in a very anti-climatic way. Yet that is not the impression that any reader, uncorrupted by Neoclassical prejudice, has ever received. The poet gives no hint that Gawain can now afford to be complacent. We follow with eagerness the progress of the story, sharing the protagonist's grim resolve. It is true that we do not really expect him to die. The reasons for that are complex; in brief, they arise out of the tone of presentation, recognition of the romance convention with its normally happy ending,[8] and the general knowledge, characteristic of traditional literature, that though the Gawain-figure is treated in many different ways, in many different adventures, by many different story-tellers, yet he does not die when young at the hands of a Green Knight. So we have the 'basic trust', (to use Bettelheim's admirable phrase in *The Uses of Enchantment*) which is characteristic of most fairy tale and romance, that Gawain will survive. But he can only interestingly survive if there is at the same time a sense of real danger that he may not, which we must feel for and with Gawain, as he approaches the climax of the test, along with our 'basic trust'. Every practical reader knows on his pulses that the art of the poem is successful here; we do feel both anxiety for and confidence in the hero. There are numerous reasons why. First, the poet in no way undermines by his verbal conduct of the story our admiration for Gawain and our sense of the danger he is to face. Second, Gawain neither expresses nor is shown to feel any confidence at all deriving from possession of the belt. On the contrary, he feels horrible. We and Gawain have only the lady's word for it that the belt is magic and efficacious. Everyone knows that 'magic' is tricky and does not always work in literary adventures, just as, in the modern world, motor engines sometimes fail and brilliant batsmen are got out without making a single run.[9] Nothing is certain. These two reasons operate at the literal, manifest level. Third, we recognise in most romances, and clearly in this one, either consciously or unconsciously, that the naturalistic laws of cause and effect between successive episodes are only superficial. We do not connect successive scenes as if the second were in all respects the product of the first. Scenes are significantly juxtaposed, but not necessarily organically connected. We do not make immediately novelistic connections of a literalistic kind. We respond to pattern rather than causality. As readers we may be conscious of the dubious belt, but we do not make of it here the principal cause of Gawain's resolve. That derives from his general character, not from detailed personal motivation. Gawain is not characterised as a personality in that way. The psychology of personality is in the story as a whole, not inside that of the protagonist-figure. Fourth, most generally of all, the mixture of confidence and fear with which Gawain approaches his test is humanly true of almost every soldier who went into battle. Almost every soldier, frightened as he is, also believes that this time it is not he but someone else who will be killed. There are some exceptional individuals who seem not to know fear, and others, at the other extreme, who know only despair, but most people, while sharing both feelings in different degrees, in so far as they go on at all, feel both 'basic trust' and real fear, a profoundly ambivalent mixture, and a clear example of how we simultaneously entertain mutually contradictory attitudes towards the same object. And we need not limit this set of feelings to the more dramatic encounters of our lives. We feel them in all the many situations, great and small, in which we have to persist against the grain of preference, do something that we ought to do although we do not want to do it. The story of Gawain's experience, apparently so remote from the actuality of life even in the fourteenth, let alone the twentieth, century, is gripping because in its non-naturalistic way it vividly models real-life experience for us. The *Gawain*-poet is particularly interested in obligation carried out against inclination, which all his poems are concerned with, and this same human internal self-contradiction was a fundamental part of the medieval world-view.[10]

The splendidly dramatic encounter with the Green Knight is a climax in every way worthy of the poem. The spot is mysterious. It is a lonely valley with a hollow mound in it which is the ominous 'chapel'. This mound, not always understood by editors, is described in sufficient detail to make it clear that it is an ancient burial mound or tumulus, hollow inside, but empty. [11] Gawain himself is shown not to know what it is, and the poet may not have explicitly recognised it, but the description, Gawain's expressed comments, and the general reputation given to the spot by the guide, make it clear that it has all the feelings about death and gloom traditionally associated with such places. That it should be called a chapel is one of the rare verbal ironies of the poem. Gawain stands on top of it and hears a dreadful grinding noise coming from a hard rock in a cliff on the other side of a brook flowing nearby. He greets the ominous sound with wry resolution. 'Though I lose my life no noise shall make me afraid' (2210–11). The poet represents him as not thinking of the belt at all, but recognising the risk of losing his life. He will not complain, but leaves all in the hands of God.

The Green Knight duly makes his terrifying appearance and Gawain leans forward, exposing the flesh of his neck to the beheading blow, behaving as if he feared nothing, refusing to shrink for fear (2257–8), with the poet clearly implying that he does feel fear though he will not give way to it, and again making no mention of the belt. Two feints he endures, dramatically spaced out, and then the third blow comes at which Gawain gives up all hope (2307–8). When the tip of the blade just slices his neck there is an explosion of released tension as Gawain springs away, swings his shield round in front of him, and whips out his sword – never since he was born was he ever so happy! (2320–1). He defies his foe. The Green Knight, leaning on his axe, looks at him and 'is pleased at heart' (2335), which is the only time that the poet comments on the Green Knight's inner state. He then explains: he is really the lord of the castle. No injury is given for the first night of the Exchange of Winnings, when Gawain had handed over all his winnings; the second similarly. The actual blow which inflicted the slight wound in the neck was because Gawain had not handed over the belt on the third night. Far from being a magic protection the belt was Gawain's only source of weakness. The belt belongs to the Green Knight. He set his wife to woo Gawain. He knows exactly what went on in the temptations because he devised them to test Gawain, and he adds that Gawain is 'the most faultless man that ever walked' (2363). Only he lacked a little, was a little deficient in loyalty (*lewte*) because he kept the belt, but is the less to be blamed because he loved his life (2366–8).

Gawain is deeply mortified, accusing himself in hyperbolical terms of both cowardice and covetousness with all the passionate exaggeration of the young, and of the hyperbolical traditional style. Cowardice, for fear of the blow to be received, he says, taught him covetousness, and so to deny his own true nature, the generosity and loyalty that pertain to knights. He is faulty, false, fearful, treacherous and untrue; his conduct *all* faulty. What does the Green Knight want him to do? (2379–88). But the other laughs, and says he has confessed completely and received the penance of the point of the axe, so that he is as pure as when first born. Burrow has made much of this second 'true' confession, but there seems no reason to take it as organically connected with the previous confession to the priest. It is a purely secular parallel. Among all the sins that Gawain confesses to there is no mention of the sin of an earlier false confession. But Burrow is right in seeing that this second informal 'confession' is important, because it relates to the latent movement of the poem, while the first confession seems to be part of the local realism by which the verbal realisation gives as vivid and recognisable a surface as possible to the story. The Green Knight tells Gawain to keep the belt as a memento, and to come back to his dwelling, where his wife, who was his enemy, shall be reconciled with him (2390–2406). But Gawain will not. He commends himself to the ladies, comments on how even famous men in the Bible were made fools of by women, and therefore he must be excused. He accepts the belt as a reminder to himself of his own humiliation, and asks the lord's name.

Then comes the most curious of rationalisations in this strangest of delightful poems. The other says that his name is Bertilak de Hautdesert, and he is what he is through the power of Morgan le Fay, the learned and all-powerful mistress of Merlin, who lives in his house, and is indeed the old lady whom Gawain met. It is she who sent Bertilak as the Green Knight to Arthur's hall to test the pride and reputation of the Round Table, 'to deprive you, the court (or you, Gawain – it is not clear) of your senses', and to distress Guinevere and cause her death, by seeing the man speak with his head in his hand. Morgan is no less than Gawain's aunt and Arthur's half-sister. Let Gawain come to his aunt and make merry with Bertilak's household, who love him. Bertilak wishes Gawain as well as any man under God, because of Gawain's great faithfulness (*trawthe*). It is all extraordinarily bland. To appal Guinevere, make mad the court, has been the plan, no apology or reason offered: now, having failed, come home and be happy with that homicidal maniac, your aunt, and her accomplices! (2445–70). Gawain declines. They embrace and kiss each other, and commend each other to God. Gawain returns to Arthur's court, tells his story, shows the belt as token of what he calls his 'untrawthe'. Arthur and the court, however, comfort him, laugh at the story, and all agree to wear a baldric like the belt. Any man who wears it shall be honoured. This again has often been taken by modern critics as a sign of the court's triviality of mind and morals, because the modern view of Gawain is that of Gawain himself, and not that of the poet or of the Green Knight, and he is considered to have failed. The poem is seen as a sort of ironical comedy of failure.

I have so far kept mainly to the manifest literal level of the poem, with certain implications, while maintaining that the directing force of the action is at a different, latent, level. If we restrict our view to the literal level and assume that it alone contains the motivations, causes and effects of the action we are bound to consider the story ill-managed, despite the vivid surface realism, because there are too many puzzles and non-sequiturs. Leaving aside the actual physical absurdity of the beheading, and of a man speaking holding his head in his hand, how does Gawain happen to find the Green Chapel? Of course he gets to it on New Year's Day by the help of the guide, but the Green Chapel is obviously an appendage or extension (annexe as it were!) of Bertilak's castle, and how does Gawain find the castle at just the right time? Then, again, if Gawain were psychologically personalised as in a novel he would surely be suspicious about the Exchange of Winnings. Where would the lord think he gets his kisses from? The chambermaid? Kisses themselves may be no great matter, but there has always been more involved. Then again, if the lord himself were characterised with psychological plausibility, what sort of a man is he to send his wife to tempt Gawain? She, certainly, seems keen enough, but did Bertilak really want to cuckold himself? In all honour-systems it is always the cuckold and his wife, never the seducer, who are dishonoured. Suppose Gawain had given in to the lady the first time! The patterning of the three temptations and the three blows makes it obvious that if Gawain had given in at once to the lady, congratulating himself on his good luck, Bertilak would have had to cut off his head at the first blow, presumably leaving Gawain two up in the matter of seductions, though dead. But anyway, if Bertilak wanted to kill Gawain, why did he have to arrange to have himself cuckolded first? Nothing in the original bargain makes the temptations necessary at the manifest level.

There may be a witty if somewhat improper structural pun, as it were, hinted at behind the Exchange of Winnings. Sexual intercourse is sometimes known as 'possession' on the part of the man. Had Gawain 'possessed' the lady how could he have handed over his gains anyway? And if he could have handed over his 'possession', would that have been counted as a faithful exchange and so earned him remission of the promised blow? But perhaps one of the many symbolic implications of this story is the proposition that sex is *not* a possession, a property. Most extraordinary of all, however, is that according to the literal rationalisation offered by the poet through the mouth of Bertilak, nine-tenths of the poem and the action are entirely irrelevant to the manifest principal cause. This principal cause, to repeat, is to kill Guinevere, drive the court mad, destroy their pride, by the spectacle of a beheaded man speaking to them. Once that had failed, there was in logic and causality no more to do. Certainly Gawain had been the instrument of the initial beheading, but it could apparently in manifest terms have been anyone else. The attempt to destroy Gawain subsequently would seem to be sheer motiveless malice. Though that also is strange, for why should the Green Knight, having failed yet again, at the ending be so genial to Gawain? The Green Knight is indeed a strange tool for Morgan to use. We are not told the source of her power over him, which in terms of causality we should like to know, because though we are told she is so powerful she apparently has no control at all over Arthur and Gawain and Guinevere. Moreover, though her ingenuity in thinking of such a device to kill Guinevere and destroy the court may be admired, it is remarkably inefficient. In wondering about her relationship to Bertilak we may also wonder about his relationship to that other lady, his beautiful and amorous young wife. How could we imagine their conversations together, both before and after her attempts to seduce Gawain in his bed? And again, what could they have said to each other had she succeeded?

All these speculations are of course beside the point. They build upon quite wrong assumptions about the fundamental nature of the poem, as do all similar interpretations that take it literalistically, on naturalistic assumptions, rather than literally, at face-value, with symbolic implications. If we take it literalistically the poem is absurd. Even if we yield to its charm, we may well, on such assumptions, judge the court irresponsible and Gawain a fool and a failure because he does not match his own absurdly high standards. We may then be led to make the historical mistake that courtesy is a pagan value in conflict with Christianity. Such a reading has intolerable self-contradictions, of a kind different from the ambivalent attitudes towards an object which are common in human experience. Everywhere the court and Gawain are repeatedly described as 'good'. The explicit values of the poem are the Christian virtues of chastity, courtesy and loyalty, which the hero exemplifies. The only way to resolve the contradictions created by an anachronistic Neoclassical literalism is to invent a Narrator so that we may say that the poet ironically means the opposite of what he says. Yet there is no more evidence here for either irony or a Narrator than there is for such in the story of Cinderella. The only reason for introducing them would be the assumption that the naturalistic structure of the story denies the face-value of the words, as must be the argument of anyone who maintains that the possession of the belt gives Gawain confidence to meet the Green Knight and is itself a sign of his total failure.

But the story has *no* naturalistic structure, as I have shown. On any naturalistic reading it is a jumble of inconsistent absurdities. Criticism based on a naturalistic reading must inevitably conclude that not only Gawain but the whole story is a failure.

Such a conclusion absurdly contradicts our response to the poem and its story, our sense of its power of joy and virtue; its feeling of 'Look, we have come through'; its optimism. Some of this feeling derives from the brilliant verbal realisation, but the fundamental source is the powerful pattern of images and of what they represent as evoked by the unfolding of the story.

It is a traditional story in the sense that the characters have names which we already know; that there is a single thread of story centred on the hero; that there is a patterning of events in triple repetition with progressive variation. The subject-matter of chivalrous romance is also familiar and the main motifs of the mutual beheading and the sexual temptations are found elsewhere, though not in conjunction. At the beginning we have a demand made upon the protagonist. He soon has to leave his base to seek an adventure which will test him severely. For reasons we have seen we expect excitement, variety, fear, perhaps love,

and a happy ending. Familiar as all this is, we are ready to hear it told
again and again in different guises because it concerns our most intimate
experiences of emergence as individuals.

Gawain is the protagonist, and we identify with him almost all the way,
the exception proving the rule. We accept him as a type, an emblem, with
a few leading characteristics such as we should like to have, to be summed
up, free of historical cultural conditioning, as moral integrity. We also
largely share his point of view. His view and experience of the Green
Knight and Bertilak are ours, and we know no more than he about his
opponent at any stage, with the possible minimal exception, already
noted, of the half-line comment that the Green Knight is pleased at heart
with him (2335). Similarly with the lady. Realistic description at the level
of verbal realisation occasionally gives us an external view of Gawain, a
brief comment on his state of mind, and reports on what he says to
himself as he comes to the Green Chapel. None of this amounts to either
an objective presentation of the protagonist, or an analysis of an in-
teriorised personality. The only exception to this comes at the very end,
after the effective action, when Gawain so passionately and hyperbolically condemns himself. Then, as Burrow and Spearing remark, we
do see him through the judgements of others, of the Green Knight, and of
Arthur and the court. In each case their judgement is in accord with what
is explicit and implicit in the rest of the story, namely, that he is the most
faultless knight that ever went. Perhaps so unequivocally high an
achievement, for a poet so sensitive to men's weakness, is too much to
allow simple identification with the protagonist, especially as it goes with
the protagonist's own strong sense of failure. So we become detached
here at the very end from our previously close identification with the
protagonist, in order to see him as the hero he truly is, and not as he feels
about himself. This re-inforces our sense of his success, and does also
slightly enrich the presentation of character. It does not imply the presentation of development of character. Gawain in his courtesy is never
conceited or over-confident, and is shown weeping for his sins on
Christmas Eve. Our final admiring, if also slightly amused, detachment
should in no way change our general impression of him as the protagonist, and our general identification with him. Because of our identification with him we see the other characters entirely in their relation to
him, and never to each other. He is present in every scene, and all the
scenes have effectively only two characters, Gawain and another, thus
conforming to the general pattern of traditional folktale narrative. (The
only apparent exception, when he is with Arthur *and* the Green Knight,
will be explained later.) We never see the other characters – there are
really only two, Bertilak and his wife – in relationship with each other in
Gawain's absence. There are no bedroom scenes of marital plotting
between them.

As a result we have the familiar situation whereby the story-structure
as a whole represents the protagonist's mind, the figure of Gawain
himself being the conscious projection of the protagonist's sense of self,

and other characters similarly corresponding to his latent mental images.

The protagonist is in conflict with a frightening but ambiguous opponent, much bigger than he, much older ('of high eldee'), whereas Arthur and all his court and *ipso facto* Gawain himself are young, even boyish. The Green Knight/Bertilak has a terrifying geniality. He is cheerfully rude, patronising, superior, and always retains the initiative and the control. He is quite clearly a father-figure. It is to be noted that in one of the French poems, *Caradoc*, which is certainly an analogue if not a source of *Sir Gawain and the Green Knight*, and which the poet may well have known, the hero undergoes a similar beheading test from a man who is indeed his father, though at that time unknown to him. And the astonishingly apt quotation from *Dombey and Son*, used as an epigraph for this chapter, wells up straight from Dickens's unconsciousness, revealing a remarkable penetration and ambivalence. We may if we wish make the parental threat more specific by adopting a Freudian interpretation, though it is not certain. We may think that the Green Knight is a father-figure who threatens castration. Cutting off the head seems usually to symbolise, to put it less dramatically, the sexual anxieties, and the more general anxieties in the struggle for identity, of the adolescent emerging into manhood. Whether or not we follow Freud so far, we have clearly entered a version of the perennial family drama.

Why does the Green Knight want to cut off Gawain's head, or whatever? Because Gawain has already cut off his. The first act of rebellion has already taken place. But it is not fair, as children say, because Father is invulnerable; he can always put his head back on, while I cannot. On the other hand, Father has invited rebellion. He is a projection of the son's fear of himself, and also of the son's own strength, derived from a strong father.

Another cause of the father-figure's hostility is also sexual; it relates to the protagonist's relationship with Father's wife, who may be supposed to be the protagonist's mother. We have no simple Oedipus situation here, if indeed we have it as usually presented even in the story of Oedipus himself. The mother-image is 'split' into her aged and authoritative and consequently (as the protagonist feels) malevolent aspects, as Morgan le Fay, and correspondingly into her affectionate and cuddly aspects, with her bare breasts, maternally and erotically attractive and kind, as the young lady. Whereas the malevolent mother-image is commonplace in traditional literature, the apparently kindly one is less so. Their juxtaposition in the same story seems a relatively rare enrichment. All the same, though the mother-figure in the form of the lady is superficially attractive, she is actually extremely dangerous. To be seduced by her is death. She is firmly under the control of the father-image, while he is equally firmly under the control of the old woman; as neat an expression of certain dualities of marital relationship from the protagonist's point of view as we are likely to come across. That the lady is married to Bertilak is sufficient evidence of her maternal status; that Morgan is Gawain's aunt is sufficient evidence for hers, since parent-figures are often replaced by substitution with other relatives. Hamlet's 'father-uncle' Claudius is a clear analogy for this mother-aunt. In so far as the mother-image is sexually attractive, the father-image is jealous and threatening. In so far as the protagonist resists Mother's seductions, the father-image cannot hurt him. But Mother and Father are in league. Mother's ambiguous attractions and threats are re-inforced by Father and their aim is to kill the Son (as in the blasphemous medieval joke about the Trinity), that is, to deny his independence and individuality. His resort is to resist both seduction and threat, to say 'no' to both, as it is said that a baby's first sign of psychic development is when it says 'no'. Thus the protagonist's independence is asserted without his own aggression; it is the older generation who are the aggressors, though they are defeated.

The only other notable characters in the poem are Arthur and Guinevere, who must be further aspects of one or other of the three main figures. They might be regarded, though marginal, as repeated parent-figures, but this seems unlikely because of the hostility to them shown by the Green Knight and Morgan. They must then share their status with Gawain, since they are also young and in his ambience of the court. Arthur is as much threatened by the father-image as Gawain, and may be said to represent the protagonist's idealisation of himself when he shall be free of parents, married to his peer, and in an independent household. We see this most clearly at the end of the story, when the protagonist, having resisted being over-mothered and reduced to infantilism by the regressive attractions of the mother-image, having defeated the over-bearingness of the father-image, and, last test of all, having declined the friendly invitation to come back home where all shall be as if nothing had happened, expressed by the Green Knight's invitation to return to the castle, naturally now returns to the achieved independence of the court, represented by Arthur, his ideal self. Being human, the protagonist has not won independence without a scar, without a minor slip, but he is received with joyous laughter, and all associate themselves with his triumph. The young adult is in a world where all wish to associate themselves with him in the same struggle and carry a similar honourable scar. It is probably because Arthur is essentially another projection, or 'split', of the protagonist, alongside Gawain, that they both appear together in confrontation with the Green Knight, without breaking the felt singleness of the narrative.

If Arthur represents the protagonist's idealisation of himself when independent, Guinevere, against whom the mother-image has shown so much hostility because she is married to Arthur, obviously represents Daughter-in-Law; she is the protagonist's potential, idealised beloved of his own age, and necessary rival to the mother-image, to cleave to whom Mother must be abandoned – a sufficient reason for Morgan's hostility.

There is another mother-image in the poem, if not exactly a character, and that is the Blessed Virgin Mother. She represents a pure maternal care which is not possessive and does not enforce regression. She consequently balances the anti-feminism implicit in the presentation of the lady and Morgan le Fay. Sexuality is what drags a man back into the bosom of the family. That controlled, he is free and independent. Sexuality causes even the cleverest men to make fools of themselves, and get trapped, as Gawain observes in a famous, though not discourteous, medieval commonplace (2416–28). The whole poem might be summed up as saying, do not lose your head over a woman; but woman has multiple meanings, and the seductive or threatening mother is dominant in this poem. In the light of this and so many other romances we can hardly doubt that the protagonist is at least as anxious to escape from the mother-image as he is to kill the father-image. Very few men wish to marry their mother. The Virgin Mother makes, in this poem, no such outrageous demand. By demanding chastity she begins to break the carnal natural bond exerted by the other aspects of the mother-image, making it possible to use energy in other ways. By implication she points to God as the true father-image, who being (in a sense) absent, is good, and is more than a father.

Arthur and Guinevere represent the protagonist's successful disengagement of ideal figures from parent-images. They show, through Gawain's adherence to the Arthurian court, that he has already made the successful transference of feeling from parents to equals. This is no doubt the fundamental latent reason why the Green Knight comes to test the pride and renown of Arthur's court – the protagonist feels that the father-figure challenges his attainment of maturity and independence. He is felt to say to the protagonist, are you really as grown-up as you think you are? Look at me, I am bigger and older! Can you do what I can? Come home and try it! Arthur's court, which Gawain represents, that is to say, which is to the protagonist the independent world of his equals, is one of the factors that helps Gawain to resist.

Arthur's and Bertilak's courts have a paradoxical similarity and dissimilarity. There is in the poet's presentation no fundamental moral distinction between them in religious and courtly values. (The lady is indeed potentially immoral, but at the literal level she fails to seduce Gawain precisely because in verbal expression she adheres to the standards of Christian courtesy, with the implicit values of chastity, honour and the moral superiority of ladies over knights. If she had explicitly abandoned those standards Gawain would have been able explicitly to reject her as making patently forbidden and immoral propositions, because all the virtues, as the pentangle shows, are interlinked. When making her tempting offers she is as much in a cleft stick as is Gawain because she has to suggest immorality in moral terms.) Arthur's court and Bertilak's are equally regular in religious observance and there is no suggestion by the poet of hypocrisy on either side. There is no hope for the critic of making Bertilak's court more evil (or more good, if one wants to be really perverse) than Arthur's. The reason is that both courts are aspects of 'home'. Their opposition can be satisfactorily explained only at the latent level – they are really struggling for the possession of the protagonist; or from his point of view, he is trying to escape from the one to the other, though he acknowledges his obligation to the former. In Arthur's court, therefore, Arthur is the protagonist's ideal of himself – a 'split' from the protagonist – and Guinevere the potential beloved. Arthur's court is 'home' transmogrified into the external world, the protagonist's *own* independent home, not Father's.

The father-images are 'split' in several ways. The obvious 'split' is between the Green Knight and Bertilak. It appears from what the Green Knight (or Bertilak?) says at the very end, when he is explaining about Morgan le Fay, that his true being is as Bertilak and that the Green Knight aspect is what he assumes in order to terrify the court and, presumably, any travellers so misguided as to pass by the Green Chapel. He represents the more archaic aspects of the father-figure, connected with the world of nature, and thus also with death. He is mysterious, magical, older than the protagonist, threatening, powerful, to be resisted if not tamed. When controlled this force of nature becomes civilised, without losing strength. We see him in a truer aspect as Bertilak, the courteous, if also powerful, enigmatic and slightly alarming lord of the most elegant of modern castles. Bertilak's three hunts, so vividly and realistically described, are nowadays normally interpreted as a kind of allegory. The perception of significance is true, but the details are unconvincing. It is usual to argue that the hunted beast is an allegory for Gawain's attitudes and success on each day of temptation. This is unconvincing because there is no inherent, and certainly no explicit, connection between Gawain's actions and the hunted beast. It would be perfectly easy to inter-change the order of the hunts and make a convincing parallel with Gawain's response to the lady. Gawain would for example be just as effectively compared with a deer (the object of the *first* hunt) on the occasion of the *third* temptation as with the cunning fox, if the poet were really trying to make the connection. Such interpretations also entirely overlook the fact that in each case the hunted animal is successfully killed, whereas Gawain escapes all three of the lady's pursuits, except for a flesh-wound on the third occasion. The sequence of hunts is much better explained in terms of narrative economy in the verbal realisation, in which the poet was much interested, though there is no space to do it justice in this chapter. Nothing in my argument denies the poet's and reader's interest in the descriptions of the material world. The poet was interested in the breaking of the deer. It would have been impossible to interpolate such a description after the climactic third temptation. It has to come after the relatively less significant first temptation scene.

Yet the hunts have symbolic associations. They represent Bertilak's association with nature and death, the domain of the Green Knight. The bond between hunter and hunted is well recognised, and in so far as he is hunting for meat Bertilak is a part of nature's world which we all inhabit – eat or be eaten. Bertilak also hunts for sport, and in the ceremonial breaking of the deer establishes himself as human, creating patterns, taming nature. So Bertilak even here is part of the courteous civilised world, and once Gawain has successfully though not entirely resisted the 'nature' aspect he finds that the truer father-figure is the still formidable but human, genial and hospitable Bertilak, who occupies a castle which presents to us the cosy family world of Christmas festivity, good nature and interesting conversation, party games and comfortable beds.

It is absolutely clear that Bertilak's castle is an image for what is at the latent level the protagonist's home. The originality of the *Gawain*-poet, and the superiority of his mythopoeic genius, is shown in a potent variation of the 'canonical' folktale-pattern. The hero does not leave his 'primary' home on his quest. He has already left. He is dragged back, as it were, though that return is also a paradoxical seeking. Gawain naturally finds his way there at Christmas, unable to resist what is also his duty, though reluctantly and painfully does he do it.

It is nowadays usually accepted that the castle appears to Gawain in immediate response to, or at least in significant juxtaposition with, his prayer to Mary. I have always felt sceptical of this as part of the poet's conscious intention, since there is no explicit or implicit verbal signal of connection, and there seems no reason why Mary should lead Gawain to what is clearly shown to be a place of danger. Had he been seduced in the castle he would have had his head cut off, is what the story 'says'. I still doubt if the poet consciously intended to make the castle an answer to prayer. Such would savour of the superficially magical. Nevertheless my scepticism was probably mistaken because the association between castle and prayer very well fits the latent pattern, since Mary is a 'mother-image' and the castle is 'home'. Gawain's essential conflict is in the family. He has to go 'home', because that is the actual place of battle. Not only his 'father' (as Green Knight) but also his 'mother' as Virgin and Temptress draws him there. She as Virgin will protect him, just as she will also try (as the lady) to smother him. The castle is full of ambivalent 'mother' and 'father' and other domestic images. Even the Exchange of Winnings has some of the characteristics of the family party game of 'forfeits'. When as an innocent party-hating small boy I was forced to play this loathsome game one of the favourite questions was 'Tell us the name of the girl you love best'. Since there was no such person (and if there had been I would have died of embarrassment to reveal it), kindly middle-aged ladies used to advise me to give the name of my mother! It was the custom to shout the name up the chimney. Gawain himself is asked by the lady what is the name of the girl he loves best. He loves none; his saving devotion to the Virgin does not come into the conversation though the poet himself invokes it.

The poem provides an example of how the basic family drama, when appropriately symbolised and realised, can provide imagery whose implication takes us well beyond the bonds and bounds of the family.

The Green Knight is a condensed image of multiple significations which extend beyond, though they are consonant with, his function in the family circle, as is, or was, natural for fathers. John Speirs pointed out many years ago his affinity with the 'wild man' of medieval demonology. It has since been shown that such wild men were monsters of erotic and destructive power, originally earth spirits, to be associated with Pan, satyrs and centaurs.[13] There is no doubt of the wild man's association with nature and sexuality (not love), and he carries a club as a redoubtable phallic symbol. Whether the Green Knight's holly branch is appropriately to be understood in the same way I leave to others to decide, but his greenness, vitality and violence, his capacity for reviving himself, all point to an association with wild nature and sex. In this respect he is also to be associated with the lawless sexuality of the lady. (Parents may well seem unduly free while imposing restrictions on their children.) Speirs understood nature and sex as 'making for life', but in the traditional view the opposite is the case. 'Where shall I find you?' Gawain asks the Green Knight. 'Just look for me and you will find me' is the reply. There is only one thing you can be sure of finding thus, and that is death.[14] Green is indeed the colour of nature, but it can be devilish: Chaucer's devil who carried off the Summoner to Hell wears green. The cycle of nature inevitably leads to death. By a pun of the language itself, the flesh of corpses is described as green in Middle English. The Green Knight, like death itself, cannot die. He lives by a tumulus, the abode of the dead, and seems to emerge from the earth itself, the cleft in the cliff. Gawain, like us all, must confront death in establishing his maturity, and he has no magic charm to save him. He puts little trust in the belt and that little is his only weakness. Neither magic nor science can save us from dying, and they may even be allies of death. If Gawain had given in to sexuality, to natural forces, he would have given in to death, at both manifest and latent levels. The sexual temptations are correlated with the blows of the axe; in so far as Gawain has resisted, he is not harmed. A general proposition embodied in the story, not far removed from the literal level, is that sexual intercourse, or at any rate, illicit sexual intercourse, is like having your head cut off. For centuries in English poetry the euphemism for having sexual intercourse was 'to die'. At a symbolic level the axe of the Green Knight may be regarded as both a phallic emblem and an instrument of death. His tumulus is also a womb, the womb of Mother Earth, to which we return when we die. From the point of view of the poem the family not only gives birth to the protagonist, it swallows him up in the same womb, now of death, if he cannot escape. (As to the associations of tumuli with the womb, the great prehistoric long barrow near Uley, Gloucestershire, has for long been known locally as 'Hetty Pegler's Tump'. Tump, when I was a boy in Gloucester, was slang for the belly. For a woman to be 'in tump' was to be pregnant.)

Gawain, like us all, partly wants to regress into the infantilism which according to the direction in which we are going means life or death. For the growing child it is first a stage of life, but for the emerging adult to return to it, or not escape from it, is death.

In this respect the story of Gawain, like so much romance, re-capitulates not only the history of the individual's struggle through a crucial stage of life but also something of the history of the race, or at least of a very general psychic struggle. Everywhere the emerging self-conscious rationalist intellect is imaged as masculine, and the womb of nature, which sustains yet also after a certain stage trammels it, is represented as feminine. The ramifications of this dilemma as traced by Bachofen, Briffault and Neumann[15] are complex indeed, with notable ambivalences within the psyche of each individual, that need not be discussed here. The Green Knight, as repressive father-figure, nature, death, who controls and is controlled by the mother-figure, and both, or all, of whom wish to swallow back the individual struggling to emerge, is undoubtedly a part of the sustaining yet menacing world of the unconscious, the mother-world, from which the rational spirit of man in his evolutionary drive must escape.

In order to survive we need first to rise above nature, make a paradoxical escape from nature. The way of escape is twofold. First, as already suggested, by a transposition of the Great Mother as it were from earth to heaven as the Virgin Mother; but second, related to the first, the protagonist rises above nature by denying its simple promiscuous biological drives; in other words, by self-control, inhibition of instinct, having power to hurt and doing none; the driving force of civilisation. Historically speaking Gawain achieves this escape and power of self-realisation through refraining; through self-inhibition and saying no, according to the highly structured and sophisticated moral and religious system of medieval Christianity, which is implicit throughout the poem, though it is in no way allegorically described. It does not need to be. The symbolic structure of the story does the work, and moreover the message is perfectly explicit at a verbal level throughout the poem, in its emphasis on Gawain's goodness and chastity. It is an historical accident that our culture now does not, in general, put the same value on Gawain's virtues as did the poet.

The triumph of rational spirituality achieved in independent adulthood is not without personal cost. Gawain will bear the marks of the struggle for ever and it will make him appropriately humble, though the best of men. Nor is it destructive of the mould from which it sprang. Once the Green Knight and all he represents of nature, death and the family in its regressive and oppressive aspects have been successfully resisted, he is not only no longer dangerous, he is quite friendly. Any interpretation of the poem must account for the absence of chagrin, let alone rage, on the part of the Green Knight, when his plot to kill Gawain fails, as he knows it must. The Green Knight through most of the poem must be accounted an inveterate enemy of Gawain. To do all he can to trick him into death is not the act of a friend. Yet failure makes him positively genial, and he praises Gawain highly. At the psychological level this is because the father, having been deprived of power by the son's successful defiance of both him and the mother, is no longer felt to be dangerous by the son. Middle English romance is notable for the warmth with which it presents reconciliation within the family, as we see in *Sire Degarre* and Malory's *Gareth*. The *Gawain*-poet does not go so far as the poet of *Sire Degarre* in associating the son with the father, but he makes clear the pleasure of the

father-figure in the son-protagonist's achievement. Even if the protagonist still insists on striking out on his own, he is not cut off from his
'origins' in the world of nature.

From a different point of view, regarding the Green Knight as a projection of the protagonist's own hostility not only to his father, but
towards himself, the protagonist can now, having demonstrated his
independence, afford through the father-image to praise himself a little,
to feel he has not done too badly, all things considered, though he need
not be conceited. More generally, the world of nature and death is
accepted for what it is, still mysterious and unknown, but less
terrifying in the light of supernature, less hostile. The sign of the baldric
may even be taken as a symbol not only of partial failure, or sin, but of the
world of nature, sin and death from which we come and of which, it is
psychological as well as moral health to remember, we are always part.
Even Gawain is human and retains the consciousness of his humanity.
The rest of the court, like all men, are justified in wearing the badge of
common humanity as a sign of both humility and honour.

CHAPTER IV

Chaucer

The work of Chaucer, contemporary with the *Gawain*-poet, deserves consideration as a largely negative example. The family drama is only marginally invoked in his stories. A test with negative results is always useful. It shows that the hypothesis I have proposed is falsifiable in specific instances: in other words, the patterns I have invoked – my own errors and confusions apart – are likely genuinely to inhere in those stories where they have been found, since they cannot be shown to inhere in other not too dissimilar stories. A hypothesis that is true of everything is so true as to be useless, indeed meaningless. We shall be able to see interesting differences between Chaucer and the *Gawain*-poet, or other romance writers, the more clearly for this test. Chaucer turns out to be much more learned, literalistic, personalised, in fact, 'Neoclassical', than the *Gawain*-poet or other medieval English writers. He is much more remote from the popular 'folkloric' mind, less archaic, less mythopoeic, less 'medieval' in this respect even than Boccaccio. Yet everyone is a man of his own times. What Chaucer was is what his times helped to make him. There was an element of literalism among some scholastic writers in the thirteenth and fourteenth centuries, as Professor Morton Bloomfield has shown.[1] More widespread is an element of popular 'materialism', which demands that we call a spade a spade, and gets a pleasurable thrill from openly naming objects for which a contrary but equally popular tendency prefers euphemisms. Chaucer was also a man of his times in a more general sense. Many of his narrative procedures are traditional and he seems to have turned at the end of his life, as Boccaccio did, to a devout piety as narrow as his earlier secularism had been broad.

There can be little doubt that very early in his life Chaucer was deeply attracted by precisely those English rhyming romances that later in life he, and the almost unanimous vote of subsequent criticism, have considered so ridiculous. The parody *Sir Thopas* in *The Canterbury Tales* shows his mature view. It is as if in all those writings of his that have survived he had passed the imaginative stages of the emergence of the individual. There is just one possibility that he did write something of that kind, if there is any truth in my speculation that the lost 'Book of the Lion' which he refers to at the end of his life in his 'Retracc:ouns' may refer to a translation of the poem *Yvain* by Chrétien de Troyes (certainly known in England in the fourteenth century, for another partial translation survives). Chrétien is the romance writer *par excellence* whom it is likely that the mature Chaucer would have ridiculed as he did the English romances.[2]

The earliest datable poem that we have by Chaucer is *The Book of the Duchess*, now known to have been written in 1368 when he was at least 28.[3] But it may be that his earliest work to survive is the beginning of the partial translation into English of *Le Roman de la Rose*, which may not be much earlier. This French poem, so vastly influential in general, and on Chaucer in particular, is an 'allegory of love'. The poem as a whole demonstrates the psychological awareness that exists in medieval literature. The poet is the protagonist who tells his own story. It is of a wonderful dream, in which he is welcomed or threatened by a variety of personifications who represent attitudes or states of mind, Idleness, Mirth, Hostility (Daungier), Shame, etc., as well as images of other people, of qualities and concepts. It very well shows how a whole work can represent the protagonist's total mind, while he himself appears in it as the leading figure, with the other characters as 'splits', projections, images of his idea of opposing forces. The story, with infinite digressiveness, tells how the youthful lover enters the Garden, encounters both helpers and opponents, and finally plucks the Rose, i.e. wins his beloved. To that extent it is indeed a romance, with strong resemblances to the psychological aspects also of fairy tale, and is a story of 'emergence'. But it is only minimally a drama of 'transference'. There are certainly superior persons (Nature and Reason) who harangue the protagonist, as well as Shame and Hostility who oppose him and may perhaps be regarded as much displaced father-figures. There is a youth and an old woman who help and advise. But the narrative is extremely thin because the concepts are extensively analysed and extended by practical or theoretical discourse which is realistic and even scientific. There is a great deal of actual scientific and philosophic discourse, and pungent realistic satire of contemporary abuses, which must have been the elements that principally appealed to Chaucer. The poem indeed turns into an extensive argument for a purely naturalistic philosophy of promiscuous sexuality, returning to imagery only at the end where sexual intercourse is lightly symbolised. Chaucer only translated the first few hundred lines of this immense poem, which give the charming image of the Garden of youth and love, though he undoubtedly knew the rest. A characteristically uncommitted attitude!

Another very early poem is *An ABC*, a translation of a French poem in praise of the Virgin Mother. This is a vernacular derivation from the clerical culture, without action, and offers us only a sweet and superficial mother-image which obviously charmed Chaucer but has nothing to do with the family drama.

In *The Book of the Duchess* the poet, representing himself as sleepless for sorrow, reads the story in Ovid of how Queen Alcyone's husband was lost to her by being drowned at sea, then dreams he meets, in a forest, a man clad in black who mourns the loss of his beloved. The poem has traditional images and modes of operation in plenty; the early birdsong, a hunt, the forest (in particular); triple repetition with variations; a hyper-bolical, setentious style, etc. It is easy to see that at the latent level the underlying protagonist is represented by 'splits', the poet-in-the-poem, Queen Alcyone, and the man in black. Through these there is a threefold, progressive confrontation with loss mainly through death, although the first of these losses is only the sorrowful poet's brief hint at the beginning that he cannot enjoy the favours of his mistress. The specific occasion of the poem was the death of Blanche the Duchess, the wife of John of Gaunt. The problem in it is how to come to terms with loss, specifically with death. But as we have noticed, the family drama does not normally in the medieval period lend itself to the confrontation with death. It usually issues in romance, in 'comedy' in the medieval sense of a story having a fortunate ending. It is about living through a successful *rite de passage*. In *The Book of the Duchess* we have already passed beyond the disengage-ment from parent-images, beyond the successful transference of feeling to the beloved, to a further stage, much more 'modern', contemplating the lack of an object for feeling, not the transference and growth of feeling. It is not the poem of a very young man. All the relationships are already essentially lateral. They are broken by accidents not in the pro-tagonist's time, but in external, 'objective', public time, and the only consolation is memory of the *past* happy time. You have come of age only to realise that you do *not* live happily ever after. The reality of absence is the topic. It is unlike most romances in suggesting that it is the past, not the future, which must console present suffering.

What is absent in Chaucer's pattern is real aggressiveness, real para-noia; in fact, real superiors. It is characteristic that when the man of great authority at last appears in his next major poem, *The House of Fame*, the poem breaks off incomplete. Chaucer can think of nothing for him to say. The schoolmasterly Eagle who carries the poet up to the skies might be considered as a father-figure, but even if he is, he is a joke. Chaucer could not personate authority.

The love-story of *Troilus and Criseyde* begins with the treacherous desertion of Criseyde's father, Calkas, from Troy, which is beseiged by the Greeks. His desire to have Criseyde with him brings about the ultimate tragedy of her departure to the Greeks and in turn her betrayal of Troilus, and to this extent Calkas performs the function of the danger-ously possessive father, whose possessiveness succeeds and thus pro-duces tragedy. But it is a vestigial function. Troilus, the protagonist, never comes into any conflict direct or symbolic with him, any more than he does with his own father or any other person in authority. Criseyde is won for Troilus by his friend Pandarus's direct negotiation with herself. She has no one to take into account but herself. Difficulties arise from Troilus's inhibitions, but they are directly presented as internal, not portrayed by figures in the action. From the point of view of the latent pattern Troilus and Pandarus may be regarded as a 'split' protagonist – Pandarus doing the dirty work, Troilus remaining spotless and suf-fering – but this is no great complexity, even if of some critical and moral significance. Pandarus fades out of the action once Criseyde is won, though he is useful later as confidant. Almost all the relationships in the story are lateral, the only exception being Criseyde's obedience to her father. Although Troilus begins like a folktale hero with a 'lack', and has to seek his beloved, he does not leave home on a quest. He is beseiged there, in Troy, and he wins the beloved half way through the story. The narrative in the poem is powerful but its course 'from woe to wele and after out of joy' emphasises that much of the interest is, as in *The Book of the Duchess*, on the later loss. Chaucer uses the story much more to explore the nature of the world of appearances than to evoke images with powerful latent associations. The interest is more on the literal level. Hence the frequent modern comment that the poem is 'the first novel in English'. It is still much more traditional than naturalistic, even in detail, while the ending, when the soul of Troilus is carried up to the skies after his death, brings in, curiously displaced, romance elements totally alien to the novel; nevertheless, the modern comment that it is a sort of novel expresses a true perception that Chaucer is much concerned with naturalistic cause and effect in the progress of the story, and is much less interested in the evocative pattern of traditional images, than is the normal medieval romance writer.

The Legends of Good Women treats traditional stories, taken from Ovid, centred on women abandoned by their husbands or lovers, their lovers having always at least promised marriage. This theme had long been in Chaucer's mind[4] and suggests that the Cinderella theme, with a feminine, domestic, basis for its story, was more attractive to him than the masculine, questing, outgoing theme more characteristic of medieval romance; but once again, the emphasis in these stories is on the pathos of the loss which follows the achieved relationship.

As he grew older Chaucer used more traditional material in a less traditional style. The result is a special quality of ambivalence, sometimes emotional tension, sometimes comedy. The most direct 'comment' by Chaucer on the theme of emergence in medieval English romances is the mercilessly brilliant parody of *The Tale of Sir Thopas*, where the hero, presented as very effeminate, dashes off to the forest in search of an elf-queen. It is extremely funny, but the story is not taken very far, and the joke is as much against the style of the English romances as against their content. Chaucer is here at his most modern and destructive, least sympathetic to archaic imagery. An index to his total contrast here with the *Gawain*-poet is his presentation of the arming of Sir Thopas, in contrast with the *Gawain*-poet's use of the same ancient motif in connection with Sir Gawain, which has already been noted (above, p. 74). No poet uses this motif more seriously and splendidly than the *Gawain*-poet; none so derisively as Chaucer.

In the Prologue to *The Man of Law's Tale* in *The Canterbury Tales* Chaucer puts into the Lawyer's mouth a mocking reference to himself and to his friend Gower, and goes out of his way to reproach Gower for telling stories of father-daughter incest, like that of Canacee. There seems no reason to disbelieve Chaucer's expression of dislike of such traditional stories about incest. They did not appeal to him. He thought they were nasty. He did not like fairy tales either. At the beginning of *The Wife of Bath's Tale* he puts into her mouth a sarcastic reference to the fact that the only fairies about nowadays are friars. Arthurian romance also comes in for sarcastic comment in this tale and elsewhere. Making all due allowance for the partially dramatic nature of these comments, they fit in too well with the general cast of his mind in his work to be ignored. If he knew Chrétien's work, I am sure that he was as convinced that it was silly stuff as was any late-nineteenth-century novel-reading scholar.

Yet Chaucer could also entertain traditional stories and not mock them, though he sometimes strained them. In *The Knight's Tale* he shows two young men in love, and makes the poem more of a romance, though a philosophical romance, than does his source, Boccaccio's *Teseida*. Of the two young men, one dies, but one succeeds and marries the lady Emily. There are some potent traditional images, such as the fight in the glade in the forest. We obviously have a 'split' protagonist, but Chaucer uses this device to show himself less tragically inclined than when younger. If one dies, at least the other succeeds, whereas loss is dominant in the earlier poems. Theseus, middle-aged Duke of Athens, brother-in-law to the lady, is something of a father-figure, and has taken the young men prisoner and shut them up in a prison for life – a powerful and original image. But he is also genial and forgiving and is not in any way contested by the young men. Chaucer's imagination is simply not bothered by father-figures.

Chaucer is more open to traditional aspects of the family drama in a religious or semi-religious mode like that of *The Man of Law's Tale* of Constance, and *The Clerk's Tale* of Patient Griselda. The protagonist is in each case a woman and there are many traditional elements. The story of Constance is the only one of Chaucer's stories that gives us a traditionally wicked mother-in-law, or rather, two of them. The strains of family life are certainly apparent in each story, but in each case the centre is in adult life, after the marriage. Constance is twice the victim of a jealous mother-in-law, is twice set adrift in an open boat upon the sea where she drifts for years. This is effective traditional repetition. Constance has a son by her second husband, and eventually through this child, after living many years with him alone in obscurity in Rome, not revealing herself to her parents, she meets again and is reconciled with them and her husband. That she chooses to live so long in Rome unknown to her parents suggests that deeply latent in the story is some hostility to parents. The repeated hostility to mothers-in-law is rational on the literal level, for they are cruel religious enemies, and jealous of their sons' love for Constance. But at the latent level the mothers-in-law may also be taken as the representation of mother-images, and may thus suggest the usual daughter-mother hostility. The ease with which husbands are disposed of suggests an ambivalence towards them on the part of the protagonist. The numerous accusations from which Constance suffers suggest externalised self-reproach. The possessive father-image is suppressed, but supplies all the latent motivations, including the setting adrift as a kind of 'accidental' search by the protagonist to find the father (and mother?) whom she also wishes to avoid. The main implausibility which needs to be explained in this story is Constance's long stay in Rome without making herself known to her father, the Emperor, and mother. They have been represented as kind and loving parents, she as a dutiful and loving daughter. Why live in obscure poverty, when the natural thing would have been to go back to them? The motif is found elsewhere, for example in the early saint's legend of Alexis. His father, a rich and noble Roman, arranged a marriage for Alexis which he would not consummate; instead he ran away and lived in holy poverty for seventeen years. Then he returned to the house of his kind and disconsolate father and was taken in as an unknown beggar. There he lived unknown for a further seventeen years, unnecessarily enduring all kinds of humiliating treatment from the servants, until, on the point of death, he made himself known to his lamenting father. The explicit reason, not unjustified on certain premises, is that a man should love God more than wealth, parents, wife. It is the ascetic anti-type of romance, which on the contrary in its secular, sensible way represents all these as goods sent by God for us to enjoy. At a latent level such stories may well represent hostility to the parents and a rather negative or perverse or alternatively religious way of establishing identity and independence, breaking out of the family circle through the love of God and the consciousness of sin. Family reconciliation comes at the point of death. This sort of semi-religious story was able to get below Chaucer's rational scientific defences as secular romance rarely could.

This was partly because Chaucer was more interested, imaginatively speaking, in being married than in getting married – a rare situation in a writer so interested in personal relationships. Thus the story of Patient Griselda also appealed to him, as it did to an extraordinary number of people for several centuries after being cast into its present form by Boccaccio. It is the last story in the *Decameron* and was translated by Petrarch, from whose later version it was turned into French. Chaucer used both Latin and French, but seems not to have known the Italian version in the *Decameron*. Griselda is the poorest of village girls, who is married by her lord, the local marquis, Walter. She makes a wonderful wife, mother and marchioness. But Walter tests her by pretending to have their two young children killed one after the other; and finally by proposing to reject her in favour of a new twelve-year-old bride, actually their own daughter, brought up secretly far away, as their son has also been. Griselda takes all in patience and is finally triumphantly restored. Chaucer realises this totally implausible story with the most beautiful restraint and most convincingly naturalistic detail. It is in consequence almost intolerable to read. There is almost no way of making sense of it at a realistic level, though if anyone could it would be Chaucer. He felt the strain himself and in consequence he explodes in a famous mocking envoy appended to the poem. The appeal of the poem arises from the way it presents a model of that undeserved suffering which is so characteristic of human life, and yet offers some hope, or at least some 'basic trust'. The point of view, being grown up, perhaps suggests latently not children's dislike of parents but the much less fashionable and equally true dislike of children by parents. The only aspect of the family drama however which is strongly suggested is Walter's proposed, though never intended, marriage with his daughter. This, however, is seen from the point of view of the mother, the grown-up, and not, as would be more usual, from the point of view of the daughter. In so far as the daughter is a projection of the protagonist we may say that part of the strange power of the story comes from the latent concept of Walter, so much the social superior to Griselda, as a kind of father-figure. This tyranny is what it would be for the daughter to be married to her father. The emphasis on filial obedience is much more painful when applied in the image of a husband, as Chaucer and the Wife of Bath knew. The direct presentation of fathers in Chaucer's poetry, though rare, tends to show them as stern and disagreeable. The latent images in the story of Griselda offer no solution in the sense of changing the fundamental situation. The father-figure merely stops being tyrannous, won over by passive obedience. The female protagonist offers no more resistance than the poet did to the Eagle in *The House of Fame*, nor are there any other characters to symbolise action or development. Chaucer's imagination is so lacking in aggression as to be completely pacifist.

As he grew older Chaucer moved more towards traditional stories, as already noted, and also towards more obviously secular ones. The bawdy folktales (the so-called 'fabliaux') are the extreme example, but *The Wife of Bath's Tale* offers an interesting intermediary stage. It is based on the folktale theme called the Loathly Lady, which expresses the universal masculine fear of women, especially old women. The protagonist, having offended against women, has to discover what all women most want (suppressed sexual joke). He can only find the answer from an old woman at the price of marrying her. The answer (of course) is domination. All women want to be mothers. The only solution in this story appears to be for men to give in, as is the case in the reverse direction with the story of Griselda. The basic folktale theme, as found for example in Gower, then produces the situation in which the protagonist, having been forced to marry the old hag who may be taken at the latent level as a mother-image, is offered the choice of having her young and beautiful by either night or day. This is fruitful in implications of many kinds not relevant to the present theme. When he gives her the choice, that is, when he surrenders completely, she says she will be young and beautiful all the time. This folktale version seems to be as regressive as that of Jack and the Beanstalk, and moreover without any father-images. Mummy will always be the same to you, Son. But one might say that the absence of aggression also allows for the mother-image to be completely transformed, and if without a struggle at least, from the imaginative point of view, quite genuinely. Chaucer enriches this implausible story first of all by putting it into the mouth of the Wife of Bath, who, however man-hungry she may be, certainly has nothing in her of the mother. He begins the story by having the protagonist committing a rape – an achieved relationship of a kind! The old woman lectures the protagonist on their wedding night on the best Christian morality. Finally the dilemma offered him is whether she remain old and ugly and certainly faithful, or young and beautiful with all the risk that that involves. Although he naturally chooses to take the risk, this does seem the more positive transference – rejecting the boring certainties of mother-love for something more exciting and suitable to his age.

The bawdy folktales or 'fabliaux' are international popular comic tales with many traditional elements – a 'split' protagonist, for example, in *The Reeve's Tale*, who as a duality makes love to both mother and daughter. The traditional contempt for a jealous old man married to a beautiful young wife, and amusement at his cuckolding, may be related at a distance to protagonists who defy possessive fathers and carry off their daughters. At any rate, the family circle is certainly broken, but it is someone else's family, for the protagonist is clearly external. Whatever the overtones, the latent forces of the internal family drama are not significantly invoked. These international popular comic tales, usually about sexual success or misadventure in adulterous affairs, are, like the similar and sometimes analogous tales in Boccaccio's *Decameron*, a product of the popular adult secular mind, for which marriage and personal independence are already achieved. They are fantasies, of sex, not love, about material physical pleasure and pain, not about the breaking and making of emotional bonds. The enviably ruthless young men who so easily persuade beautiful amorous young women to go to bed with them may feel affection but are essentially free. In this respect they belong to the world of cause and effect which Neoclassical theory would have all stories be images of, rather than to the symbolic world of pattern and unconscious bonds. But it is worth remarking that these popular comic tales do not require too much sympathy for the characters from the reader. If the plight of victims is too vividly realised such stories take on an inappropriate pathos, as happens for modern readers who sympathise, quite mistakenly, with the elderly cuckolds who are duped by their randy young wives in *The Miller's Tale* and *The Merchant's Tale*. Interesting as Chaucer cannot but be, therefore, he shows himself much less akin to the characteristic writer of romance who evokes the resonances of the unconscious mind than he does to the modern analytical mind.

CHAPTER V

The story of Gareth

I

The story of Gareth in *Le Morte Darthur*[1] is one of the most memorable parts of that book, or books, and if not the greatest, yet among the most characteristic of Malory's tales. It has for long been thought to have been Malory's own invention, until a possible lost source was deduced.[2] We do not know how far Malory changed his source, but at least it is clear that the tale of Gareth is more purely a 'romance' than are any of the other main sections of *Le Morte Darthur*, and has a single dominating thread. We are not for the moment concerned with how Malory wove that thread later, after the tale of the Grail, into the more complex tragic pattern of the latter parts of *Le Morte Darthur*.

The single dominating thread of the tale of Gareth is obvious, and sympathetic minds have always enjoyed its instructively repetitive simplicities and successful outcome. We recognise the pattern instinctively. It is that general story-pattern which has come to be called 'The Fair Unknown', and which is at the centre of a number of European romances.[3] The relationships between different tellings of the 'Fair Unknown' theme are complex but the outline of the story is simple enough and easily recognised. At the most general level it is the story of the 'canonical' fairy tale hero, from David to Dummling, of *The Golden Goose*, who setting out from obscure origins overcomes difficulties and wins the Princess.

Yet critics have found difficulties. 'Incoherencies' have been found in the conduct of the story. Dr. Mills refers not without justification on the literal level to the 'Tale of Gareth' as a 'curious jumble'. The most penetrating and sympathetic account so far, which rightly minimises the degree of confusion that really exists in the story, is that of Professor L. Benson.[4] He shows that the story is one that sets out to establish, quite literally, the hero's identity. The narration embodies a process of education, testing, self-realisation, and at last the acceptance of the proved young adult into society. Benson notes a trace of the 'male Cinderella motif' which often attaches itself to 'Fair Unknown' romances.

My purpose in the present chapter is to show at the deeper level of story-pattern why the apparent inconsistencies of a simple story do not worry the reader who reads the story with the assumptions it clearly calls for, and how some of the apparent inconsistencies are structurally significant. The underlying pattern will be familiar by now to the reader, yet the repetition has its own interesting variations.

II

The story begins in Arthur's court, at the High Feast of Pentecost, when Arthur has the custom of not eating until a marvel presents itself, as of course immediately happens, or this would not be a story. We know that we are in the land of imagination because our act of reading has been a choice to enter it, just as when we enter a church we choose to invoke certain conventions and types of behaviour, and to exclude others. We also easily recognise that Arthur is not the protagonist. Arthur's court is where all the action starts from and returns to; it is therefore in the latent sense 'home'. But when the protagonist enters, as he immediately does, 'home' is seen to be ambiguous. The tall, broad-shouldered, handsome, unknown young man enters, leaning weakly on the shoulders of two others, accompanied by a dwarf. He asks for three gifts from Arthur. One is food and drink for a twelvemonth; two more he will ask for at the end of that time. He conceals his name and lineage and we are never told why he so enters, though it is soon clear that there is nothing wrong with him. It seems that he devised the strange appearance himself, because he left his literal home, his parents' court, well armed and provided for, as his mother later indignantly explains to Arthur (339–40). The protagonist, whom we eventually know as Gareth, himself later explains in rather vague terms that his asking for food at Arthur's court was to test his 'friends' (313). Since the only people he knew at Arthur's court were his elder brothers Gawain (the eldest), Agravain and Gaheris, none of whom recognises him, we may understand the word *friends* in the older sense of *kin*, *relations*. As far as they are concerned, therefore, it is a clear symbolisation of the protagonist's sibling rivalry at home, himself being the youngest. His siblings' failure to recognise their youngest brother is at the latent level a projection of that sense in the young protagonist of not fully existing, and of his consequent resentment against siblings for not doing him justice, which is a basic *donnée* of the family drama. His simulated weakness is equally a view of his own childishness, which is emphasised by the request for food and drink; all of it a sort of 'wilful' expression of childishness – if *that's* what you think of me, that's how I'll behave! – which easily co-exists with the protagonist's even stronger sense of his own beauty, wealth and great potential. It is an excellently complex image in human terms of, so to speak, the chicken just as he is breaking the shell, as ancient as the presentation of David.

To say so much is not in any way to make a character-study of Gareth at the literal or manifest level, such as one might deduce from a presentation in a novel. Gareth's 'character', in the sense of personality, is barely developed or individualised. At the literal level he is extraordinarily handsome, brave, strong, courteous, polite, meek and mild to ladies, devoted to his beloved; in other words, he is a conventional chivalric hero, good and brave, with whom it was easy, at any rate in any age but our own, to 'empathise', without for a moment confusing oneself with him. The underlying feelings and attitudes just described are latent within the beginning of the story as a whole, and they too are not individualised but common to everyone. They are given a vivid imaginative life by the detail and art of Malory's manifest verbal realisation, which are not here directly my concern. As already noted it is the *whole* of the story which represents the latent drives of the protagonist's *whole* mind. The protagonist-figure *within* the story is thus the leading manifest image of the whole protagonist, but nevertheless is only a partial image.

The ambivalence with which the protagonist as it were regards himself is emphasised by the nickname which the traditionally scornful Sir Kay the steward gives him; Beaumains, 'Fair-hands', 'Beautiful hands'. We have already been told that he is the fairest and largest-handed person ever seen, and his mother much later in protesting at his treatment makes a kind of pun, saying he is 'as fair an handed man and well disposed as any is living' − fair-handed referring I take it to his generosity and justice (340). The nickname, as everyone in the story recognises, is meant by Kay as a kind of irony, given scornfully. Sir Kay believes the Fair Unknown to be not a gentleman but a 'villein', and condemns him to the kitchen. The kitchen, as with *Cinderella*, is an ambivalent but mainly bad image here. Such goodness as it has derives from being the very heart of the home, and thus the protagonist is sent back as it were to origins. But since the protagonist wants very strongly to emerge from what are now the constrictions of home, the kitchen, like the womb, once good, is now bad: it is dirty and degrading. There may even be an insinuation, though this is not explicit, that Beaumains has to do kitchen-work, will therefore be actually 'dirty hands'. The lady Lynet later complains that he stinks of the kitchen. But the nickname, though scornfully meant, is in fact true. At the latent level the protagonist sees himself condemned by the adult world for what is in truth a good and desirable quality, both physical and moral, which he really possesses, though it may be rare. (How many of us adults can truly claim to have entirely 'clean hands'?) There may be other historical reasons behind the nickname, but this is how it seems to work for Malory. That Beaumains when he comes first to court refuses to disclose his own true name and lineage is part of the characteristic anonymity and quest for identity of the protagonist who has yet to establish his maturity, as Benson has shown. Beaumains, as he himself later says, intends to prove himself (313). Although there is much explicit, manifest and literal reference in the tale to the importance of noble blood, being a gentleman born, etc., product of Malory's fifteenth-century class-consciousness, there is deeper in the tale a feeling that differs from respect for inheritance or lineage. There is a feeling that you have to achieve worth (worship, honour) by earning it; that 'gentil is as gentil does' − the lesson of *The Wife of Bath's Tale*. The two strands, of inherited and of achieved nobility, are united by the importance of establishing one's identity. One has not only to know oneself who one is, but make sure that the world knows too, and that a proper respect for oneself emerges.

These considerations arise out of the Fair Unknown's arrival at Arthur's court in a manner not naturalistic but profoundly natural. The court is ambiguous in a latent sense because it both is and is not 'home'. It is 'home' in that now the protagonist lives there, is fed, is in an inferior position, and must get away to prove himself. But he is already at one remove from the childhood home, since he has come there from his actual childhood home. Arthur's court is thus part protective, part constrictive, part the source of opportunity. It is the shell at the moment of breaking.

After twelve months, at the next Pentecost Feast, a lady comes to ask King Arthur for a knight to succour her sister, who is besieged by a mighty enemy, the Red Knight of the Red Lands. But she will not divulge her sister's name (nor is she asked her own) so that King Arthur says he will allow none of his knights to undertake the adventure. At the manifest level of verbal realisation this is a narrative device to allow Beaumains to ask for the adventure. No explicit reason is given for the lady's refusal to tell her name, which makes her request for succour apparently self-defeating. Any latent reason must be sought in the pattern of story as a whole, centred on the protagonist and his passage through difficulty and isolation to maturity and a beloved of his own age. There is in the story at this stage an absolute necessity that the protagonist and no one else shall seek the adventure. We have noted the ambivalence of the protagonist, the emphasis on his childishness, as well as the desire, implicit in his very coming, to grow up. At this stage, furthermore, the story will not yet truly envisage the beloved. It is only a mysterious message from her as an unknown that invites the protagonist. No need to emphasise the archaic and profound sense that the name *is* the person, shows that the person truly exists, for Beaumains himself illustrates this. The story plays a good deal with name and identity (and kin) later on. The besieged lady's anonymity here then corresponds at the latent level to that of the protagonist. Who is she? Not surely a mother-image! He does not yet know. He will take the adventure.

The besieged lady's anonymity is to be associated at the latent level with the manifest hostility to Beaumains of the damsel her sister, who is not pleased to have the kitchen-page as her knight, even when a splendid set of armour (though no spear and shield), a horse in cloth of gold and an attendant dwarf immediately appear for his use. We meet 'split' characters including beloved ladies in plenty of folktales and romances. The sister is at this stage a 'split' image of the as yet unknown besieged lady; a foreshadowing of her. She has to be partially differentiated, so that her coming and going, which is the message from the beloved, may be quite unhindered by the Red Knight of the Red Lands. This works at both manifest and latent levels.

On the other hand, as she mercilessly derides Beaumains through adventure after adventure, the sister also represents that aspect of the protagonist which feels (as so often in this story) that people are 'against him', do not think well of him. She is decidedly superior in attitude and emphasises his apparent status as a kitchen-boy. She therefore also represents yet another aspect to the protagonist; she is a projection of a *derisive* mother-image, which has to be shown to be false, and this derisive mother-image has eventually to be expunged from the total image of the heroine which the protagonist entertains.

In contrast to the wavering, multiple, and mainly hostile image of the female element so far in the story, there is a clearer *pro* and *con* among the male images. Sir Kay is hostile, and there will be a series of downright hostile male enemies; on the other hand Lancelot and to a lesser extent Gawain are friendly. Lancelot is in particular benevolent. Beaumains is devoted to him and asks Lancelot to knight him, revealing to him therefore his true name and impressive lineage. (The devotion between Gareth and Lancelot is very important in the economy of the overall narrative of 'the whole book' of King Arthur and his knights, but that is not my concern here. In the final books Lancelot is himself the protagonist-figure and tragically kills Gareth.) In this 'Tale of Gareth' Lancelot may play something of the role of a benevolent father-figure, a 'split' of the father-image which compensates for the other 'splits' of the composite father-image who represent the hostile elements. From the point of view of the protagonist Lancelot is also the guarantor of his achievable potential. He is the protagonist's faith in himself as it were personified.

Beaumains, led along by the sister (later known as the Savage Damsel!), defeats Kay and takes his spear and shield, kills two more bad knights, and also the Black Knight, whose armour he then wears, and in succession defeats the Black Knight's brothers, the Green, Red and Blue, all of whose names begin with P for no reason that I can see, concluding with Sir Persant of Inde. This patterned colouring is delightful, but seems in itself no more than decorative. Malory's genius for narrative repetition with variation reveals itself in the progress of Beaumains' relationship with the damsel, not in personal terms, but as indicative of the protagonist's growing self-confidence. This is revealed in delightfully dramatic speeches and interesting sentiments in the verbal realisation which are a main source of the artistic merit of the tale, but which I have to neglect here for lack of space. The damsel's continuous derisive slander is eventually defeated by the heroic achievements of Beaumains, and she finally begs his pardon. Beaumains says that her contempt was useful to him, firing him to do even better, since he is out to prove himself (313), which is a nice psychological sidelight about the need to please contemptuous parents which ardent children feel; but it must be said that Beaumains does no worse when she is polite to him.

The episodes of derision are peculiar because the damsel speaks as if she were on the side of what are, after all, on the manifest literal level, her own and her sister's enemies. This does not (or should not) worry the reader, who recognises that at the governing *latent* level all relates to the protagonist. We are not in the least concerned in these perilous passages with the damsel's relationship with the successive enemies, but only with how she, and they, relate to the protagonist with whom the reader so closely identifies. The knights and the damsel are allied in so far as they are against him, and if the successive enemies may count as shadowy father-figures, so she, at this stage, is in the aura of the hostile mother-figure. As in dreams (and in some medieval literature, like *Piers Plowman*), one image may have several different significations, just as several different images may convey the same latent signification.

But the lady is forgiven when she apologises. She apologises because Beaumains does so well. We may say that the protagonist has now confidence enough not to denigrate himself, and not to feel that females will think poorly of him. Similarly the Green, Red and Blue knights once defeated become friendly and treat Beaumains as their superior. At one latent level their hostility has been a projection of his own attitudes: as characters they are projections of his own aggressiveness; once they are overcome, the protagonist has defeated that aspect of himself which they represent, and there is no reason for them to continue their hostility, no reason for resentment on either side, just as there was no rational, material, manifest (as opposed to real, latent) basis for the enemies' original opposition.

The overcoming of the opposition of the series of 'coloured' knights marks a clearly defined stage, whereby Beaumains has passed all the 'perilous passages', as they are called. It culminates in Sir Persant's genial hospitality to Beaumains for the night, of which the high point is Sir Persant's extraordinary command to his daughter to go to Beaumains' bed, so that he wakes up to find her naked beside him. Hospitality could scarcely go further! (314–5). No doubt this is part of every young man's dreams, but Beaumains, like the hero of *Sir Gawain and the Green Knight* in a similar situation, gently repulses her, on the grounds that if he should defile her it would be a great dishonour to her father (her views being taken into account by neither). There is a complex intersection of social bonds concerning sex and male and female honour here which can be only briefly analysed.[5] The essence of the matter is that a man's honour is founded primarily on his bravery, and a woman's on her virginity, or, if she is married, on her marital faithfulness. But a man's honour also depends on the honour of his wife and close female relatives. Thus it would not be dishonourable for *Beaumains* if he and the daughter had sexual intercourse, but it would be for *her*, and by extension for her father. It is not dishonourable to deprive another man of honour – it is done, for example, by defeating him in jousting – but it is decidedly unfriendly. Beaumains does not wish, at the literal level, to deprive his new-found friend and host of honour through his daughter. This shows what a decent man Beaumains is. As Sir Persant says, it shows that he comes of noble blood. Furthermore, that he can refrain sexually also shows that he is not a casual lecher, which is important later in the comedy of his and Lyonesse's frustrated attempt to anticipate the joys of their wedding-night, where his sexual eagerness is not in doubt but is seen to be clearly the product of his romantic love for Lyonesse. But no explanation at the literal level can account for Sir Persant's action, going so far beyond the call of duty of a host. What kind of a man is Sir Persant, so freely to offer his daughter? In a purely naturalistic, literal, reading he would be in the social and moral context of England from the earliest times until at least very recently at best silly, at worst tyrannous and corrupt. But Sir Persant is presented as a great gentleman. We respond to the latent significance of the whole episode, seeing it from the point of view of the protagonist and the maturing organisation of his emotions towards other people, not as an objective characterisation of Sir Persant. We therefore easily accept the manifest literal, though apparently irrational presentation of Sir Persant as a good man, because he is good to the protagonist. We see him only in this relationship and not for himself as an autonomous character. What concerns us is the protagonist's (like the Pilgrim's) progress. The protagonist is sexually tempted, and refrains out of his own goodness of feeling. The capacity to refrain from casual sexual intercourse was regarded in medieval English literature as a high and mature virtue. The episode shows the hero's developing maturity. Furthermore, the story has not yet progressed so far that the protagonist can image a young woman as his beloved, especially when she is so closely associated with even a demoted father-figure like Sir Persant. As in the best literature, the manifest level and the latent levels of imagery run together.

This little episode having illustrated the developing maturity of the protagonist, we are now in a position to learn that the name of the damsel who has been guiding Beaumains so ambivalently through these perilous passages is Lynet, and her sister's name is Lyonesse (315). This emerges in an important conversation with Sir Persant, who thinks he knows Lynet; but it emerges without any of the fuss about the need for anonymity which has been expressed by Lynet in Arthur's court, and which is never explained. The underlying reason is that now at the latent, non-naturalistic level the protagonist is able to identify and focus on the lady more clearly.

Sir Persant in this same conversation tells us more about the ultimate adversary, the Red Knight of the Red Lands, about whom he is well informed, though he is by no means, as might have been supposed on naturalistic grounds from his initial enmity to the protagonist, an ally. We are told that the Red Knight has maintained the siege of the Lady Lyonesse for two years, though he might have foreclosed many a time, because he wanted to have the opportunity of doing battle with Sir Lancelot, or Sir Tristram, or Sir Lamorak, or Sir Gawain. Now, this is a very elaborate device for procuring such battle. Why should he not have gone straight to King Arthur's court and asked for a fight? 'Here fayles thou not to fyght' as Arthur, in *Sir Gawain and the Green Knight*, may be taken as saying for all representations of that sporting institution, his court. The latent reason, which we easily absorb when we are reading in the appropriate state of mind, for the Red Knight to remain at the siege, is that the protagonist is working his way towards the image of the ultimate distant adversary who bars the way to the beloved. The Red Knight of the Red Lands, as the ultimate adversary, can only be so in so far as he is associated with the lady, who herself has to be seen in relation to the protagonist, yet separated from him. The beloved *can* only be conceived of in the first instance as being barred up against the rescuing prince (and

Beaumains is son of a King). We later learn, moreover, that the Red Knight is at least fifty years old, having had experience as an armed knight for thirty years, as he himself says (337). Not much doubt about whom he represents! He is a father-figure. The explanation given by Sir Persant of the Red Knight's actions, and later elaborated by the Red Knight himself, that he behaves as he does at the request of a lady whom he loved (325), is a perfectly good rationalisation according to the non-naturalistic but actually natural rules of what Professor Vinaver calls 'the mad world of Arthur'. We accept Sir Persant's account, both for the literal conventional reason, and because the conventions, for all their strange-ness, constitute a model which at bottom has powerful rational connec-tions with the world we all live in. The Red Knight at no time expresses love for Lyonesse, or a wish to marry her; in terms of latent significance he is in exactly the same position as a king who makes anyone who wishes to marry his daughter first joust with him. We need not bother to identify the Red Knight's own lady, since she is only once and casually referred to. From the protagonist's point of view the Red Knight's desire to meet and kill particularly Sir Lancelot and Sir Gawain expresses the Red Knight's hostility to those with whom the protagonist identifies himself, and whom he wishes to emulate. It thus repeats the hostility between father-figure and protagonist, for these other knights are ideal expressions of the protagonist. If, says Sir Persant, in the important conversation out of which most of these clarifications arise, Beaumains can 'match' the Red Knight, he will be the fourth knight of the world, effectively as good as anyone. The Red Knight, who can be 'matched' only by Lancelot and Gawain, is thus himself seen by the protagonist as a very great man. To conclude this conversation, which began by identifying Lynet, Lyonesse, and the Red Knight and also includes a listing of some good knights of King Arthur, Beaumains reveals that he himself has been knighted by Sir Lancelot and that he is Gareth of Orkney. So the pieces of the pattern are being progressively identified and placed. Yet Gareth (as I shall now call him) wishes the identification to be kept secret, and emphasises that Arthur and Gawain do not yet know 'what I am'.

The Red Knight is very ambivalent. When he defeats an enemy he hangs him, and has so served nearly forty knights. On the other hand, this is felt to be a great pity, because otherwise he is a good knight, 'a full lykly man, and a noble knyght of proues, and a lorde of grete londis and of grete possessions' (320). But Gareth defeats him, his evil habits are dismissed from the mind, and all is forgiven. He is again forgiven at Arthur's court, where it is emphasised that Arthur still does not know who Beaumains is, though Lancelot, bound by law of secrecy, vouches for his noble blood.

Obstacles overcome, it would be natural for Gareth simply to marry Lyonesse, but there is a further sexual comedy to be played out which emphasises that the story is very much about the establishing of appro-priate sexual, social and familial relationships, as well as a full identity. The artistry of Malory's verbal realisation, his structural powers (whatever his debt to any source), are at a high point here within the conventions of romance. Much interesting detail and several curious episodes must because of lack of space be left aside so as to concentrate on the main narrative, which involves some use of magic.

Gareth and Lyonesse, each being young and tender of age, so burn in love for the other that Lyonesse advises Gareth to insist on sleeping in the hall, where she will later join him. And so she does, and they begin to make love. But neither has practised such crafts before, and their youth betrays them. Lynet is much displeased. She thinks her sister a little over-hasty, and that they should wait until they are married. So now an armed knight appears and fights Gareth. Eventually Gareth kills him and cuts off his head, but not before the knight has smitten him, where else but in the thick of the thigh, and cut many veins and sinews (333). The noise brings out Lyonesse's brother, with whom she has a defiant conversation. Lynet then appears, takes up the severed head, and having anointed it and the body at the neck, glues the two successfully together, so that the knight is whole, and Lynet puts him in her chamber. Gareth says he hadn't expected this, but Lynet assures him it is for his honour and worship and that of them all. Gareth and Lyonesse try again, a few nights later, and the same things happen, except that Gareth hews the head into a hundred pieces and throws them out of the window into the moat. But Lynet collects them all and repairs the knight as before. Gareth and Lyonesse remain reluctant virgins.

These episodes operate mainly at the level of the verbal realisation, but they have latent symbolic implications. There are still impediments to a fully mature enjoyment of sex and marriage. Gareth's thigh-wound symbolically represents a sexual anxiety, as does the beheading of the armed knight who may well also represent the protagonist's inhibitions. Lynet as usual may be seen as a 'split' of the beloved, this time representing for the protagonist not, as before, Lyonesse's eagerness to be sought, but her partial last reluctance to give herself sexually to the protagonist. We are not interested in any possible relationship between Lynet and the fantasmal knight, independent of the protagonist. Lynet and the knight, images female and male, are not absolute, but represent inhibitions still not overcome. The protagonist is still not fully mature.

He is however now identified to King Arthur in his absence by his mother, who sweeps into Arthur's court and indignantly asks, as any mother might, why her son was not better looked after. 'Where have ye done myn owne dere son that was my joy and blysse?' (339) (a wonderful verbalisation of a doting mother's attitude to her youngest son!). There is further emphasis on sustenance as well as lineage. The emergence of the 'true' mother in the pattern will free the protagonist to marry his beloved, and a final tournament is arranged, by Gareth's instructions, to be held by Lyonesse at her castle, on the Feast of the Assumption of the Blessed Virgin, the day which commemorates both the recognition and the removal (by ascension) of the great mother-image of medieval England.

Gareth does supremely well at the tournament, but still remains for much of the time anonymous. Tournaments are the great image of enmity and reconciliation for Malory, but there is still a final stage to go. Before the tournament is properly concluded Sir Gareth, now constantly so called by Malory, as he carefully was not in the earlier part of the story, goes off to further brief adventures, proving himself in various ways, and at last meeting an armed knight with whom he instantly fights. The battle is not described in detail but lasts for two hours, before Lynet suddenly turns up and cries out to the unknown knight, 'Sir Gawayne! leve thy fyghtynge with thy brothir, sir Gareth!' (357). They cease and there is an ecstatic reunion. Even more striking is how rapidly King Arthur is summoned and would have spoken but can not, and falls into a swoon for gladness. Then he makes great joy: 'And many a peteous complaynte he made to sir Gareth, and ever he wepte as he had been a chylde' (358). Here Arthur's vital residual role as in so many romances is invoked – he is the ultimate reconciled father-figure to the now mature protagonist. He is the father whose son has outdone him. He is joyous, even grateful, a little pathetic, all power transferred. He is at the literal level Gareth's uncle, as he is Gawain's, and this is referred to and is important. No sooner have we had this satisfying image than no less a person than the Queen of Orkney, Dame Morgause, Gareth's actual mother, appears; she too swoons, but recovers and makes good cheer. The family party is complete and happy. Lyonesse is then summoned. As so often in English medieval romance the 'heroine', though vital to the pattern, is a figure secondary to the reconciliation of the protagonist with the now powerless and therefore beloved actual parents. There is a moving and charming declaration of everlasting love each for the other by Gareth and her. The family drama is brought to a successful conclusion.

It is particularly satisfying in this romance, which has dwelt so much on food and drink, that the conclusion should be a feast. When Gareth has finally established his identity, but just before the final reconciliation scene, he is lodged in the castle of the Duke de la Rowse, and is set to supper 'and full knyghtly he ete his mete and egirly. Also there was many fayre lady by hym, and som seyd they nevir sawe a goodlyer man nothir so well of etynge'! (354). At the final feast the coloured knights and others that Gareth has defeated all beg to be his servants during the feast; his chamberlain, chief butler, sewer-chief, wine-waiter, culminating in the Red Knight of the Red Lands as his carver. What simpler, yet more effective, demonstration that the protagonist is now successfully at home, so fed by assiduous and humble defeated father-figures!

Malory's handling of the story shows that he understands very well what it is about, and the nature of the conventions involved. There are all the same some interesting innovations, probably due to his own genius in this specific verbal realisation rather than to his source, if such there were. The most notable technically is the occasional brief switch of the point of view. The first of these occurs when the castle of the third of the coloured knights, the Red Knight, is being approached by the hero. 'And the lorde of the towre was within his castell, and loked oute at a wyndow and saw a damesell, a dwarff, and a knyght armed at all poyntis' (308). For a rare moment we see the hero small and solid, from the outside. It is a foretaste of a different, more objective (in one sense more realistic) manner of story-telling, which will become more pronounced in the later section of *Le Morte Darthur*, where, though Lancelot is the protagonist, and Arthur and Guinevere are to some degree displaced parent-figures, there is a more various division of sympathies and a greater sense of autonomous character.

Another development in Malory's telling of the story of Gareth is in the presentation of time. In the earlier part time is essentially the protagonist's. All is measured by his actions. Even when Lynet wishes to hurry on to her sister it is apparently quite all right that Beaumains and she should remain to accept hospitality overnight from Sir Persant. But after the defeat of the Red Knight of the Red Lands there is a clear though not detailed period of two months to the Feast of the Assumption (which is the 15th August), and then to Michaelmas Day, early in September, when the wedding takes place. The protagonist in his mature identity has emerged as it were into public objective time, out of his own private time.

III

Malory's art becomes even greater and more complex in his last two major sections, Parts Seven and Eight of *Le Morte Darthur*, and there is a notable degree of objectivity in his narration. Yet the basic procedures even of the great last tragic story are traditional, and the latent forces remain those of the family drama. There is repetition with variation in the narrative rhythm, as in Lancelot's three (and what other number could it be?) rescues of the Queen, extending like a bridge from Part Seven to Part Eight. There is repetition in the presentations of family rivalry. The most obvious presentation of the protagonist-father-mother tangle concerns Mordred, literally Arthur's son by Morgause, who is Arthur's sister and also mother of Gawain and his brothers by King Lot. Mordred, when Arthur is conquering Rome, carries off Guinevere, Arthur's wife, to marry her; and eventually kills, as he is killed by, Arthur. No doubt about the theme there! It is that of Oedipus in the Sophoclean version. More complicated, more 'displaced', and therefore more interesting, is the situation of Lancelot. We are never told his age, but as he comes on the scene when Arthur is well established, and Arthur is his lord and king, he is in a son's position. We are never told Guinevere's age, but her authority over Lancelot and his obsession only with her makes his tragedy – at the deep latent level of these images – that of the man who cannot escape the mother-image in the family triangle, cannot break out of his own original family in order to found another. Guinevere, like a possessive mother, will not let him go – witness her rage when he has sexual intercourse with Elaine and begets Galahad. But Lancelot only sleeps with Elaine because he is tricked into thinking her Guinevere; he never loves her, and never becomes in his own right an effective father-figure in this latter tale. In terms of the total pattern of the whole tragedy, and in his relation to Arthur and Guinevere, Lancelot at the latent level never grows up. He is always the brilliant youth. Our own latent recognition of this is the reason why we are never bothered by the implausible presentations of Lancelot's physically as well as morally heroic feats when by any naturalistic reckoning he would be well into his sixties, any more than we worry about Guinevere's ageing beauty. The situation is permanent. Lancelot's failure to break out of the family triangle is not of course 'a fatal flaw' in his character as a personality presented on the literal level; it is part of the fundamental pattern of that particular story. The protagonist (of whom the figure of Lancelot is the main exponent), if he wins the mother-figure, is in conflict with the father – here is indeed the archetypal oedipal situation. In Malory's version of a theme older and broader than just the version by Sophocles, Lancelot is betrayed by the hostile sibling-figures – Gawain with his brothers Agravain and Gaheris, and half-brother Mordred. Gareth (the other sibling) and Lancelot are devoted to each other, but that the protagonist kills the beloved sibling-figure is significant. It is, as children say, 'accidentally done on purpose'. The protagonist *wills* to be alone. True, Lancelot has his followers, Bors and the rest, at the literal level, and well realised they are, but at this deeper level they are only appendages to him.

Lancelot's is the characteristic medieval love-tragedy, but as Anne Wilson in *Traditional Romance and Tale* has shown, the full story of Tristram is another set of variations on the same theme. Malory, it may be noted, does not follow out the full implications of the Tristram story. He takes only a weakened form of it, much interspersed with other material, to leave Tristram happily established with Isolde in Joyous Gard – essentially an episode, for all its length and variety, in the general history of Arthur that he is writing. Thus one section only of a given story may be taken by a traditional writer, and from a tragedy a 'comedy' may be abstracted. Most medieval romance is deliberately orientated towards 'comedy', in the sense of achieving a happy ending. The story of Gareth is yet another working out of the initially contradictory feelings arising within the family drama; the successful achievement of the main passage of life, from childhood to adulthood, shaking off parental bonds, becoming reconciled to parents, and establishing new equal relationships on a mature basis of self-realisation and responsibility.

CHAPTER VI

Some examples from Shakespeare

I

As You Like It

Le Beau: There comes an old man and his three sons –
Ceilia: I could match this beginning with an old tale.

As You Like It (I (ii) 104–5)[1]

And indeed Shakespeare matches this fairy-tale beginning with the whole play. Orlando is the third and youngest son. Rosalind, the heroine, is driven from the court that is her home by her uncle, the bad aspect of a composite father-figure. Accompanied by her cousin Celia, her bad uncle's daughter, she finds another home in the forest, where she is wooed by a handsome stranger. When the good and bad aspects of the father-figure, her natural father and uncle, are reconciled, which happens for no very good reason, she goes back to court and will there be married.

The play is more complex than a fairy tale or than the usual romance because Shakespeare complicates the protagonist's character and situation and takes more interest in the protagonist's future mate. He does this in part by telling two stories simultaneously, weaving two fairy-tale themes together, one of a heroine, one of a hero. Rosalind's Prince Charming is not just a handsome stranger. He is also the hero of his own fairy tale. Orlando is, we are not surprised to find, the third and youngest son; his father is dead; his eldest brother both tyrannises over him and neglects him. But, says Orlando, in the very first scene of the play, which is where we are told all this, 'the spirit of my father grows strong in me' (I (i) 60–7). In other words he is beginning to grow up and identify himself with the good aspect of the father. After successfully wrestling with the powerful and deadly wrestler Charles (instead of some more usual hostile father-figure like a giant, black knight, or dragon) Orlando goes off with his ancient servitor Adam. We have already several 'splits' of the father-figure. The dead good father, Sir Rowland de Boys, with whom the hero identifies himself; the tyrannous elder brother who as sibling of the same sex represents paternal oppression; Charles the wrestler, representing a simpler physical threat; and Adam, an old man indeed, and therefore inferior physically as well as socially, but because inferior not dangerous. He is partly a hindrance but his company is invaluable to Orlando in helping him get to the forest, to which also the female protagonist is hurrying. The forest is dangerous but for Orlando it is a place free of dominating parents and full of opportunity. For Rosalind, the forest is a place mainly of freedom and opportunity, though as a girl her freedom is more limited and she is more tied to her base. It is true that her father the Duke, who has been displaced and banished by his younger brother, is also in the forest, but as the good aspect of the father he is weak and ineffectual (or he would not have been defeated). He has lost his natural authority and, in addition, Rosalind has disguised herself so that he does not know her and has nothing to do with her.

The spinning out of the story depends on Rosalind being disguised as a boy, so that she can meet, know and test Orlando by acting in apparent jest the part of his beloved. The ambiguity of this boy/girl situation (further complicated on the stage because a boy acted the girl's part anyway) pleased Shakespeare. It derives not from the European fairy tale but from traditional romance going far back into antiquity. It is totally unconvincing in naturalistic/novelistic terms, but it is imaginatively satisfying because it allows Shakespeare both to present the fluid ambiguities psychologically present in all character, especially at the time of late adolescence, and to create an intriguing if highly improbable plot. As he makes even greater use of it in *Twelfth Night* it will be discussed further in that connection.

In *As You Like It* Orlando's elder brother Oliver then also comes to the forest, for no reason given us, as 'a wretched ragged man o'ergrown with hair' (IV (iii) 105ff). Such an appearance suggests an abandonment of adult self-responsibility and a rejection of the norms of society. While he is asleep under a tree, we are told, a green gilded snake wreathes itself about his neck and is poised to enter his mouth, but Orlando happening (by an agreeable coincidence that does not offend us) at that moment to pass by, the snake slips away. Danger still remains, for by further co-incidence a lioness with udders dry is waiting for Oliver to awake, when she will eat him. Twice does Orlando turn his back to abandon Oliver to his fate, but kindness and nature, that is, the instinct of family, prevail, and in what is effectively the third impulse, he kills the lioness. This scene is recounted to Rosalind by Oliver himself, who is converted from his wicked ways by Orlando's self-sacrificing brotherly love.

Preposterous as the incident is, it is the key and pivot of the action as it concerns Orlando and thus Rosalind, and we must return to it for its latent significance. It must not be dismissed. To resume the story: the reformed Oliver immediately loves Rosalind's cousin Celia who as instantly returns his love. They then being 'in the very wrath of love' are to marry incontinently next day, or they will be incontinent before marriage. Their marriage is the opportunity for Rosalind to declare herself to her father and suitor and to marry Orlando. We immediately hear of the usurping uncle's repentance (with no cause recounted, or seen in the present action) and all can go home as a united family. There has so far been no mention of a mother.

The action exemplifies a pattern and is not controlled by causality. The two protagonists are attracted, solve problems, come together. The driving force is the magnetism that naturally exists between boy and girl. They are eager to meet and must leave home to meet in a free environment. Father-figures are a constriction on freedom at home and a reason to seek freedom elsewhere. Another way of putting it is that the protagonists need hostile father-figures as a projection of their own inhibitions and also as a reason for going away. Once away they feel guilty and frightened but also excited by being free. In relative freedom each protagonist must test the self by independence and conflict, and test the reliability of the other. The tests are confronting oppressive aspects of the father, enduring danger and experiencing self-sacrificing love. Once the boy has fully grown up, that is, shown himself capable of bold independent action by killing the lioness, and of finally identifying himself with the father, as he already has done in intention by self-sacrificingly defending the hostile aspect (Oliver) of the father-figure, thus turning the father-figure into a friend of inferior status, all difficulty between boy and girl simply drops away. What has changed and developed is the psyche, not material external circumstance.

The snake and lioness that threaten Oliver are not allegorical representations of some potentially explicit factors but must be taken as symbols. Very obviously they are images of hostility, of poison and devouring animality, and it may be enough to leave them at that. But one must recognise that though there is no permanent, stable, unambiguous set of correspondences between any images and their significances, snakes *are* often symbols of feared or undesirable or unmastered sexuality – phallic symbols of a sinister kind. By driving the snake away from Oliver Orlando may be said to expel from his family, and from his own psyche, a poisonous sexuality. The lioness is more unusual. Why a lioness rather than a lion? It is possible that the lioness is a very much displaced image of possessive and thus predatory mother-love which will not let the boy go free to find his girl. The dried udders might be thought to represent her now dried-up uselessness. Once she is destroyed nothing holds him back.

The male protagonist has thus destroyed the evil in his image of parenthood and family, an evil which was as much or more within the totality of his own multiple psyche as in the external world. Now he is free from threat. Oliver, the elder brother/father-image, takes a position junior to Orlando, and thus symbolically demoted and improved from tyrannous father-figure becomes in effect a younger brother and a 'split' of the protagonist. Since Rosalind's cousin Celia must be regarded at the latent level as a 'split' of the female protagonist represented by Rosalind, her projected marriage with Oliver is an earnest of the marriage of Rosalind with Orlando which can immediately be arranged so that both marriages take place together – a repetition with variety which emphasises the triumph. So much for the latent action from the point of view of the male protagonist.

When the female protagonist has both tested the lover and recognised that the gross animality in him and the threat of the possessive mother have been destroyed, she can envisage her marriage through the marriage of Celia and Oliver, the minor 'splits' of each main protagonist. She can now develop beyond the neutral sexual ambiguity, girl dressed as boy, in which she had taken paradoxical refuge after the alarming step of leaving home (though she has always kept a firm anchor in femininity through the female 'split' character, Celia). It must also be said that boyishness is no bad image of sexual enterprise on the part of the feminine. Adolescent boys and girls notoriously tend to have ambivalent sexual characteristics before they are to some extent – never completely – polarised as one sex or the other. But as the pattern has worked out and the male protagonist is fully identified and unified in himself, Rosalind as female protagonist can now fully accept the woman's role and is ready for marriage.

Neither of the protagonists, since they have effectively come to an understanding of themselves and each other, now needs to confront a hostile father-figure. The male protagonist has already got rid of his. That of the female protagonist simply fades away. We hear in a charmingly perfunctory rationalisation how, having gone to the trouble of gathering 'a mighty power' to kill the rightful Duke, the usurper Frederick (the hostile father-figure) at the edge of the forest met 'an old religious man' and

> After some question with him, was converted
> Both from his enterprise and from the world.

> (V (iv) 154–6)

The ease with which we accept this, as the play hastens to its foreseen and desired conclusion, shows that we unconsciously accept its appropriate function at the latent level and need little causality of motivation to justify the pattern.

The protagonists have acted vigorously out of their own dash and energy and spirit, and have – especially the female – re-acted only mildly against parent-figures. Once the usurper has withdrawn, the rightful Duke, Rosalind's father, comes easily and mildly forward. It is notable, in Shakespeare's extremely paternalistic imaginative world, that Rosalind, when she discards her boy's disguise, first 'gives' herself to her father and only then to Orlando, and in identical words. Orlando has identified himself *with* his father (as Hamlet does): Rosalind is appropriately dedicated *to* hers: and the two protagonists are united in an everlasting bond under the aegis of the benevolent father-figure. The spirit of family reconciliation is as strong in Shakespeare as in medieval English romance. By uniting families he expresses the image of a wider reconciliation in society as a whole.

This general account of the play concentrates on the core of inner action. There are many other aspects of the play that in the full discussion, which space does not allow here, could be related to this central pattern at a lower level of generality. The variations played on the theme of love in the characters of Touchstone and Audrey, Silvius and Phœbe, are all interesting variations on the same theme. The life-refusing melancholy Jaques also deserves consideration as a minor 'split' of the male protagonist who represents the possibility of rejecting all love of women and family, living entirely to himself alone, without social, sexual or religious support, an egotistic nihilist – melancholy indeed! The humour, the portrayal of nature, and the many other aspects of the verbal realisation have inevitably been left aside in this discussion, not as unimportant in themselves, but as secondary in this anatomy of the play. The symbolised central pattern as thus disengaged is however the only kind of account of the action that makes sense. The desire to take *As You Like It* as a seriously intended imitation of possible actual life, of material cause and effect, realistically represented as they appear in their circumstances and settings, with rational, autonomous, plausible characters, is self-defeating; it makes the play and Shakespeare himself seem merely silly. And that, self-evidently, they are not. Any account of the action of the play is therefore bound to take it as symbolic. That does not mean that it is an allegory, and it certainly does not mean that we should disregard the literal level. We can only come at the inner meaning through the literal level, which we must read properly and give its full value, including a proper historical understanding of the possible meanings of Elizabethan English and of the historical culture. The verbal realisation is rich in pointers to its own further significance. Everything that I have argued in my interpretation of the latent implications of the literal level is based on the literal level, taken first literally not allegorically, and supported by quotation from the text, which is indeed a version of the story adequate to itself. Only by reading the text, or watching the play, in accordance with its own rules and conventions, historically based and sympathetically understood, can we properly understand it. There are implications here for staging. The notion of the 'sub-text' has been fashionable among producers – the 'sub-text' being 'what the play *really* means', a version of a symbolic interpretation. In practice this has often meant that the 'sub-text' has denied what the literal level asserts. That is not my argument at all, and does injustice not only to Shakespeare, which cannot now matter to him, but more importantly to ourselves, by denying us what Shakespeare meant. We have also seen heavily symbolical productions, with fantasticated settings robbed of all possible realism of presentation and cluttered with the bric-à-brac of adventitious physical 'symbols' – as if we *needed* ugly modernistic ironwork to show us that life is hard, or skulls to bring home to us the significance of death. Such superficial clutter violates the Shakespearean play. Settings must not attempt an overall naturalistic imitation of ordinary life, but there is every reason why producers should accept the literal text and, for example, when it refers to doublets and hose, dress the actors in them, and let them behave with the decency and decorum that Shakespeare everywhere requires except when consciously and rarely violating it for comic or tragic effect.

II

Twelfth Night begins with a shipwreck, thus symbolically delivering the emerging adult into the romantic, puzzling, painful, above all promising brave new world of those who are almost grown up. Such is Illyria. It is not exactly the world of the fully mature. Personal relationships are all; there is no work to do. Orsino is the Duke, but we never see him governing the country. The situation corresponds to that of Arthur in *Sir Gawain and the Green Knight*. Unlike the medieval poem, or *As You Like It*, Illyria is entirely bereft of overt parent-figures and there are no problems of origin and identity. Viola and Sebastian are identical twins of opposite sex, a thing impossible in nature. The basic action is comprised of a series of instant loves of desperate intensity which can nevertheless at a given revelation be switched to someone else with no suggestion of fickleness on the part of the noble lover. The central figures are Viola, Sebastian, the Duke Orsino, and the lady Olivia. All four are of almost equal age. Viola is described, when in male attire, as not old enough for a man nor young enough for a boy (I (v) 161–2). Her twin, Sebastian, is therefore the same – perhaps seventeen. Orsino is older than Viola (II (iv) 28) yet is 'of fresh and stainless youth' (I (v) 267), a virgin like Sebastian (V (i) 265), and might be thought of as eighteen. Olivia is younger than Orsino (I (iii) 111) thus a seventeen-year-old girl of about the same age as Sebastian. The youthfulness of the protagonists must not be disregarded. They are noble, virtuous, high-spirited, on the brink of adult experience.

The implausibility of the story hardly needs emphasis. By Neoclassical standards of naturalistic plausibility it is hopeless. We early note the lack of organic connection between character and action which is a feature of the aesthetic structure of traditional stories, especially in Shakespeare, and which derives from the fact that characters are secondary to actions and events, not prior to or creative of them. Thus Viola is obviously a good, modest, beautiful, intelligent, loving, unaggressive girl, gently brought up. Yet we see her first of all having just been shipwrecked, an adventure which leaves her unshaken, and then shrugging off without much feeling the probable death of her beloved twin brother and only relative. She does not know the name of the country on whose shore she has been shipwrecked, which is rather extraordinary, since everybody else on board seems to have known it, and when she asks she is promptly told by one of those companions. As soon as told, she asks who is the ruler of the land, makes sure he is a bachelor, and decides to serve him as a eunuch. Were we to judge her character in terns of her actions and decisions, as in a novel, we should think her a heartless man-hungry hoyden, with an implausible mixture of stupidity and crazy cunning. Of course we do not, because of Shakespeare's skilful management of style and imagery at the literal level of the verbal realisation, and, through its poetry, our immediate recognition of the fundamentally symbolic nature of traditional story. The shipwreck is a traditional event in romance, symbolising transition to a new sphere of action. The effect of the brief practical speech in this scene, the second in the play, following the high romantic style of the short first scene, which has set the general tone, allows us to accept the action because we know the sort of story it is. (Modern producers sometimes reverse the sequence of the two scenes. They lose the vital tone-setting contribution of the first scene by a mistaken zeal for bustle and an appearance of logical cause and effect, thus denying the audience the opportunity of immediately responding to the proper essence of the story and foreseeing its natural outcome.)

The story, with four principals, is even more enriched than in *As You Like It*, for the principals have more equal parts to play. Yet there is a dominant emphasis clearly placed upon Viola. When there are twins in a fairy tale they are obviously a composite protagonist, even when of opposite sexes (like Hansel and Gretel). Looked at from one point of view, then, we have an emerging composite protagonist, both male and female, with Sebastian a 'split' of the protagonist representing a minor masculine element. (It will be seen that Olivia, whose name is almost an anagram of Viola, may be thought of also as an element of the protagonist, but more of that later.) At the beginning of the play, especially when Viola takes on male attire, the protagonist has a male/female nature, a potent ambivalence which needs to be sorted out by the action of the play both externally and internally. The problem for the protagonist is to divide his/her ambivalences and attach them to appropriate objects. It is easy in the uneasy stages of puberty to love someone of your own sex, but unsatisfactory. There is no promise of fruit. Thus Viola disguised as a boy but really a girl loves the Duke Orsino, while the lady Olivia loves Viola thinking her a boy. In each case they can come to no issue because, for different reasons, there is no appropriate difference of sex.

The male/female protagonist loves/is loved by a male and female in the wrong order. This might suggest that Orsino and Olivia are displaced parent-figures, but that does not seem to work, since they neither protect nor oppress and do not need to be cast off. They are themselves, if I may put it so, a composite Prince Charming, both male and female, needed to meet the double necessities of the dual main protagonist. Since Viola is the dominant element in the protagonist it is inevitable that in order to correspond to her femininity the masculine element, Orsino, must dominate in the composite Prince Charming. Nevertheless there are some delightful paradoxes. Orsino is not very positive, while though Olivia may at first be seen as a princess locked up in the tower of her own self-indulgent grief, it needs only the appearance of the male aspect of the protagonist, Sebastian, for her to break out with admirable vigour. Even more than in *As You Like It* the objects of the protagonist's love have their own dramas, but in *Twelfth Night*, as in many a fairy tale, it is the feminine element which dominates, and with less of the self-pity or misfortune of fairy-tale heroines. In *As You Like It* Orlando, though not dominant, is at least able to act for himself and so bring about the dénouement, but Shakespeare does not repeat himself. In *Twelfth Night* it is Prince Charming himself who is the one who has to be rescued. Orsino thinks he is deeply in love with Olivia. Yet he does not go on a quest to win her. He remains at home in his palace and sends messengers, until Act V, when his reason for coming is to confront Olivia with Cesario, whom Olivia loves, and to destroy Cesario whom Orsino also loves. In other words, when Orsino eventually moves Cesario/Viola is the motive force. In this final scene Sebastian also appears. As soon as all four are present together the ambiguities are resolved obviously enough at the literal level. What we need to account for is the easy switch of objects of love, though Shakespeare's mastery of story and language makes it easy for the unsophisticated and sensible reader or audience to accept it without difficulty.

No serious problem can be made of Olivia, since she has always loved Cesario, the masculine aspect of the protagonist, and Sebastian does no more than fill out the clothes more appropriately. However that then produces a more interesting switch in the play of images, whereby Sebastian and Olivia interchange their emotional significance in relation to the main protagonist, Viola. Sebastian ceases to be a 'split' of Viola, for he has now achieved his own independent masculinity in relation to Olivia. He has become a version of Prince Charming, who can in the end be only masculine. Sebastian, married to Olivia, thus becomes a 'split' of Orsino. Olivia, formerly an aspect of the beloved to the ambivalent protagonist, now herself becomes an aspect of the protagonist; she is now a 'split' of Viola, and the protagonist has lost her ambivalence and become entirely female. An aspect of growing up is identifying oneself as male or female, outgrowing the sexual ambiguity of adolescence. The close similarity between the names Viola and Olivia is remarkable. Structural anthropologists who study myth find such anagrammatic repetitions with variation significant.[2] Viola and Olivia have each had an antithetical relationship both to Orsino (one loves, one hates) and to each other (Viola repels Olivia who loves her as Cesario). As the story progresses these antitheses are re-arranged and the heroines are brought closer together and now function as a composite purely female protagonist. At the end of the story they show how the female protagonist can love both the brother within the family and the beloved, the Other from outside, thus reconciling the family circle with the new, desired, external Other, the 'intruder'.

Olivia quite clearly demonstrates how the family relationship must be sorted out by the protagonist, first in experiencing the confusion by excessive love for her brother, then in resolving it. Her reason given at the beginning of the play for not seeing any man is that she is mourning the death of her brother (I (iii) 1ff). The inner significance of this is that she is refusing to grow up and refusing to accept both death and a lover from outside the family circle, wishing as it were to remain in pre-sexual childhood with her brother. The absence of parents emphasises that the refusal is her own decision, not forced on her by parents, and thus with little prospect of tragedy, because it is obviously within her own will and depends on what offers. Orsino is unacceptable, we may say, because he is too passive for Olivia; he does not seek her energetically, and as soon as Cesario appears as a mere messenger Olivia is ready enough to love 'him'. From Olivia's point of view Cesario is of course a 'split' of the later-to-appear Sebastian. Cesario is the unknown mysterious much desired summons from the outer world.

To turn to Orsino, it may well appear that his longing for Olivia is at the latent level a passive yearning for a mother-figure. He wants *her* to come to *him*. He wants comfort, though the yearning is negative, as it were idle, not perverse. Everyone notes that his passion is self-indulgent but not dynamic or demanding. As soon as Olivia is obviously unattainable because about to be married to Sebastian, Orsino's unfulfilled potential for love is easily seized by Viola, the main protagonist, who has long sought her Prince Charming. This play is notable for the way in which the female protagonist, as either Viola or Olivia, takes the initiative in obtaining her/their mates. Orsino obviously does not *really* love Olivia with love *paramours* or he would go and seek her of his own initiative. He is genuinely in love, but confused as to the object. Unlike the active female protagonist, whether Viola or Olivia, and the usual Prince Charming of fairy tale and romance, he is at it were trapped at home, not yet quite grown up, wanting to get out yet unable to. Not the princess but the prince in this fairy story is shut up in the tower. Luckily the princess comes to rescue him. A story like this, though it follows the modes of fairy tale, operates at a higher level of culture than the popular. At a higher level women, unlike those in a peasant culture locked in little more than subsistence farming, are not trapped at home. They are educated and enterprising, especially when there are no parents about to hold them down. Women seem in general in Shakespeare's personal mythology (and not only there) to be able, when adult, to be emotionally and spiritually self-sufficient; able (contrary to some still popular beliefs) to achieve a profound self-reliance, to generate their own identities. But men in order fully to realise themselves need, it would appear, to identify themselves with their fathers, that is, with the conscious, intellectually self-aware, controlling element in their culture – even if this identification takes partial form in conquering, or mastering (metaphorically 'killing') some part of that element, the 'father' in it.

In *Twelfth Night* the feminine aspect of these complex major processes is presented through the energetic, self-sufficient, delightful, female generative forces of the story. All the initiative comes from the girls. Perhaps because it is feminine, and apparently self-generating, there seem to be no parent-figures at all in the story. If the main protagonist were male there would certainly be stiffer opposition, as it were generated by masculine aggressiveness. Yet even in *Twelfth Night* there is one aggressive, oppressive, senior masculine force – Malvolio. If there is one thing more than another that parents, and especially fathers, are likely to say to us, it is, 'Be quiet, and go to bed early'. This is Malvolio's constant refrain. He is surely a much displaced father-figure. Malvolio is shifted out of the main *plot* and is put in action mainly against that overgrown delinquent schoolboy, Sir Toby Belch, who gets that juvenile thrill from staying up late by no means unknown to otherwise adult men, and who demonstrates his boyish bravado in an equally familiar continuous irresponsible drunkenness. The everlasting childishness of Sir Toby meets the equally unyielding paternalistic authoritarianism of Malvolio and neither yields. For this reason the situation is comic, though not a romance because there is no outcome, no resolution of conflict. But when Malvolio is shifted back into the main action, though in a marginal way, and shown to be in love with Olivia, the story does progress towards a resolution. He is shown to commit the father-figure's greatest crime, that of loving the heroine – that is, Olivia, in her aspect of a 'split' of the female protagonist – far too much. Of course his pretensions are never taken seriously, and that for a social reason, good enough in Shakespeare's hierarchical world. He is Olivia's social inferior, her steward, and being inferior is thus not dangerous. He is bound to fail, and so the story is a romance, a comedy. We look at him from the protagonist's angle and need spare no tears for the suffering of this highly respectable, honest, intelligent, well-educated, rational, authoritarian, Puritan father-figure. We rightly regard him as ridiculous. But it should be added especially to the present interpretation (which makes no claim to be a full evaluation of the play) that Shakespeare as usual gives him at least a touch of autonomous freedom as a character, beyond the controlling interest of the protagonist, and represents Malvolio as not acknowledging his role. 'I'll be revenged on the whole pack of you!' (V (i) 364). Most of Shakespeare's characters might say, as does Parolles, also at his moment of supreme discomfiture, 'Simply the thing I am shall make me live' (*All's Well that Ends Well*, IV (iii) 310–11).

The consideration of Malvolio may remind the reader that a considerable part of *Twelfth Night* at the literal level of the verbal realisation is concerned with various sorts of by-play showing the antics of Sir Toby and his friends, which have only superficial connections with the underlying movements of the psychic drama. A full consideration of the play as a whole would require more attention to this element, in itself apparently Shakespeare's own invention, but in type being jest-book material going back pretty well to the beginning of recorded time. It is harsh, derisive, traditional, popular comedy, abusive heartless horse-play, dependent on the toughness of the victim and a popular lack of sympathy for suffering on the part of the audience. It slots in well enough, if only by contrast, with the progress of the family drama, giving time for psychological developments and allowing the illustrations of significant facets of the protagonist's roles – for example Viola's (as Cesario) physical cowardice, by no means felt to be shameful to a woman, and Sebastian's bravery. The fooling in general adds laughter and an objective physical boisterousness which gives both relief and embodiment to the otherwise highly internalised emotional drama of youthful love and psychic development. But all this specific comedy is dependent on, and to that extent secondary to, the basic structure of the working out of this particular variant of the family drama.

III

Twelfth Night gives us an imaginative world with no significant parent-images. By contrast *Hamlet* and the late Romances are obsessed with them. If any one has trouble with parents Hamlet has. He is the only protagonist (Horatio is a shadowy 'split' and certainly not a sibling-figure). As usual, the general point of view being from protagonist to the rest, the emerging adult is central and parent-images marginal to him. It is unusual for Shakespeare that the story figures a mother-image. It is less unusual that there are two father-figures, as the actual literal level of the text makes clear, when Hamlet, mourning his dead actual father, refers to Claudius, his father's brother now married to his mother, as 'uncle-father'.

The nature of Hamlet's problem is made clear in the very first interchange between him and Claudius. Claudius in his oily, odiously conciliatory manner says

> But now, my cousin Hamlet and my son. . . .

Hamlet comments bitterly

> A little more than kin and less than kind.

> (I (ii) 64–5)

By 'more than kin' Hamlet refers to Claudius's being more than just a family relation – he has usurped the father's place. 'Less than kind' means 'unnatural', and also, perhaps, 'unkind' in the modern sense, but the word-play *kin-kind* emphasises the confusion and the perversion of role that Hamlet perceives in the father-image. Marriage (such as Claudius's) to one's deceased brother's wife was regarded by law and general feeling in the Elizabethan period as incestuous. Incest is almost universally felt to introduce the most fundamental and therefore disturbing confusion of roles and categories within the essential family. (It may be that much of our sense of category difference in the world is produced by our extraordinarily early sense of differentiation between mother and father, which has historically in Western culture been elaborately enriched until the present general collapse of the stability of marriage.) Hamlet, at any rate, bitterly plays upon the parental confusion which does not indeed require any reference to outdated Elizabethan law to be understood.

Both Claudius and Gertrude, Hamlet's mother, go on to reason with Hamlet. The King in particular emphasises that while mourning is proper it is inevitable that fathers should die. Not to accept this inevitable process is

> a fault to heaven,
> A fault against the dead, a fault to nature,
> To reason most absurd; whose common theme
> Is death of fathers, and who still hath cried,
> From the first corse till he that died today,
> 'This must be so'.

(I (ii) 101–6)

Claudius as always speaks truth and sense, which of course does not make him in the least more lovable. He accuses Hamlet of failing to accept the first principle of adult reality; in effect, of failing to grow up, to accept maturity and responsibility. He is undoubtedly right in this. Hamlet is a young man distinguished in birth and talents, with the instability of highly gifted young men on the brink of maturity.

Why will not, or cannot, Hamlet grow up? Basically it is because of the confusion of identities in the family circle caused by his mother's incest. That is, the substitution of uncle for father, the perversion of the nature of the father from good to evil, makes it impossible for him either to identify with or clearly to reject the general image of the father because it is too mixed. He thus cannot recognise and accept his father's death, and this prevents his own emergence into independence. Symbolically this means that the father is dead and not dead. Apparently killed, he has come symbolically alive again in a totally unacceptable way, Hamlet's original father being to this new uncle-father as 'Hyperion to a satyr'. That is why Hamlet cannot get over his death, and why he is so obsessed by his mother's wickedness. It is in effect she who has done this to him: she is the occasion of the death of his father (as the elder Hamlet) and yet in marrying Claudius she will not let his father die. She has corrupted the father-image. Her corruption is the latent cause of Hamlet's grief and the literal cause of his anger at her. There is no concealed, no displaced, latent, love for his mother in Hamlet. After the play-scene he tells himself he must use no violence towards her, only 'speak daggers'. There is no 'oedipal' desire (even if there is in Oedipus). Her corruption extends to Claudius. Hamlet when sent to England says mockingly but revealingly to Claudius

Farewell, dear mother.
King. Thy loving father, Hamlet.
Hamlet. My mother: father and mother is man and wife: man and wife is one flesh; and so, my mother.

(IV (iv) 49–52)

So the confusion of the family circle is compounded. The uncertainty of feeling thus created extends to Hamlet's view of the ghost of his father. Since the audience sees and hears this figure he has objective existence, as far as Hamlet and the play are concerned, at a literal level. Shakespeare does not present him as a figment of Hamlet's disordered imagination, nor does the Ghost tell lies. Claudius undoubtedly did murder Hamlet's father. The ghost is not a devil, as Hamlet fears he may be (II (ii) 594–5), and the play-scene proves it. But Hamlet still cannot bring himself to carry out the Ghost's clear orders to revenge because he can neither accept the death of his true father, nor thrust off from himself the sense that after all his uncle *is* his father. In other words he cannot identify with an adequate father-figure, which in Shakespeare's culture, as in the New Testament, is the mark of full maturity ('I and the Father are one').

Another result of the trouble caused by an errant mother is that she arouses in Hamlet that disgust with physical sexuality that is never far below the surface in Shakespeare, though by a familiar reversal it often issues in its comic aspect as bawdy joking. Hamlet accuses his mother of a raging sexuality that is itself unnatural (III (iv) 65 ff). She has much offended 'his' father, and 'would you were not my mother' (III (iv) 10 ff). He dwells on the incestuous sweaty love-making with disgust, though in logic incestuous sexuality should be no more sweaty than legitimate conjugal love-making. Hamlet attributes Gertrude's corruption to all women, including Ophelia, whom he undoubtedly loves, but whom he rejects in the scene with her which Polonius and the King spy on, and whom he makes the subject of degradingly coarse jokes during the play-scene. Even more, Gertrude's corruption extends to Hamlet himself. Unable either to hate or to love the father, he feels, as part of his incapacity, that he himself is deeply corrupt and accuses himself passionately (III (i) 121 ff).

The course of the play shows Hamlet's terrible struggle to achieve the paradoxical necessity of the male protagonist to do what we have seen done by the heroes of medieval romance, that is, both to kill the father-image and to identify himself with it and be reconciled with the parent-images. He is frustrated by the confusion which has been created in the father-image by his mother's treachery. The hero never kills the *true* father-image, so that the true father is as it were the eternal father imprisoned within the protagonist's psyche, yet not identified with him. Hamlet's true father returns from the grave to tell him to kill the false, the hostile, father-image, who is Claudius. (A dead father is good, a living father is bad; a variant of the weak but good, or strong but bad, pattern.) The story shows Hamlet killing Polonius, hidden behind the arras, thinking that Polonius is Claudius. The action is direct, vigorous. But that is because the father-figure is unseen. That is, Hamlet cannot kill him openly, as he cannot kill Claudius openly when he finds him apparently praying, though in the latter case Hamlet gives an unconvincing ration-alisation for his failure. Hamlet disobeys the clear orders of the Ghost (his true father) to kill Claudius, thus revealing an ambiguity towards the good father-image similar to his ambiguity towards the bad father-image. And in each case the mother's confusing relationship to the father is the cause of the ambiguity and confusion.

Hamlet fails to clarify the confusion, to identify himself with the true and good, to reject the evil and false. The confusion, the failure to establish a mature identity, drives him nearly mad, and Claudius sends him to England.

Nothing happens in the course of the story that clearly accounts for the new-found decisiveness that is reported by Hamlet himself of his voyage, when he so easily despatches the father-surrogates and hostile sibling-figures Rosencrantz and Guildenstern. But as soon as Hamlet leaves the centre of the stage two significant figures of his own age come to the centre of the action and at the latent level develop the pattern. These are Ophelia and Laertes. Ophelia is shown as mad in the scene immediately following Hamlet's last appearance on his way to England, and later in the very same scene her brother Laertes appears leading a revolt to avenge the death of *his* father, Polonius, upon Claudius. Of course Claudius easily deflects Laertes's purpose. At the symbolic latent level we may see Laertes as a 'split' of the protagonist, and the baleful father-figure easily foils him. At the literal level of verbal realisation Laertes is given a shallow character which makes the management of him easy. More significant is the much more extended scene, both before and after Laertes's irruption, of Ophelia's madness, which is marked by pathetically indecent songs. This must be associated symbolically with the sexual disgust felt by Hamlet at his mother's remarriage. Her madness sym-bolises the death of Ophelia as a possible beloved for Hamlet and it is soon followed by her actual death. It is the death of the feminine element. The problem of distinguishing the image of the beloved from that of the mother which is so obvious in so many medieval romances is given no prominence in this play, which is why an 'oedipal' reading of *Hamlet*, though it brings insights, must be unsatisfactory. Yet the problem exists as it were in a negative way. The taint that Hamlet finds in Gertrude extends to Ophelia and all women. Not only does the mother-figure impossibly confuse the images of the father, she makes undesirable any image of the peer or mate who must be found outside the family circle. Hamlet is trapped by the mother-image in a peculiarly horrifying way.

Yet there *is* always an escape, even from the family circle. There is always death. Ophelia dies. If Gertrude by extension taints, for Hamlet, Ophelia, Ophelia's death is the death of all women, and thus, symbolic-ally, of Gertrude, of the mother-image itself. (In most Western tales the literal death of female figures is not by any means so frequent as that of male figures – women are less physically threatening than men, giants or dragons and therefore do not have to be eliminated.) Were the mother-image alone to die, or be got rid of, that would of course remove the tragedy and turn it to romance. But that is not the case. She only dies in the form of the young girl, and it is with the young, not the old, that life and the future live. So Ophelia's death, being that of the young, ensures the tragedy. Yet since it implies the whole feminine element, including Gertrude, *the paralysing element in Hamlet's story, the corrupt feminine, is also dead*. Since the feminine element is also the generative element of life that cannot turn Hamlet's course towards success. But it allows him to act when he wishes to act, *if* he wishes to act.

In the scene immediately following the last of Ophelia's madness Horatio is shown receiving a thoroughly business-like letter from Hamlet describing his adventures. From now on Hamlet is a different man.

He is not however a man of action, successfully emerging into the adult world. In a way he *has* emerged, but at the cost of all he holds dear, all that makes life purposeful and valued. On his return, apart from the quarrel with Laertes at Ophelia's grave, his last outburst of youthful emotion, of which he shows himself ashamed, he expresses nothing but calm resignation, all passion spent. There is a paradoxical maturity here. Gertrude is no longer significant to him – he totally ignores her at the grave-side while he expresses his previous love for Ophelia as greater than that of forty thousand brothers. It needed, alas, Ophelia's death, to clarify to the protagonist the height and depth of his love for the 'princess', and now it is for ever frustrated. Yet death has at least swept away the poisonous mother-image; Ophelia's death has paradoxically and symbolically re-deemed Gertrude. Gertrude being insignificant, Hamlet is less confused about Claudius. Hamlet is burnt out, but Claudius will, in his own time, die. Hamlet has grown up and accepts the fact of death – all men's death, and thus that also of his father, and of himself:

> there is a special providence in the fall of a sparrow. If it be now, 'tis not to come; if it be not to come, it will be now; if it be not now, yet it will come – the readiness is all. Since no man owes aught of what he leaves, what is't to leave betimes? Let be.
>
> (V (ii) 212–16)

In the acceptance of death, including that of fathers, Hamlet has grown up. In so far as he has gone one stage further and already associates his own death with that of all men in the providential order he has been tragically forced to omit his own central period of maturity. He will die without having married Ophelia and without himself becoming a father-figure for whom death is appropriate. He dies too young, his promise unfulfilled.

> For he was likely, had he been put on,
> To have proved most royal
>
> (V (ii) 389–90)

says Fortinbras. Royalty is the normal image in fairy tales for achieved maturity, for being grown up. (Hamlet has earlier reckoned that he could be bounded in a nutshell and count himself *king* of infinite space were it not that he has bad dreams. Denmark is a 'prison' to him, and for Hamlet as later in *King Lear* the prison may be taken as a latent image for the stifling bonds of family relationship (II (ii) 240–58).) Hamlet's maturity then is only paradoxical, not unequivocal, and this is one source of the multiple impressions the play makes on so many readers, its almost infinite plasticity.

Hamlet is killed by the father-figure and does not achieve the princess. That is tragedy. The protagonist is at it were tricked into killing himself, for Laertes at the latent level may be regarded as a 'split' of Hamlet. Laertes's hostility to Claudius is easily deflected so as to cause him to kill Hamlet – an apt image (since one aspect of the protagonist kills the other) of the protagonist's failure completely to unify and identify himself, a counterpart of his failure to sort out the confusion of the father-image. That the young protagonist should be inveigled into self-destruction is the most painful tragedy.

Yet the paradoxical if barren maturity of Hamlet is exemplified by the way that he, like Samson (another folktale hero), brings down all in ruin about him. The protagonist does succeed in killing the father-image as he has already in effect shrugged off the mother-image. Claudius is killed by Hamlet and to that extent Hamlet is successful. Gertrude dies appropriately in error by the poison set out by Claudius himself. The mother-figure is rarely directly killed by the protagonist – a hard tradition still treats women in this respect less harshly.

The tragedy is more equivocal than most of Shakespeare's other tragedies but it is to be remarked again that Shakespeare's plenitude of power endows many characters with sometimes paradoxical life and is rich in ambiguities and ambivalences. If ever the multiple points of view of Gothic art are seen in literature it is in Shakespeare, even though this multiplicity sets in one general direction and is never purely relative or totally self-contradictory. There is always a hierarchy of values, an ordering of multiplicity, even where Shakespeare admits the possibility that no such objective order may exist ('for there is nothing either good or bad, but thinking makes it so', *Hamlet* II (ii) 249–50).

In *Hamlet* as in some other plays of Shakespeare, the inner story has many levels and aspects which are realised at the literal verbal level with extraordinary liveliness. Particularly noticeable is the wealth of traditional 'sententious' style full of proverbial or semi-proverbial human wisdom and reflectiveness, not meant ironically, and an unparalleled wealth of serious word-play, or puns. These traditional aspects of style, like the Gothic variety of story, have been constantly condemned by

Neoclassical critics up to and including T. S. Eliot. As usually in Shakespeare, and especially in *Hamlet*, the traditional poet really is the spokesman of the traditional culture. There are in consequence many points about the play which have not been considered here; what has been analysed is the essential core.

IV

King Lear

The story of the old man who makes extreme demands for expressions of love from his daughters occurs in many variants, ultimately to be linked with the story of Cinderella. It had been told in relation to King Lear many times before Shakespeare's version as part of the pre-Anglo-Saxon history of Britain. It was well known in outline to his audience, in other words, a traditional story. It is normal for such a story that amongst the various versions names, circumstances, even segments of the plot could be changed within broad limits. In versions by Shakespeare's immediate predecessors Cordelia succeeds in restoring Lear to his throne and he dies happy. Only then is Cordelia herself overthrown; she dies in despair by her own hand. Such might indeed – give or take some oddities – be the arbitrary course of history, but Shakespeare gives us a tighter pattern, and draws it back more firmly within the family drama, to follow up what became almost an obsession with him.

Until *King Lear*, in the course of those plays in which the central core is some working out of the family drama, the protagonist is always the developing child (in the early sense – not an infant but a person seen in relation to parents). In *King Lear* Shakespeare's infinite variety gives us the *father* as protagonist, so turning the traditional pattern of the family drama inside out in an astonishing way. The tragedy of so aged a man can hardly be the failure to become adult! Or, to put it another way, his significant personal relationships cannot be with parent-figures. His tragedy is that of one who kills the thing he loves. His own death at so great an age is merely incidental. Cordelia is therefore the point at which the tragedy aims, just as, in the related but opposite case of Cinderella, Prince Charming is the point at which that story aims. But the tragedy is not the tragedy of Cordelia, any more than the happy outcome of the Cinderella story is the success of Prince Charming. The protagonist is all. The winning of the Prince is the sign of Cinderella's success, and the loss of Cordelia is the sign of Lear's tragedy. In Shakespeare's *King Lear* Cordelia is not the protagonist.

It *would* be possible to conceive of Shakespeare's version of the story of *King Lear* with the youthful protagonist normal to fairy tale. In this case we should have to think of the three sisters as a multiple protagonist, and we should have to give them personalities different from those with which Shakespeare has endowed them. We should see how the oppressive father makes an unwarrantable demand on the inclusive love of the protagonist. Two of the daughters equivocate, but the third, in her innocence or folly, answers according to truth and nature, and in the spirit of the Biblical injunction (Genesis II, 24) that a man shall leave father and mother and cleave to his wife. Though Cordelia is condemned by her father, she finds a Prince who marries her, as do her sisters. Thus all the daughters have escaped. This is a kind of version of *Catskin*, a success story. The oppressiveness of the father however is not so easily evaded. He sets up disharmony between the daughters, who may be seen as the various aspects of the protagonist, as Claudius does between Hamlet and Laertes. Yet two of the daughters successfully resist the father and imprison him. That aspect alone of the protagonist which is represented by Cordelia falls his victim, is won over to him, is imprisoned with him, and, like him, dies.

This version is not too far from the bare bones of Shakespeare's version, and is not unrelated to some modern productions that claim to be of Shakespeare's play; but it is enormously different in spirit. Every version must be taken in its own terms and Shakespeare has realised the story in *King Lear*, it need hardly be said, with a most significant change of perspective, by making the father-figure the protagonist. It is this shift of the general angle of approach which makes all the difference. We thus see the other characters from Lear's general point of view, as is normal in traditional story. I do not mean that we see them literally as he sees them. We, the audience, always have a fuller view of the whole, we see more, than any character, even (or especially) the hero, in a traditional story and especially a Shakespeare play. We always know, as Lear does not, that Cordelia is supremely good and that Goneril and Regan are wicked. We see characters intriguing together when Lear is not present. That does not alter the basic principle that the characters must be interpreted in relation to Lear, and not as if they were fully autonomous rounded characters acting in their own right. Thus Cordelia is supremely good and her sisters irredeemably wicked from the generalised point of view of the protagonist which is spread throughout the play and confirmed by the ending. We see only that aspect of Cordelia's character which is significant to the protagonist and for the inner pattern of the story. Shakespeare, as is his way (like the tellers of fairy tales, the *Gawain*-poet and the rest), normally makes it abundantly clear at the literal level which characters are good and which bad. A 'naive' reading of the literal level of traditional literature is the correct one. There are no moral puzzles based on character. Just as we are told that Cinderella is good, and as the *Gawain*-poet tells us that Gawain is good, and we must believe this or fundamentally misunderstand the story, so we must take Shakespeare's word for it that Cordelia is good. To present her as in any way hard-hearted, immorally inflexible, foolish, stupidly unwilling to humour the foibles of senile Daddy, is a violation of Shakespeare's traditional art, produced by unconsciously debased Neoclassical realism and literalism.

The literal level must not be taken literalistically. The result may be a dangerous version of the tolerations of liberal humanism, when critics blame Cordelia for telling a deeply human truth, and palliate the vile crimes which her sisters do literally commit.

To avoid such distortions we return to the naive, the obvious, traditional reading, accepting the traditional principle of the centrality of the protagonist and the natural interpretation of other characters in relation to him, which does indeed mean accepting what Shakespeare writes (unless obviously ironic) at the literal level, without falling into literalism. It is always worth reminding ourselves that no symbolic interpretation may violate the direct literal meaning of the text. The only apparent exceptions are when there is clear evidence in the immediate context that irony is being used, or when a villain is speaking who can be shown to be lying (as with Goneril, Regan or Edmund). This principle is particularly important for the historical understanding of Shakespeare's plays, where in order to carry on the story, or to give basic information that in non-dramatic narrative is given by the author, the speeches of some characters must sometimes convey a considerable amount of information that is not a part of naturalistic characterisation or a naturalistic imitation of any ordinary interchange between two people. This kind of non-personalised narrative extends to descriptions of a given character's own state of mind, or moral quality, even when such description is put into the character's own mouth, that is, when it is self-description. The outstanding examples are soliloquies. We may take it as a further rule that characters always describe themselves truly, and do not mislead the audience. Yet there is little or no modern introspection, or moral confession, as an aspect of the character's own dramatic personality, in this convention. When Richard Duke of Gloucester, afterwards Richard III, says 'I am determined to prove a villain' (*King Richard the Third* I (i) 30) he is not engaging in subtle self-examination or special cynicism or modern nihilism. The words are no more part of his character than the blank verse in which he speaks reveals him to be a poet. Both the manner of expression and the metre are like the music in opera, part of the medium. In other words the character on the stage speaks always as it were with two voices, one his own, and one the narrating author's, and part of the experience of a reader versed in traditional narrative is concerned with distinguishing which of these two voices is at any moment predominant. For our purposes here it is enough to say that when a Shakespearean character describes himself the authorial voice is dominant, and thus what the character says, be he never so villainous, is true. When Gloucester says he is going to be a villain, that is the case and the author wants to make sure that we, the audience or readers, know it unequivocally. He is not telling us that Gloucester is especially cynical, or even, as some modern actors now play the line, so delightfully and humorously self-aware that we may forgive him anything. Equally, to return to *King Lear*, when Cordelia describes herself as 'true' and disdains to answer her enraged father's accusation of 'untender' (I (i) 105–6), we are to believe her, but not construe her self-description as a precocious self-awareness or, least of all, as a hard-hearted pride. To do so is to apply the inappropriate assumptions of Neoclassical naturalism. That Cordelia is neither proud nor hard-hearted, but true, is the whole point of the story. The audience or readers know it all the time, and the unfolding of the story is in part the narrative of how Lear also comes to acknowledge it. I am not arguing that Shakespeare makes no attempt to give light and shade to a character's personality. Cordelia herself, and the King of France, with a slightly more realistic touch, describe her personality further a little later in the scene, as one who is not only not a liar and flatterer but one who does not with ease express her deeper feelings. Shakespeare has indeed a genius for characterisation at the level of the verbal realisation, but it is often less naturalistic, more related to the underlying pattern, than we may at first realise, swept away as we are by the power of his art. The part of the pattern that we are concerned with in this episode is so powerful that we easily overlook the fundamental implausibility of the actual scene as presented. Far from worrying about the naturalistic presentation of a family row, we respond to the ancient spectacle of a father reluctant to let his daughter grow up and away, and the daughter's determination, in this case, to do so.

Cordelia has said:

> Good my lord,
> You have begot me, bred me, lov'd me; I
> Return those duties back as are right fit,
> Obey you, love you, and most honour you.
> Why have my sisters husbands, if they say
> They love you all? Haply, when I shall wed,
> That lord whose hand must take my plight shall carry
> Half my love with him, half my care and duty.
> Sure I shall never marry like my sisters,
> To love my father all.

(I (i) 94–103)

Lear's response is totally to reject her, but this is not a disaster for her at the latent level and it is significant that at the literal level the King of France immediately comes forward to accept her without a dowry. Cordelia has already symbolically broken away from the family circle even before an actual Prince Charming is supplied. Cordelia needs an actual mate no more than Gawain in order psychologically to grow up, though in the situation of resident suitors in the court we may detect the vestiges of a testing by the father of various suitors, and when the Duke of 'wat'rish Burgundy' refuses to accept her without a dowry it is a kind of failure of a test. Cordelia thus, as the King of France says, has only lost 'here' (i.e. at home) 'a better where to find' (I (i) 261), to find, like Catskin, a better home.

Lear's other daughters have equally clearly made the same transi-

131

tion, even though they hypocritically pretend not to have done so. As the story unfolds they ill-treat their father progressively worse. Although this is highly deplorable and merits the strongest condemnation in the play, it would not in itself constitute a tragedy even for Lear; it would be pathos, sorrow, the way of the world, wicked hypocrisy, and so forth, but not tragedy, and though in the working out of pattern and plot the part played by the wicked daughters is crucial we may leave them out of consideration in the central tragedy.

What then is the central tragedy in Shakespeare's *King Lear*? Although Lear is the protagonist, and does indeed develop more self-awareness, humility, and care for others, he dies. It might be enough to say that the death of the protagonist is sufficient to allow us to define a story as tragic, and as far as that goes it is true. But the death of so aged a man cannot be felt like that of one who is young, and cannot account for the deep emotional power of Shakespeare's story. Moreover, Lear is more than just an old man. He is a father and the story has centred on the family drama, although from an unusual angle. In the family drama death of parents is the happy ending; it is the death of children which is tragedy. We return then to Cordelia, but in a different light. The play is not about Cordelia. Her death is not *her* tragedy, but it is Cordelia's death which is *Lear's* tragedy. In a sense he kills her and in so doing kills himself.

We may express the tragedy at the symbolic level by saying that it lies with Cordelia's returning to her father, her voluntary rejection of her emancipation. On the literal level Lear does not ask her to return, but his plight calls her. She says

> O dear father
> It is thy business that I go about

(IV (iv) 23)

The Biblical echo, one of several in this play, does not establish Cordelia as a Christ-figure, or suggest any regular allegorical parallel in the action, but emphasises the seriousness and virtue of Cordelia at the literal level at this moment. She identifies herself with her father, as Christ did with his, and that is one of the supreme virtues for Shakespeare. Virtue is essential to tragedy. Moreover it is only as little children, we are told, that we can enter heaven. But we are not concerned centrally with Cordelia's virtue, only with the tragic recognition that it destroys Cordelia when the battle is lost and she and Lear are imprisoned together – a highly symbolical situation. The tragedy is the death of Cordelia, but her death is not a tragedy for her because she is not the protagonist. Her death is the tragedy for Lear because all the time she is what he wants and cannot have. He causes to be destroyed what he most values, and it is indeed a tragedy that he over-values his daughter's love. He will not let go when he must. It is characteristic of

Lear that he only pretends to let go, as we see very clearly at the literal
level when he first divides his kingdom:

> Only we shall retain
> The name and all th'addition to a king:
> The sway, revenue, execution of the rest,
> Beloved sons, be yours.

(I (i) 134–7)

Lear will retain the honour (*name*) and glory, and others can do the hard
work. He gives up the practical reality of power while wishing to retain
the prestige and personal advantage it gives. Life is not like this: he sets
up a fundamental self-contradiction in political terms. He does the same
in personal family terms, wanting love without responsibility, above all
wanting to keep what cannot live if he retains it. That is Lear's tragedy
at the latent and indeed at the literal level.

To say that Lear wants too much of his daughters is not at all to deny
in Shakespeare's or in Christian or in general human terms that
children should honour their fathers and mothers and do their duty to
them. It merely asserts the ineluctable order and sequences of the
family drama: that parents are older than their children and should
behave accordingly. Disturbance of such order will lead to tragedy if it is
not corrected or redeemed.

VI

Cymbeline

Shakespeare had by no means exhausted the potential of the family
drama with *King Lear*. On the contrary he became obsessed with it. It
even invaded his historical and political interests in *Coriolanus*. The
late Romances, *Pericles*, *The Winter's Tale*, *Cymbeline*, *The Tempest*,
highly traditional and extremely non-naturalistic stories, all work in
various ways at the problem we see first clearly formulated in *King
Lear* – how to reconcile the fate of the father-figure with the successful
survival of the young on whom the future depends. Shakespeare became
less and less interested in general naturalistic plausibility as he mined
the rich vein of the symbolic reality of these themes in his last plays. The
wealth and variety of the material is too great for me to do more than
suggest some of the many possibilities, and concentrate on only one play
which has often given difficulty, *Cymbeline*. Some themes must be left
almost totally aside, as for example the subordinate and at best ambivalent attitude to mothers, as in *Coriolanus*. The emphasis in the later
plays on daughters as opposed to sons may perhaps be accounted for
quite simply by the fact that Shakespeare was himself an elderly man

with daughters, though to posit such a close connection between the actual existence of a writer and his work would be challenged by much modern criticism.

Broadly speaking the plots of the late Romances, rightly so called, seem to be a series of attempts to convey a pattern of reconciliation within the family circle after an apparently tragic breakdown. *Pericles*, based on the medieval romance by Gower, bluntly confronts the horror of a father's incest with his daughter, first in actual fact (within the fiction) which is not very interesting, then in a more disguised way which shows difficulties and transferences of feeling more subtly, though in a rambling version not all by Shakespeare. *The Winter's Tale* shows disharmonies between two families and between parents and children which are repaired by the love between the children. *The Tempest*, where the protagonist is again the father, shows fraternal treachery and disharmony repaired by reconciliation effected through a daughter. All these plays are full of romance and folklore themes. Shakespeare cared little for naturalism at any time, and by the end of his life he seems almost completely to have given up bothering even about local realism, or poetic verse, so interested was he in working out possible permutations of family relationships within the nuclear family, and in presenting families reconciled after being divided for many years by faults, jealousies, angers, mutual offence. This too is traditional, as I have shown, with the medieval English romances, but Shakespeare comes back to the topic from different points of view and enriches the story-structures in a remarkable number of ways, articulating them sometimes through many inter-linked events, weaving in themes, general concepts, descriptions, characterisation, local motivation, 'sententious style', wit, etc. etc. He even adds a touch of pantomime at times, and occasionally has a sort of detached fun with these stories as he does not with the tragedies. It is as if he takes seriously, and can therefore afford not always to be serious about, his own message in these plays, that all shall in the end be well, that there is a providential order, and joy cometh in the morning.

The stories are absurd from a Neoclassical and naturalistic point of view, and even in his own time drew Ben Jonson's criticism in his Prologue to *Every Man in his Humour*. No story is more absurd than that which centres on Imogen in relation to her husband Posthumus Leonatus, who makes the extraordinary bet with his Italian friends on his wife's chastity and is so easily deceived. Yet it is also worth recalling that even such a hardboiled and cynical story-writer as Boccaccio liked this story enough to use it in the *Decameron* (Day 2, Story 9), and the audience there calls it 'beautiful'; though it is also true that after the coarse and brutal tenth story the ladies agree that the hero in the ninth corresponding to Posthumus was in comparison to the ruthless hero of the tenth a blockhead.

There is a sense in which all art, and thus all stories, should be regarded as 'play'. Within this general quality some stories are more playful than others, either because they are in fact comic, which is not the case with *Cymbeline,* or because they have something extravagant or schematic, together with a happy ending, which allow us, and often the author, to be interested in the story without as it were worrying about it. Romance, with its deliberate artificiality and such well-recognised conventions as girls disguised as boys, lends itself particularly well to such playfulness, without losing its capacity to articulate our interests and our necessary daydreams. In his late plays Shakespeare exploited this romance element, allowing himself much casualness of execution and perhaps occasionally a touch of mockery.[3]

All these elements have to be accepted when we read or see *Cymbeline.* How disastrous the wrong assumptions about a work of literature can be to its understanding is illustrated by our greatest critic's summation of the play:

> This Play has many just sentiments, some natural dialogues, and some pleasing scenes, but they are obtained at the expense of much incongruity.
> To remark the folly of the fiction, the absurdity of the conduct, the confusion of the names and manners of different times, and the impossibility of the events in any system of life, were to waste criticism upon unresisting imbecillity, upon faults too evident for detection, and too gross for aggravation.

(*Johnson on Shakespeare*, ed. Walter Raleigh, London, 1908, p. 183.)

Johnson's own comments sum up implicit Neoclassical criteria that are often still with us, even in productions which make no attempt at that degree of local realism which Shakespeare's own stage practised. But the play can be taken as a traditional story and found not merely interesting but a penetrating analysis of aspects of the family drama as part of the human situation.

There are two main strands in *Cymbeline,* each based on a version of the family drama, and one of the chief purposes of the story is to draw these two strands together. The first concerns Imogen and the second the unknown princes Guiderius and Arviragus. All three are the separated children of Cymbeline. Cymbeline is not himself the protagonist, rather surprisingly since he gives his name to the play, and since Lear, Prospero, Pericles – all fathers of daughters – have such dominant parts. Cymbeline's folly and anger, of which he repents, are the motive forces of the action, and perhaps this was in Shakespeare's mind. Furthermore, although as the story turns out the centre of the action lies with the young people, of whom the most important is Imogen, the audience is given to know so much more than she that the exposition itself has a sort of paternal omniscience.

Even a blow-by-blow account of the action of the play at the most literal level would show how close it is to fairy tale. A more summary account emphasises this quality, though doing injustice to the plethora of event and intricacy of narration. There are naturally variants. At the opening of the story Imogen is already married, but it is against her father's will and her husband, Posthumus Leonatus, is immediately banished. So Prince Charming is already identified, and the story is to be how the union is validated. It is important for this version of the family drama to note that Posthumus has been bred up by the King himself as Imogen's 'playfellow' (I (i) 40–54 and 145) and so he has been almost as a brother to Imogen. Although in every way noble he has one deficiency, which though not personal will need to be remedied. He is without a family. This alone would show that he is not the protagonist, but in order to be fully integrated within the whole story he will eventually have to be established in a family setting, like any hero in a medieval English romance.

We are immediately made aware that there is a wicked stepmother, who deceives and manipulates the King. Shakespeare uses the simplest devices of asides and soliloquies to make us aware of her wickedness, and also to show us that all the other characters, except Cymbeline, are aware of it. Thus the poison she procures from the Doctor and gives to Imogen's servant is not what she thinks it is, because the Doctor knows she is wicked and has made it innocuous. Although Cymbeline rages at Imogen and the Queen is courteous, Imogen is not deceived by her, and we immediately recognise the basic pattern of the fairy tale with a female protagonist: wicked stepmother, father under her influence, innocent heroine oppressed at home.

There is a development in the number of characters. The Queen has a son, Cloten, by a previous marriage, who is in every way as ignoble as Posthumus is noble. Cloten is also a suitor to Imogen and pursues her even though she is married. He too is in a sort of 'brotherly' relationship to Imogen, again not by blood, but in his case by his mother's marriage to her father. I return later to his place in the family drama as it centres on the protagonist.

Imogen is now forced to leave the court. The causal mechanics of this at the manifest literal level are brought about by the Italian intrigue which enmeshes Posthumus Leonatus, but the fairy-tale pattern of heroine forced to leave home is clear, and Imogen, under threat of Cloten, feels that she has no choice but must even try to leave Britain (III (iv) 130–9).

Although Cymbeline says later that she is 'the great part of his comfort' (IV (iii) 5), and he has been enraged by her marriage, his anger was because she had evaded Cloten, and we obviously do not have here the Catskin-pattern in which the protagonist has to escape a danger-ously doting father. The father is manipulated by his wife, whom he loves, but who hates the protagonist, and the protagonist is escaping from the wicked Queen, her stepmother. From the protagonist's point of view she is fleeing the hostile mother-image and seeking her mate. The pattern is close to that of *Snow-White*, although the overt rivalry in beauty between the Queen and the protagonist does not appear. I am not arguing that we have in *Cymbeline* an actual analogue to the interesting folktale of Snow-White; only for a certain similarity of deep pattern and effect, and I hope the lover of Shakespeare will forgive me if I also argue for a similarity in the play to the Seven Dwarves.

Imogen flees to Wales in hope of meeting the Roman ambassador Lucius and becoming his page. This will also bring her closer to her still beloved husband. Wales is also the abode, though Imogen does not know it, of yet more brothers. Guiderius and Arviragus have already been introduced into the narrative by Shakespeare as boys living in wild Wales with their father Belarius. Belarius tells them, as he has told them many times before, his history: that he was once Cymbeline's best general but was the subject of false accusations of treachery which Cymbeline immediately believed, and so Belarius was banished twenty years ago. The boys run up a mountain and Belarius immediately explains to himself that they are really the sons of Cymbeline whom he took with him in revenge. Samuel Johnson remarks of this passage:

> Shakespeare seems to intend Belarius for a good character, yet he makes him forget the injury which he has done to the young princes, whom he has robbed of a kingdom only to rob their father of heirs.
> The latter part of this soliloquy is very inartificial, there being no particular reason why Belarius should now tell to himself what he could not know better by telling it.

Johnson on Shakespeare, ed. Raleigh (p. 182.)

This notes both the incompatibility frequently to be observed between action and character in the re-telling of traditional stories, and the 'conventional' authorial nature of much speech in Shakespeare. We must read with acceptance of the author's evident intention, that Belarius is a good character, and look for patterns rather than material causes. The pattern of the Belarius episode is not naturalistic, but will soon be recognised as illustrating a very widely held concept of the self. Although Belarius has moralised at great length in Shakespeare's favourite sententious vein on the superiority of the simple rustic life, Shakespeare has given him a deliberately artificial tone, for though what he says is true it has only a limited truth. Belarius has also told the young men about his own experience of the world, and as Belarius acknowledges, their royal nature expresses itself in eagerness to leave this dull quiet life and to win honour and fame. They rightly object to being kept in this 'cell of ignorance' as Guiderius, the elder, calls it. Arviragus complains that 'We are beastly' (III (iii) 33 and 40). The situation of the two youths is a beautiful and simple representation of what Rank called 'the family romance of neurotics' – the notion many people have when young that our *real* parents are persons much more distinguished than those poor old souls who have the honour of bringing us up.[4] The difference within this particular fiction is that 'the family romance' is not a mere fantasy, it is true. The youths really are sons of a King, and superior to their apparent father. Although the young men feel no hostility towards Belarius Shakespeare makes it plain that they are straining at the leash and must soon be away. They are at the point of emergence into adult life. It is characteristic for Shakespeare that the wife of Belarius, whom the young Princes at the moment believe was their mother, is dead. Being dead, her memory is loved and revered.

To this all-male family comes Imogen alone, in a boy's clothes, lost and deadly tired. The young men take her for a boy, but feel instant friendliness, being in fact her siblings of the opposite sex. Notwithstanding Imogen's apparently male sex it is agreed that when the men go hunting the 'youth' will stay at home to be their 'huswife', and it turns out that 'he' is an excellent cook! Snow-White too kept house for the Dwarves, to whom Guiderius and Arviragus are the equivalent. The Dwarves however in the fairy tale are insignificant in their own right, not to say comic, while these sibling-figures in *Cymbeline* have their own significance and contribute to the general pattern of children and parents in the play beyond their immediate relationship to the protagonist – which is however their primary function in the pattern.

We now come to the crucial episodes in the protagonist's story. The Queen had prepared poison for Imogen which she entrusted to the ever-faithful Pisario as sovereign remedy. Imogen has been carrying this, and takes it to revive herself after the rigours of her journey. It is not poison, but it casts her into a death-like trance. So far we are still close to the story of Snow-White, whom the Queen discovers in her retreat and to whom she gives a poisoned apple. In the fairy tale the Prince eventually moves the beautiful corpse, dislodges the piece of apple and so brings Snow-White into adult life. It is a pattern also reflected in *The Sleeping Beauty*. In *Cymbeline* the story-line is more complicated and subtle, though at the deepest and simplest level it is similar.

It is Cloten, not the fairy-tale Prince, Posthumus, who now comes into the picture. He has followed Imogen to Wales, and is disguised in Posthumus's clothing. Just after Imogen has met her unknown brothers, and has received succour from these disguised siblings, Cloten appears and in a soliloquy expresses his brutal lust for Imogen, whom he intends to rape and 'spurn her home to her father, who may, haply, be a little angry for my so rough usage; but my mother, having power of his testiness, shall turn all into my commendations' (IV (i) 23–7). Besides this brutality of sexual desire Cloten has also expressed the intention of killing and decapitating Posthumus. Since we know Cloten to be a fool and a coward we do not worry unduly about his threats, but they provide a deeply interesting symbolic pattern, which we can follow with interest even if at the level of subconscious response.

I shall argue in a moment that Cloten's murderous lust is the deepest element in the whole drama, the knot which the whole story sets out to disentangle, though of course at a level deeper than that of characterisation and plausibility on the level of verbal realisation, which Shakespeare has to sacrifice. The full demonstration depends on

slightly later scenes, but here it is important to recognise first that
Cloten represents the Queen's hostility. The absence of any intention to
marry Imogen, even were Posthumus dead, and the strange intention to
return the violated Imogen to her father, express the mother-figure's
powerful determination not to let the protagonist escape from home.
That Imogen would have been raped shows how Shakespeare, like many
traditional writers, including the *Gawain*-poet, does not consider that
physical sexual experience is in itself significant of maturation. Gawain
is mature, has escaped, without it, while Imogen, having been forced
into it, would nevertheless still be entrapped within the family circle.
That the mother-figure's hostility should be expressed in such powerfully male symbolism as rape reveals a strange ambivalence that I do
not fully understand.

We proceed however to the deeper aspects of what Cloten represents,
which are clarified by the immediately following events in the story.
Cloten meets and challenges Guiderius and is killed and beheaded.
Since he has boasted to Guiderius that he is the Queen's son (thus
symbolically expressing that aspect of himself which embodies the
Queen's hostility), Guiderius remarks

> I have sent Cloten's clotpoll down the stream,
> In embassy to his mother: his body's hostage
> For his return.

(IV (ii) 185–7)

Symbolically, the Queen's hatred returns upon herself. Imogen's
apparently dead body is then brought in, is mourned, and laid side by
side with the headless Cloten's, which, it will be remembered, is wearing the clothing of Posthumus. Immediately all leave and Imogen wakes
to think that Cloten's body is that of Posthumus. It is a grotesque
situation. The speech in which Imogen expresses her nightmarish
recognition, as she thinks, of her dead husband is surely one of the most
difficult to play in all Shakespeare, for such is the balance of feeling that
it is hard to avoid inappropriate laughter. Shakespeare's task was to
make us sympathise with Imogen while knowing that there is now no
real cause for grief. The death of Cloten has removed the essential
danger. Why does Shakespeare run this extraordinary risk, create this
apparently 'unresisting imbecillity'?

Abandoning hope of plausibility we also rightly abandon ourselves, in
this scene, to relief as well as sympathy, along with detachment. Something is in process of being solved, and the audience's attitude to
Imogen, from its superior point of view, is that of a father who may smile
at a child's present suffering because he knows that it will be brief, not
damaging, and even good for it. What then is in process of being solved?
It is clearly good that Cloten is dead, and we should follow the play's own
lead that identifies him, with a difference, with Posthumus. Each has a
sort of brotherly relationship with Imogen. They are obviously physic-

ally alike, and each loves Imogen in his own way. Cloten is all bad to Posthumus's all good; he is the mirror-image of Posthumus. At the deeper level of symbolic interpretation it is obvious that he is a 'split' of Posthumus. *In the latent sense Posthumus and Cloten are the 'joint' Prince Charming at the beginning of the play*. This is where Cloten's murderous lust is so important. If at the deepest level of symbolic interpretation we regard the whole story from the point of view of the female protagonist, we can see that murderous sexuality is for her an aspect of love, one that she cannot accept, that she has banished, but which she must come to terms with. Or, to put this complex matter in another way, sexual love has an aspect of aggressiveness which has to be tamed, or got rid of. To put it yet another way, the virgin has to learn to become a wife. This is an entirely traditional theme, represented in such stories as *The Frog Prince* and *Beauty and the Beast*. Chaucer puts the traditional attitude in his own more literal way:

> For thogh that wyves be ful hooly thynges
> They moste take in pacience at nyght
> Swiche manere necessaries as been plesynges
> To folk that have ywedded hem with rynges
> And leye a lite hir hoolynesse aside
> As for the tyme – it may no bet bitide.

The Man of Law's Tale, The Canterbury Tales II (B) 709–14

The point is made in the very text of *Cymbeline*. That is why Shakespeare uses the absurd story from Boccaccio about the chastity-bet. Implausible as that story is, it is a paradigm about the need to trust love to control the natural savagery of sexual desire. Posthumus himself says of Imogen (when raging against her apparently rapid betrayal of him with the villainous Iachimo, a mere acquaintance whom he has after all encouraged to try to seduce his own wife and whose word he immediately accepts):

> Me of my lawful pleasure she restrain'd,
> And pray'd me oft forbearance; did it with
> A pudency so rosy, the sweet view on't
> Might well have warm'd old Saturn: that I thought her
> As chaste as unsunn'd snow.

(II (iv) 8–12)

One could hardly have it more clearly expressed in humane and civilised terms. Shakespeare in no way implies that this is false delicacy on Imogen's part, yet the story takes us, and her, beyond it. When we realise that, at a latent symbolic level below the level of literal consciousness, Cloten represents what is to the female protagonist the untamed, or unacceptably aggressive, sexual element in the lover's love for her, we can see that the daring, dangerous, confusion Shakespeare apportions to Imogen in lamenting the dead Cloten as if he were the dead Posthumus shows a progress in deep human relationship that could hardly be made otherwise. As usual in traditional art we are presented with significant juxtapositions placed in a pattern, not with a chain of material cause and effect, for these are movements of the mind and feelings. Least of all, of course, is there any attempt at discursive analysis, which must always be, like the present effort, secondary to the multiple effects of creative art, laborious, single-stranded and simplifying. At the deep level of symbolic interpretation which we are considering here we have to leave aside other elements of the play, including consideration of detailed characterisation at the level of verbal realisation. But it is the deeper level which ultimately controls the other elements.

Brotherly and lover-like relationships of the protagonist's are being explored and clarified. Her true brothers will foster her tenderly but without sexual feeling, and for all their love she is dead to them. Yet she has in a sense found them, and it is immediately after their appearance and rescue of her that Cloten appears, a false brother at the opposite extreme, a brother in the aspect of brutal sexual desire. True brotherly love kills him. The protagonist has not really lost her beloved, though she thinks she has. She has lost her fear of his aggressive sexuality. The decapitation of Cloten also suggests that the complex beloved has overcome his own sexual aggressiveness. This is made clear when Posthumus appears in the scene after next, lamenting his own previous angry command to Pisario to murder Imogen. There has been no sequential build-up of causal motive, no view of Posthumus which has led to this sudden repentance. We do not need it. Motivation and the analysis of character in its presentation is the function of the novel and Shakespeare rarely presents character through such means. We see his people in violently changed moods which are part of the general pattern he presents. The pattern now allows, indeed requires, Posthumus to repent of his anger towards Imogen, and this is natural, though not naturalistic, after the death of Cloten who represents the beloved's intemperance, greed and cruelty. Once these natural but morally reprehensible aspects of love are purged Posthumus can also repent of his possessiveness and self-regarding pride which his bet with Iachimo expresses. Absurd as that story is, it exposes, in its schematic way, an anatomy of husband's love as unduly proud, possessive, and egotistic – all counterparts of Cloten's mere physical desire without true love. But now Cloten is dead and in the pattern of the action these untoward elements of love are being purged.

It is also a part of the pattern that before Posthumus's repentance is shown, in the scene of Imogen's fainting over Cloten's body, she is taken up by the Roman Senator Lucius. We should expect a father-figure here, and lo, Lucius, who in terms of probability has taken to the 'boy' with astounding speed and trust – but who minds that? – says to Imogen that he will

And rather father thee than master thee.

(IV (ii) 398)

It is equally a part of the pattern that with the sexually hostile, false-brotherly element in the beloved killed, and with the re-establishment of a genial father-figure for the protagonist, the very next scene, only a few lines further on, should show us Cymbeline's court and immediately tell us that the Queen is so ill that her life is in danger. Cymbeline's own grief for Imogen is apparent. The death of Cloten symbolises the end of the Queen, for he is an aspect of her hostility, and a genial father-figure is correspondent with the wane of her powers.

Thus at the beginning of the long Act Five the ground is cleared for a satisfactory outcome and a grand reconciliation. Although the core is the relationship between protagonist and beloved much else happens.

Cymbeline has, on his Queen's advice, rejected the payment of tribute to Rome and Lucius is now at Milford Haven with a Roman army and a bloody battle is toward. Posthumus has come to fight with the Romans against his own countrymen, but in the same speech in which he expresses his repentance for what he has done to Imogen, he says

> 'Tis enough
> That, Britain, I have kill'd thy mistress; peace!
> I'll give no wound to thee.

(V (i) 18–20)

He says he will disguise himself as a British peasant

> so I'll die
> For thee, O Imogen, even for whom my life
> Is every breath a death.

(V (i) 25–7)

Imogen and Britain are associated. There is a strong and agreeable patriotic element in the play which is more subtle and more closely connected with the inner theme than may at first appear.

As well as Posthumus, Belarius and the sons of Cymbeline also fight marvellously well in the ensuing battle, and it is largely owing to the bravery of these four that the battle is won and the Romans soundly defeated.

Posthumus however is assumed by the British to be a Roman and is cast into prison, where another most extraordinary scene (or what would be so if plausible appearances and naturalistic assumptions were the basis of the story) now takes place. He is visited by the apparitions of his dead father, mother and younger brothers – a splendid demonstration of family solidarity – who one by one reproach Jupiter, king of the gods, for allowing Posthumus to be banished because of his marriage, to be tainted by Iachimo, and now to be 'in miseries'. Thus is

142

the integration of Posthumus within his own family circle expressed. He is not the protagonist, and so has no inner psychic drama portrayed for him, but he is shown now to be fully worthy of the protagonist because a full sense of his own family has been openly established within the story. He is fully himself. This interest in hereditary identity is strong in medieval English romance. Posthumus says

> Sleep, thou hast been a grandsire and begot
> A father to me; and thou hast created
> A mother and two brothers.

(V (iv) 123–5)

It is true that they have now vanished, but Jupiter has left a tablet on his breast containing a symbolic prophecy, that a 'lion's whelp' (Posthumus's full name is Posthumus Leonatus) shall be embraced by a piece of tender air, that previously lopped branches shall grow on a stately cedar tree (obviously Cymbeline), and that Britain shall thrive. All shall be well. Posthumus has been shown as united with his family, but he does not need, even if he must lament the absence of, his family. Fathers need heirs, but heirs, once established, do not need fathers. Furthermore, Posthumus has been fully established as from a different family and not in any sense a brother to the female protagonist. Brothers are excellent helpers and protectors but a female protagonist no more wants to marry them than to marry her father. Exogamy is the fundamental rule of traditional stories (E. R. Leach sees exogamy as the basic 'motive' for many Old Testament stories[5]). No doubt part of the horror of Cloten's sexual desire is his 'brotherly' relationship, and his death kills that element too in the general image of the beloved.

We proceed immediately to the great reconciliation scene, where all the persons of the drama are brought face to face, and proper family relationships are restored. The final necessity before all can be unravelled is the death of the Queen, source of all the woe. Of this we are immediately informed, as also that, with glorious improbability, she has in dying confessed all her past and even her intended future misdeeds. Cymbeline of course immediately believes what we all know to be true, and the unravelling and knitting up begins. Imogen, naturally enough, being now successful, sets the action going, though she is still disguised as a boy. She controls Cymbeline – a docile, rejoicing, no longer dangerous father-figure – and then brings Iachimo to confess his crime. We are not surprised to find that Iachimo is glad to confess, for that re-inforces the underlying pattern.

A word must be spared at this stage for Iachimo's role. On the level of the verbal realisation he is a thinly sketched character playing a role familiar in a schematic folktale. His unmotivated lust and malice are sufficiently matched in life, alas, to allow us to accept his treachery towards both Posthumus and Imogen without looking for further cause or deeper characterisation. His unmotivated repentance is equally acceptable in this final scene when all is being revealed and when repentance and pardon are the themes. In other words he fits well enough into a verbal realisation of a folktale kind. At the deeper symbolic level, adopting the principle that most characters are 'splits' or aspects of the three or four main characters, it is plain that Iachimo is another aspect of the beloved's aggressive sexuality, as Cloten is. Unlike Cloten, he is not brutal, but he is sly, dishonest, seductive, untrusting, cynical, sociable, superficial. He represents even on the literal level the jesting about private matters of psychic as well as physical integrity to do with sex that young men are seen to be prone to, with the easy degradation that it brings. This does not call for extirpation, like Cloten, but for repentance and after repentance, pardon. His repentance is called for by the protagonist and at the latent level we may say that the beloved now rejects, or is purged of, the more ignoble, untrusting, self-seeking elements of his love. At the literal level Posthumus's pardon of Iachimo re-inforces our sense of his manifest noble nature. At the latent level, taking Iachimo as a 'split' of the beloved, we may say that from the beloved's point of view it is important for people not only to repent, and forgive others, but also to forgive *themselves*, to forgive that aspect of the self which has sinned.

To return to the literal level, which is not inconsistent with this, Iachimo's praise of Posthumus's nobility allows us to accept Posthumus as good without priggishness, and Iachimo's revelation provokes Posthumus to reveal his own identity and in his own person to express the deepest repentance. This is what is needed. The beloved must repudiate all the hateful aspects of his love, for he too needs pardon. Imogen intervenes to moderate Posthumus's rage against himself, and thinking that 'he' scorns or mocks his desperate self-condemnation Posthumus knocks 'him' down. It is an aptly paradoxical last expression of his aggressiveness towards her, his beloved wife, or of what, at the deepest level, we may say that the protagonist feels is the beloved's aggressiveness towards her. The blow is a repetition, so to speak, of his previous offence. It also produces the full revelation that the 'boy' is his own wife in disguise, and the aggressive deed now made again explicit and conscious can be finally and fully recognised, repented of, forsworn, and pardoned.

The episode with Posthumus allows us to note again, as with the case of Belarius, the general point that in traditional stories the moral quality of the character and that of his actions may not at the literal level exactly co-incide. There can be no doubt that Posthumus, like Belarius as Johnson notes, and like such other Shakespearean characters as Bassanio in *The Merchant of Venice*, Claudio in *Much Ado about Nothing*, Prince Hal at the beginning of *Henry IV, Part I*, even Bertram in *All's Well that Ends Well*, are meant to be taken as good men. The literal texts constantly tell us so. Yet if their actions are taken as proceeding from them by their own volition, as if they were characters in a nineteenth-century novel, they may be seen as 'blockheads', hypocrites, or worse. We must recognise that the stories have their own schematic structure, and that the personality of the character is added on the literal level 'inorganically', even, by naturalistic standards, inconsistently. In many cases the personality of the character, at the level of verbal realisation, is only slightly etched and shaded. The character is primarily a role, as in Posthumus's case. The richness of psychological insight lies in the presentation of several such characters which add up to what the twentieth century can understand as a fuller and truer psychic whole, with a mixture of good and bad. This is why we must insist that Posthumus himself, as a character in the action, plays fully the role of paragon, is essentially ideal, noble, brave, even if in his actions temporarily tainted by the wicked Iachimo, for which he must repent; and this is why we may also insist that, at the latent level, Iachimo and Cloten are both, like Posthumus himself, elements in the total image of the beloved, though these others are elements that need to be repudiated.

To return to the story, the revelation and reconciliation concerning the protagonist and the beloved lead to a sequence of others. This is one of Shakespeare's most exciting final scenes. It is an admirable example of the narrative interest of a traditional tale, where the audience knows the whole story and finds pleasure in seeing how the characters within the fiction learn its realities, so that eventually both audience and characters share the same truths of relationship. The image of the united family is dominant in the text. Cymbeline says of the recovery of his two sons and of Imogen:

> O what am I?
> A mother to the birth of three? Ne'er mother
> Rejoic'd deliverance more.

(V (v) 368–70)

The image of the mother which is adopted by the father validates re-birth and re-union. Cymbeline also recognises Imogen's devotion to Posthumus, and sees her, as we must, as the central rock, the protagonist, round whom all the characters are ranged:

> Posthumus anchors upon Imogen;
> And she, like harmless lightning, throws her eye
> On him, her brothers, me, her master [i.e. Lucius], hitting
> Each object with a joy; the counterchange
> Is severally in all.

(V (v) 393–7)

Each reciprocates. Cymbeline calls Belarius 'brother', and Imogen calls him 'father'. Posthumus is recognised as brother to Guiderius and Arviragus. Jupiter's symbolic tablet is interpreted, the 'tender air'

145

being in Latin 'mollis aer', a word-play on 'mulier', 'wife', which signifies Imogen. It is towards this full recognition of Imogen as 'wife' by both Posthumus and Imogen herself, with all the many ramifications of that acceptance within the family, that the whole story has been working. This family drama is the web into which the woof of all characterisation (such as it is), and all the other elements, including the religious and the political-national themes, is woven.

It is worth then asking why the absolutely last action of the play should be religious and political. Why are we not left with the family? Important as such public themes are, they are not in themselves central to the essential personal drama and have been given only marginal treatment in the deployment of the story. The scene of Iachimo in Imogen's bed-chamber, for example, is far more extensively treated than these apparently grander, more general themes. Even more re-markable, it may seem, is the light-hearted manner in which, after much strongly-expressed patriotic sentiment about Britain's freedom from the Roman yoke, and so many deaths incurred in procuring it, independence should now be jettisoned, and Cymbeline proclaim his intention of paying tribute despite his victory. The rationalisation is that Cymbeline was persuaded to revolt by his 'wicked Queen'. This is satisfactory in that it brings the political element in relation to the fundamental motivation of the inner drama, but does it fit into the deeper pattern?

The patriotism is genuine, but it is subsumed, not negated, in a higher ideal of equal alliance with Rome which publicly repeats, extends and validates the personal pattern of reconciliation and peace. That pattern is repeated again in the religious references. Cymbeline is a pagan, but a devout one, and his intention of praising the gods and his reference to 'our bless'd altars' are easily assimilated to Shakespeare's ordinary Elizabethan Christianity, which is a cultural *donnée* for all his plays. Religion and country, in Shakespeare's time normally, and even nowa-days still for some, are closely identified, and are a normal extension of the family. A king may easily be thought of as 'the father of his people'; he was thought of in Shakespeare's day as God's vicegerent on earth; God himself is 'Our Father'. These generalities lie behind the images of re-birth and re-union worked out through the family drama, and com-plete them with a sense of universal peace, that extends from the inner psyche to the furthest stars.

VII

These examples of the family drama in Shakespeare by no means exhaust his treatment of the subject. Beside the other late Romances and the mature comedies there are other examples to explore. The subject is strongest in romance, which gives most play to inner drama and to the devising of patterns of action; in the history plays, in so far as they depict what appears often to be so desultory, inconsistent, arbitrary and wasteful in ordinary life, the family drama is at work, but more interruptedly, and we are less close to the type of folkloric and mythic narrative, nearer to superficial appearances. But in some of the history plays the family drama plays a part. *Coriolanus* has been already mentioned, and the two complementary father-figures of Prince Hal, Henry IV and Falstaff, will be easily recalled. The family drama hardly appears in the Roman plays, nor in *Othello* or *Macbeth*. The notion of the family drama is not a universal key, and Shakespeare's infinite variety takes up other human interests in many plays. It is this absence in some which re-inforces our sense of the truth of the appearance of the family drama in those plays where it can be seen.

CHAPTER VII
Mainly on Jane Austen

I

Both the novel and the romance are extended fictions about characters in action. The novel is distinguished by its greater emphasis on plausible appearances and on the action of material cause and effect. This emphasis develops in English in the eighteenth century, and the novel supersedes the prose romance.

Many eighteenth-century novelists continue to take as their main arena the personal relationships at play in the family drama, centred on the emerging adult and his or her efforts to break out of the family circle and establish a permanent relationship with a peer. The most extended and realistic treatment of this drama is that immense and remarkable book *Clarissa Harlowe*, where it is hardly latent at all. The family drama has also a large place in Fielding's *Tom Jones* and other novels. Scott treats the subject in *Waverley* and *Rob Roy*, where the protagonist is an admirable young man who is foolish in the way that young men so often are, and comes into conflict with his parents. In these novels the family drama, though basic to the plot, is only one element in the total effect. Scott does not appear closely to identify himself, as teller of the tale, with his hero. His largeness of mind, his luminous historical and social vision, his humour and great breadth of sympathy, all make him genuinely a novelist of the finest type. While it would be of the greatest interest to examine the play of tensions within the family drama in all these, and other, eighteenth-century and early-nineteenth-century novelists, a sharper illustration of the play of the pattern of fantasy within the naturalistic world of the novel is offered by Jane Austen, whose more restricted range also lends itself to exemplary treatment within a chapter. Even here, such is her richness that detailed illustration must be limited to her most characteristic, as it is her most extreme, novel, *Mansfield Park*.

II

Jane Austen is traditionally regarded as the novelist of realism, creating rounded believable autonomous characters who, impelled by plausible motives in a plausible way, initiate events that produce results which themselves cause further effects. She wrote only about those aspects of life she personally knew. Some distinguished contemporaries, unlike Scott (who publicly praised her work, so different from his), saw only her 'naturalism' – mere 'dishwashings' according to Carlyle, unconsciously foreseeing 'kitchen-sink drama'. Charlotte Bronte describes *Pride and Prejudice* as 'An accurate, daguerreotyped portrait of a commonplace face; a carefully fenced, high-cultivated garden, with neat borders and delicate flowers.' She says that Jane Austen is 'only shrewd and observant,' and concludes the letter in which she says all these things to one of Jane Austen's admirers by writing that 'Miss Austen being, as you say, without "sentiment", without *poetry*, maybe *is* sensible, real (more *real* than *true*) but she cannot be great.'[1]

In fact, Jane Austen as patently deploys the fantasies of the family drama as does Charlotte Bronte, whose isolated and oppressed heroines are always running away from home to be at home and either marrying father-figures rendered impotent (the blinded Rochester in *Jane Eyre*) or failing to marry them because, as in *Villette*, the ending cannot be faced. Charlotte Bronte's power obviously lies in the presentation of a family drama with a female protagonist. No less fascinating is the way Jane Austen welds her naturalistic surface by moral warmth to yet another version of the underlying pattern. The novels are driven by a powerful passion, powerfully controlled. Without in the slightest undervaluing the importance of the literal manifest level of the stories, or seeking any ironical reversal of their face-value meaning and values, we can recognise the tensions of the family drama at work. Though they are disguised they are not buried so deep that their latency requires deep search. Once one has accepted that the family drama is an inexhaustible subject with many facets its normal tensions can be seen without much difficulty, and the symbolic implications of the delightful literal level are seen to be a natural extension of the latent level.

At the heart of Jane Austen's supremely novelistic novels is an interesting variant of the traditional pattern (*true*, but not in her case *real*) concerning the irredeemable awfulness of mothers and the need to improve and capture a father-figure. This fantasy is constantly repeated in her novels. The protagonist begins by being a modified Cinderella. There is an occasional rather ambivalent Fairy godmother. But eventually Cinderella will be shown to be less of a Cinderella than she seems.

The traditional pattern is given a characteristic personal configuration by Jane Austen which was established in its general structure when she was very young and is found in her first attempt at fiction.[2] This work is mainly parody, but is the more revelatory of her mind. The story is *Catharine or the Bower*, from the manuscript called *Volume the Third*, written in 1792 when the author was sixteen, though copied out by herself in the present manuscript in later years, and begins thus:

> Catherine had the misfortune, as many heroines have had before her, of losing her Parents when she was very young, and of being brought up under the care

of a Maiden Aunt, who while she tenderly loved her, watched over her conduct with so scrutinizing a severity, as to make it very doubtful to many people, and to Catharine amongst the rest, whether she loved her or not. She had frequently been deprived of a real pleasure through this jealous Caution, had been sometimes obliged to relinquish a Ball because an Officer was to be there, or to dance with a Partner of her Aunt's introduction in preference to one of her own Choice. But her Spirits were naturally good, and not easily depressed, and she possessed such a fund of vivacity and good humour as could only be damped by some very serious vexation.– Besides these antidotes against every disappointment, and consolations under them, she had another, which afforded her constant relief in all her misfortunes, and that was a fine shady Bower, the work of her own infantine Labours assisted by those of two young Companions who had resided in the same village –. To this Bower, which terminated a very pleasant and retired walk in her Aunt's Garden, she always wandered whenever anything disturbed her, and it possessed such a charm over her senses, as constantly to tranquillize her mind & quiet her spirits – Solitude & reflection might perhaps have had the same effect in her Bed Chamber, yet Habit had so strengthened the idea which Fancy had first suggested, that such a thought never occurred to Kitty who was firmly persuaded that her Bower alone could restore her to herself. Her imagination was warm, and in her Friendships, as well as in the whole tenure of her Mind, she was enthousiastic. This beloved Bower had been the united work of herself and two amiable Girls, for whom since her earliest Years, she had felt the tenderest regard. They were the daughters of the Clergyman of the Parish with whose Family, while it had continued there, her Aunt had been on the most intimate terms, and the little Girls tho' separated for the greatest part of the Year by the different Modes of their Education, were constantly together during the holidays of the Miss Wynnes; [they were companions in their walks, their Schemes & Amusements, and while the sweetness of their dispositions had prevented any serious Quarrels, the trifling disputes which it was impossible wholly to avoid, had been far from lessening their affection].[3] In those days of happy Childhood, now so often regretted by Kitty this arbour had been formed, and separated perhaps for ever from these dear friends, it encouraged more than any other place the tender and Melancholly recollections of hours rendered pleasant by *them*, at one [sic] so sorrowful, yet so soothing! It was now two years since the death of Mr Wynne, and the consequent disperson of his Family who had been left by it in great distress. They had been reduced to a state of absolute dependance on some relations, who though very opulent, and very nearly connected with them, had with difficulty been prevailed on to contribute anything towards their Support. Mrs Wynne was fortunately spared the knowledge & participation of their distress, by her release from a painful illness a few months before the death of her husband.

(Ed. R. W. Chapman, Oxford, 1951)

There are five elements here that are fundamental to Jane Austen's works and the shape of her mind. First, the protagonist is a lonely girl. Second, the parents are dead. Third, there is an ambivalent mother-figure both fostering and oppressive, who attracts both love and hate. Fourth, home, as the place where one actually lives, is very important but also insecure – an insecurity produced by death and the ambivalent mother-figure. Fifth, there is a place of refuge, a place of inner resource, where the protagonist can indulge solitary thought; it is made by herself and her friends, is her responsibility, yet is also natural, 'given'. It is subjective, yet has independent existence. It is the equivalent of Cinderella's ashes; an alternative home, yet not home. It is what home should be, in the heart, yet is also a place of solitude. The first four elements are constants in Jane Austen's novels, with only superficial change. The fifth, image of the self-possessed, self-aware soul, finds its most striking physical equivalent in the chilly ex-schoolroom, the East room which is the heroine's refuge in *Mansfield Park*, but is also in the novels moralised into the protagonist's self-possession and self-knowledge which has profound though implicit religious inspiration and reliance. The story of *Catherine or the Bower* gives us more, although it is not finished. Prince Charming turns up, but it seems likely that in the story as planned he was to be revealed as a deceitful would-be seducer, so that Cinderella would reject him. That would be natural enough, perhaps, for a sixteen-year-old girl not yet anxious to leave home, but it is an element which is only partially qualified later.

Sense and Sensibility was begun in November 1797, five years after *The Bower*, worked on intermittently, and not published until 1811. By this latter date her father had indeed died, but as we see from *The Bower* the death of a father had already been established as a datum of story-telling during her father's life, and in later novels the death may be imaginatively transposed into incapacity for action – if a good man, then weak and ineffectual; the normal fairy-tale pattern.

After her father's death Jane and her mother and elder sister were in a position similar to that of the heroine Elinor, with her mother and sister, in *Sense and Sensibility*. In the novel, because of the father's death they lose the parental home (its fundamental insecurity thus evident). They stay with the inheriting son, whose wife makes what was once their home unpleasant to them. But here in the novel the autobiographical resemblance ends and the fairy-tale pattern has taken over. Jane's brother in real life was as kind as Elinor's is selfish and unkind. The novel, being *true* rather than *real*, needs to isolate the protagonist. Elinor is the typical early Jane Austen heroine, the only character in the story who is seen from the inside; resourceful, intelligent, loving and lonely.

> Elinor, this eldest daughter whose advice was so effectual, possessed a strength of understanding, and coolness of judgement, which qualified her, though only nineteen, to be the counsellor of her mother, and enabled her frequently to counteract, to the advantage of them all, that eagerness of mind in Mrs. Dashwood, which must generally have led to imprudence. She had an excellent heart; her disposition was affectionate, and her feelings were strong: but she knew how to govern them: it was a knowledge which her mother had yet to learn, and which one of her sisters had resolved never to be taught.
>
> (Chapter I)

This is indeed a princess! The failure to note in the slightest her physical appearance emphasises the inward point of view. Elinor's qualities are a fine summary of Jane Austen's conscious moral and civilised values, and the whole story is designed to recommend them. Elinor represents the sense of the title. Yet however enthusiastically one may support such values, if the story represented only this zeal for order, successful in the protagonist, it would be less than true to life. Much of the success of the novel derives from the presentation, in effect, of a 'split' protagonist. Elinor's sister Marianne, who is the one referred to as determined never to learn to control her feelings, represents sensibility. She is obviously not a marginal sibling-figure (represented at the latent level by the vulgar Miss Steeles, who are not related at the literal level but are rivals of the same generation). Elinor and Marianne, considered as a 'split' protagonist at the latent level, present when considered as a unity a fuller picture of life than is allowed for by the admirable but exclusive virtues of Elinor. We are *told* that Elinor has strong feelings, but we *see* Marianne's. Marianne gives us the strength of feelings that Elinor has to control, and a more living centre to the novel than could be given by the perfection of the nineteen-year-old Elinor.

There are four mother-figures in *Sense and Sensibility*, three of them silly, one full of ill-will. Elinor's mother is foolish and imprudent, and although she is not jealous of her daughter's suitors, her approval is so silly as almost to be worthless. Lady Middleton is marginal, the wife of the good-natured, honest, stupid neighbour, Sir John. But in so far as Lady Middleton appears she is represented as a foolishly indulgent mother to her very tiresome small children. Her mother, Mrs. Jennings, is almost equally silly, and with a touch of vulgarity, but she is so remote that she can be more indulged. She is genuinely loving and has a touch of the Fairy godmother, for it is she who brings Elinor and Marianne to London, where several crucial events are worked out, and helps look after Marianne in her illness. Even there, however, is a comic satiric touch, for Mrs. Jennings, good person as she is, is convinced that Marianne will die. The fourth mother-figure, more remote still, is the mother of the hero, if such he can be called, Edward Ferrar. She is capricious, mean and tyrannical, and though she is never actually presented on the scene her acts and intentions influence the action.

What is rather striking at first sight is the absence of father-figures. The most interesting men constitute varieties of Prince Charming, and there are three. The principal one is the young man designed for Elinor. He is a confessedly quiet inexpressive young man whom Jane Austen has gone out of her way to deprive of all interest and sparkle.

Edward Ferrars was not recommended to their good opinion by any peculiar graces of person or address. He was not handsome, and his manners required intimacy to make them pleasing. He was too diffident to do justice to himself; but when his natural shyness was overcome, his behaviour gave every indication of an open, affectionate heart. His understanding was good, and his education had given it solid improvement. . . . All his wishes centered in domestic comfort and the quiet of private life.

(Chapter III)

Beside Edward Ferrars there is Colonel Brandon, a sober, sensible, rich man of thirty-six, who eventually marries Marianne (aged seventeen). In so far as Ferrars and Brandon are 'splits' of the composite hero they represent a decidedly mature Prince Charming. The third, Willoughby, has all the dash and charm of which the other two are deprived, but though basically good-hearted he has been brought up badly and has acted the part of a selfish libertine, eventually losing Marianne and condemning himself to a loveless marriage. He is both condemned and forgiven by Elinor, who hears his long confession when he comes to what he has feared is Marianne's death-bed. That it is Elinor, not Marianne, who actually meets the repentant Willoughby well illustrates the fundamentally composite nature of the latent protagonist.

Though Willoughby is pitied and forgiven, he is repudiated, having removed himself by his self-seeking but unhappy marriage. Colonel Brandon is relatively old, has goodness, power and authority, but is a subsidiary hero. Edward Ferrars is deliberately presented in unemphatic terms, and even with a kind of weakness, since he gets entangled with the designing Lucy Steele. It is as if the Cinderella-figure did indeed marry a father-figure, but a weak, good father. Indeed, the protagonist is so strong, and Prince Charming so feeble, that it is almost as if he becomes not so much an equal as an inferior, a kind of son-figure. At the end of the story Cinderella makes only the smallest of removals to a place that is closely connected with home, and continues to dominate the story.

Pride and Prejudice had been begun in October 1796, even before *Sense and Sensibility*, but was revised and published two years later, in 1813. Here the portrait of the mother, Mrs. Bennet, though comic, is almost savage. In Jane Austen's world, it is true, the great vice of mothers is their extreme silliness, not any ill-will. Silliness is however a serious matter for Mr. Bennet, for it has deprived him of all companionship with his wife. The wonderful reception given by Mr. Bennet to the pompous Mr. Collins's proposal to marry Elizabeth is a masterpiece of comic yet severe comment on this aspect of the total family drama, to which the mother-figure is crucial, and which as usual in Jane Austen results in the emotional isolation of the protagonist.

Two marginal women reflect images of the mother. One is the snobbish Lady Catherine de Bourgh who tries to prevent Elizabeth from marrying Darcy, and by her attempt brings about the event she wished to avoid. She is a rather more important figure in both pattern and plot than may at first appear. She is also a rather rare example (for Jane Austen), at the latent level, of jealousy on the part of a mother-figure of the protagonist. Her hostility is partly countered by Mrs. Gardiner, a more remote mother-figure still, but having like Mrs. Jennings a touch of the Fairy godmother (and like her being connected with 'trade' rather than gentility) because it is she who takes Elizabeth for the tour of Derbyshire where they visit Darcy's fine house.

The protagonist is 'split' mainly into two 'heroines', the lively Elizabeth who is dominant, representing the prejudice of the title, and the very subsidiary sweet-tempered Jane, her elder sister. The friendship between the two mitigates the isolation of the heroine at the story-level, if not at the level of latency. Charlotte, Elizabeth's other friend, is another subsidiary 'split' of the heroine, being a girl in much the same position, who takes the alternative course open to Elizabeth of marrying the pompous Mr. Collins. The other sisters are more characteristic siblings of the same sex, treated with scorn, but on the other hand, though a disadvantage as social connections, too inferior in personality to carry much weight of malice. The function of jealous siblings is fulfilled by Bingley's two sisters, one of whom is also in hot pursuit of Mr. Darcy. They express contempt for Elizabeth, for example when she walks over in the rain to look after the ailing Jane and gets the bottom of her petticoats muddy. The pattern of the story is very close to traditional folk-narrative, since it is focussed on the principal heroine and events are seen through her eyes. Events that have taken place elsewhere, for example the pursuit of Lydia and Wickham to London, undertaken by Mr. Darcy and Mr. Gardiner, are told to her, and thus channelled through her to the reader.

The Prince Charming image is likewise 'split' into at least three, or maybe four. Mr. Darcy is necessarily the principal, and is older than the heroine. He too has to progress towards self-knowledge and overcome his pride, but except for the 'confession' he makes to Elizabeth when they become engaged, we see him entirely from outside, and even this self-revelation is mediated through the heroine. His younger friend Bingley, rather more sprightly but less well-read and judicious, who marries the gentle Jane, gives us another aspect of ideal masculinity. Wickham, like Willoughby in *Sense and Sensibility*, represents the charm, the aggression and the sexuality of which the more respectable 'splits' of Prince Charming are deprived. Whether Mr. Collins can be rightly included in the composite may be wondered, since he is so amusingly satirised at the literal level. At the latent level he perhaps represents a dark or threatening aspect of Prince Charming, though he is never a serious danger. It is however notable that the hostile Lady Catherine is his patroness, while as cousin to Mr. Bennet and inheritor of his estate he is in a perverse kind of filial relationship to him and so a brotherly relationship to Elizabeth. He and Lady Catherine thus correspond – at considerable remove! – to Cloten and his mother in *Cymbeline*. But the greed and aggression of Mr. Collins are financial and social, not sexual, and instead of being defeated are partially successful, though deflected from the heroine. 'Tis thus the world its veterans rewards!

As in the other novels, images of home are very important in *Pride and Prejudice*. The Bennet home suffers from characteristic insecurity since it is entailed on male heirs only, and at Mr. Bennet's death must go to Mr.

Collins. Cinderella fortunately finds even better homes in this novel, which are more secure.

Between beginning *Sense and Sensibility* and *Pride and Prejudice*, 1796–8, Jane Austen also began and never finished *The Watsons* and *Lady Susan*, which have only been published in modern times. *The Watsons* is about a poor girl, isolated in a vulgar family, who is clearly intended to reject the suspect Prince Charming and marry his dull friend. *Lady Susan* presents a severe portrait of an extremely predatory mother who is punished by marrying the odious Prince Charming she designed for her poor sad Cinderella of a daughter. This is a remarkable but characteristic revenge on both mother- and father-figures!

Mansfield Park continues the Cinderella theme, but changes it.[4] The novel was begun when *Sense and Sensibility* was published, and was itself published only three years later in 1814. The protagonist, Fanny Price, is now entirely on her own. As a very young child she is taken from her real parents, who live in relative poverty and disorder in Portsmouth, to live with her rich uncle and aunt – the essential family romance, but again in reverse.

Mansfield Park marks a development in widening the narrative point of view and the range of characters, but it is still based on the essentially fairy-tale fantasy of the family drama. Fanny is treated as inferior, is almost completely morally isolated, and is morally superior to everyone else. She is the focus of the story, everything is told with reference to her, and almost everything is seen through her eyes, or by an extension of her point of view. When the objectionable play is toward,

> Fanny looked on and listened, not unamused to observe the selfishness which, more or less disguised, seemed to govern them all, and wondering how it would end. For her own gratification she could have wished that something might be acted, for she had never seen even half a play, but everything of higher consequence was against it.

(Chapter XIV)

The amusement, the moral judgement, the interest in the actual event, exactly reflect the attitudes of the novelist. Despite a few detached gently satirical comments on her eighteen-year-old heroine, the novelist's partisanship comes through very clearly right at the end, in Chapter XLVIII: 'My Fanny indeed at this very time, I have the satisfaction of knowing, must have been very happy in spite of everything'. She is always as blameless as Perrault's Cinderilla.

It has long been observed that Fanny is a Cinderella-figure. She is in a painful situation, from some points of view, in Mansfield Park, where as niece to the owner, Sir Thomas Bertram, who is married to her mother's sister, she has been taken in from pity, to make it her adopted home. But within it, though she has to fetch and carry for, listen to and comfort her Aunt Bertram as no one else will, including Aunt Bertram's two daughters – Beautiful Sisters, which is perhaps worse than Ugly – Fanny is isolated. In the preparations for the play to be put on by the family party in Sir Thomas's absence, of which he would, and Fanny does, disapprove,

> Everybody around her was gay and busy, prosperous and important . . . She alone was sad and insignificant; she had no share in anything; she might go or stay; she might be in the midst of their noise, or retreat from it to the solitude of the East room, without being seen or missed.
>
> (Chapter XVII)

Her other aunt, Mrs. Norris – sister to Lady Bertram and an officious busybody who frequents the house – says to Fanny, who is the most reserved, shy and inconspicuous heroine in English literature,

> I do beseech and intreat you not to be putting yourself forward, and talking and giving your opinion as if you were one of your cousins – as if you were dear Mrs Rushworth or Julia. *That* will never do, believe me. Remember, wherever you are, you must be the lowest and last . . .
>
> (Chapter XXIII)

Classic expression of the Cinderella syndrome! But we should not be too sorry for her, for we are told a few sentences later that 'She rated her own claims to comfort as low as even Mrs Norris could', and a couple of pages later of 'her favourite indulgence of being suffered to sit silent and unattended'. This Cinderella is not sorry for herself.

Fanny has, with all her sufferings, a remarkable power of inner resource. Mrs. Norris notices it, though on an occasion on which she accuses Fanny quite unjustly and is even indirectly rebuked by Sir Thomas for doing so:

> – but there is a something about Fanny, I have often observed it before, – she likes to go her own way to work; she does not like to be dictated to; she takes her own independent walk whenever she can; she certainly has a little spirit of secrecy, and independence, and nonsense, about her, which I would advise her to get the better of.
>
> As a general reflection on Fanny, Sir Thomas thought nothing could be more unjust, though he had been so lately expressing the same sentiments himself . . .
>
> (Chapter XXXII)

Mrs. Norris is quite right, and Fanny has just demonstrated her independence to Sir Thomas himself by refusing to marry Henry Crawford, to Sir Thomas's annoyance, during their discussion in the chilly East room. The powerful symbol in the book, which corresponds exactly to Catharine's Bower, is the East room. The description of this room is so complete a realisation of Fanny's mind in solid objective terms, with so full a statement of association with friendship and the transmutation of affliction into charm, that it must be quoted in full.

The East room, as it had been called, ever since Maria Bertram was sixteen, was now considered Fanny's, almost as decidedly as the white attic; – the smallness of the one making the use of the other so evidently reasonable, that the Miss Bertrams, with every superiority in their own apartments, which their own sense of superiority could demand, were entirely approving it; – and Mrs Norris having stipulated for there never being a fire in it on Fanny's account, was tolerably resigned to her having the use of what nobody else wanted, though the terms in which she sometimes spoke of the indulgence, seemed to imply that it was the best room in the house.

The aspect was so favourable, that even without a fire it was habitable in many an early spring, and late autumn morning, to such a willing mind as Fanny's, and while there was a gleam of sunshine, she hoped not to be driven from it entirely, even when winter came. The comfort of it in her hours of leisure was extreme. She could go there after any thing unpleasant below, and find immediate consolation in some pursuit, or some train of thought at hand. – Her plants, her books – of which she had been a collector, from the first hour of her commanding a shilling – her writing-desk, and her works of charity and ingenuity, were all within her reach; – or if indisposed for employment, if nothing but musing would do, she could scarcely see an object in that room which had not an interesting remembrance connected with it. – Every thing was a friend, or bore her thoughts to a friend; and though there had been sometimes much of suffering to her – though her motives had been often misunderstood, her feelings disregarded, and her comprehension under-valued; though she had known the pains of tyranny, of ridicule, and neglect, yet almost every recurrence of either had led to something consolatory; her aunt Bertram had spoken for her, or Miss Lee had been encouraging, or what was yet more frequent or more dear – Edmund had been her champion and her friend; – he had supported her cause, or explained her meaning, he had told her not to cry, or had given her some proof of affection which made her tears delightful – and the whole was now so blended together, so harmonized by distance, that every former affliction had its charm. The room was most dear to her, and she would not have changed its furniture for the handsomest in the house, though what had been originally plain, had suffered all the ill-usage of children – and its greatest elegancies and ornaments were a faded footstool of Julia's work, too ill done for the drawing-room, three transparencies, made in a rage for transparencies, for the three lower panes of one window, where Tintern Abbey held its station between a cave in Italy, and a moonlight lake in Cumberland: a collection of family profiles thought unworthy of being any-where else, over the mantle-piece, and by their side and pinned against the wall, a small sketch of a ship sent four years ago from the Mediterranean by William, with H.M.S. Antwerp at the bottom, in letters as tall as the mainmast.

(Chapter XVI)

To this 'nest of comforts' more spiritual and mental than material Fanny resorts for inner strength and consolation. It is represented in no sense as an allegory. It is itself and nothing else, and *because* it is so it is a powerful symbol of Fanny's moral and intellectual nature. Despite the deep and undisguised religious inspiration of *Mansfiled Park* there is no attempt whatever to represent spiritual and moral values of the highest kind through any ecclesiastical or religious imagery or language. The East room is never invested with any religious significance, nor is Fanny ever represented in prayer, though all the family go to church and hear sermons. The only explicit reference to churchy matters is the sarcastic one when Lady Bertram has heard an affecting sermon and has cried herself to sleep in the sitting-room (Chapter XLVII).

The East room is the inner core of the home for Fanny and in it Fanny is normally solitary. Although in some ways it corresponds to Cinderella's ashes, it is also in profound contrast because Spartan as it is (even after Sir Thomas, towards the end of the novel, belatedly discovers how cold it is and orders a fire), it is a comfortable place, like the Bower. There is no desire to leave it and it is not ambivalent.

Home is a larger, more complex entity and decidedly ambivalent. It is here that a perception of latent drives reveals more of the complex pattern of the novel, and even of the protagonist. There are two images of the home quite specifically on the literal level. One of them is Mansfield Park, the modern, airy, well-situated mansion of Fanny's uncle the rich Sir Thomas, with its shrubberies, lawns, and plantations (Chapter XLVI), all of which are so beloved by Fanny, inside and out, and are themselves a source of strength as well as pleasure. The other is the house of Fanny's real father and mother, the 'small house' in a 'narrow street' with a 'trollopy-looking maidservant' (Chapter XXXVIII). It is a home

– Fanny could not conceal it from herself – in almost every respect, the very reverse of what she could have wished. It was the abode of noise, disorder, and impropriety. Nobody was in their right place, nothing was done as it ought to be. She could not respect her parents as she had hoped.

(Chapter XXXIX)

When her suitor, the rich, charming, unreliable Henry Crawford calls on her there,

to her many other sources of uneasiness was added the severe one of shame for the home in which he found her. She might scold herself for the weakness, but there was no scolding it away. She was ashamed, and she would have been yet more ashamed of her father, than of all the rest.

(Chapter XLI)

This is her 'real' home, at the idea of returning to which, 'Had Fanny been at all addicted to raptures, she must have had a strong attack of them' (Chapter XXXVII). The 'evils of home' (Chapter XL), its 'daily evils' (Chapter XLVI), are what she becomes painfully aware of, and evil is a strong word. Fanny is not at all fitted for home, any more than her younger sister Susan (Chapter XLIII).

The juxtaposition of these two images of home in the novel is an explicit symbolic division of the ambivalence of home in all the novels. It relates to the underlying ambivalence of home in all fairy tale, and clarifies the tension admirably. Home is at once a place where as you grow up you become progressively more uncomfortable, the primary home; and the place you most want, the achieved home. The solution in most fairy tales, for both male and female protagonists, is the same. Home is transformed. The male protagonist leaves home and sets up with the Princess, usually in her palace. Such is the case with Sir Gareth and Sire Degarre. For Gawain, Arthur's court, not where he was brought up, becomes his home. The female protagonist marries to go and live with her Prince, as Cinderella does. It is the same only different with Jane Austen, and we begin to detect further variants from the Cinderella theme.

Home is indeed transferred.

> When she had been coming to Portsmouth, she had loved to call it her home, had been fond of saying that she was going home; the word had been very dear to her; and so it still was, but it must be applied to Mansfield. *That* was now the home. Portsmouth was Portsmouth; Mansfield was home. They had been long so arranged in the indulgence of her secret meditations; and nothing was more consolatory to her than to find her aunt using the same language . . .

> (Chapter XLV)

Fanny's real parents do not care a bit where she lives, while as for her, we are told a few paragraphs later, 'Could she have been at home, she might have been of service to every creature in the house. She felt that she must have been of use to all'. Her full establishment at Mansfield, after Portsmouth, is the crucial transition in the book, the pivotal growing up, the main passage. Fanny's eventual marriage and setting up of house is dealt with in a few sentences, and when she is finally in the Parsonage the concluding sentence of the whole book can give her marital home no higher praise than that it was 'as thoroughly perfect in her eyes, as everything else, within the view and patronage of Mansfield Park, had long been'.

This transformation is effected, both literally and latently, by Fanny herself, in 'her own secret meditation', by the activity of her own mind and judgement, and not by the activity of any other person, except, indirectly, Sir Thomas. It was he who had originally brought her to Mansfield Park. It was he who, after her refusal of Henry Crawford, had sent her back for a while to Portsmouth, not merely to enjoy the company of her brother and family, but wishing her 'to be heartily sick of home before her visit ended' (Chapter XXXVII), so that she would see the value of the domestic permanence and comfort that she had been offered and had declined. In this respect, since he is also in a sense trying to drive her out of Mansfield Park, or at least wishing her to feel its insecurity because she can never be its mistress, his action emphasises the general insecurity of home, wherever it is, to any but the most tenacious heroine. He learns the error of his ways. Fanny is always right.

But to what extent can Fanny be regarded as the totality of the protagonist-figure? There are a number of figures of comparable age who, if we accept the principle that at one latent level there are only three characters in the family drama – protagonist, mother, father – must be symbolically associated with Fanny. Her younger sister Susan is obviously so associated, and explicitly becomes her substitute. Susan, William and Fanny herself, we learn on the novel's last page, give Sir Thomas every reason to rejoice, as they demonstrate in later life 'the advantages of early hardship and discipline, and the consciousness of being born to struggle and endure' – the obvious yet profound truth which the Cinderella fable above all imparts.

Sir Thomas's own daughters, Maria and Julia, demonstrate the opposite. Beautiful as they are, they easily fall into the pattern of the Ugly Sisters, spoilt and indulged especially by Aunt Norris. Sir Thomas's severe attitude to them has on the literal level only made them worse by contrast with the spoiling of Aunt Norris and the mindless good-nature of their mother. With Maria's adultery and Julia's elopement they deeply disappoint the family and are barely forgiven. Their fates illustrate the moral toughness of the novel and the harshness of the protagonist towards herself.

The most interesting characters in relation to the protagonist are the rich brother and sister Henry and Mary Crawford whose attitudes and behaviour move the plot. They repeat the family-pattern of Fanny and William with only minor variation. Their mother is long dead, their father not mentioned or accounted for. In other words, as with Fanny, the real parents are rejected. As with Fanny they have been brought up by a rich uncle and aunt. So at a symbolic level they offer another hypothesis for the protagonist, and re-inforce the protagonist-pattern by giving a mirror-image. The Crawfords' uncle and aunt, far from being moral and severe, have been immoral and indulgent. The Crawfords in especial lack respect for their parent-figures – Miss Crawford for example gives pain to Edmund by speaking 'freely' of her uncle (Chapter VI). The crucial difference between the Crawfords and the main protagonist of any Jane Austen novel, and especially Fanny, is that the Crawfords pay no respect to parent-figures, whom the protagonist, often deeply against the grain, always honours. This is also their paradoxical similarity with Fanny who, as already quoted, cannot respect her real parents, though she nevertheless behaves dutifully towards them.

Of the two Crawfords it is naturally only Mary who is as it were the shadow-image, the obverse, of Fanny. Henry is part of the Prince Charming figure, who will be discussed in a moment. Mary, along with the Bertram sisters, is also one of the same-sex siblings, and the most obvious rival, being everything that Fanny is not, beautiful, lively, amusing, energetic, ambitious, cold-hearted, etc. This rivalry-with-similarity is underlined by their both being in love with the same man, Edmund. Mary fails because she is not enough in love, but it is also worth noticing that she has left home. This is not her own fault, in that her uncle-father, the Admiral, as soon as his wife is dead, brings his mistress into his home and gets rid of his niece, who is consequently seeking a settled abode. Her restless brother will not accommodate her on his own estate and remain with her. She seeks a husband. But this misfortune attracts no pity for her from the novelist. She is only seen from outside as an image of corrupted nature, and she represents all that the novel rejects in character and action as superficial, worldly and immoral. She nevertheless avoids the fate worse than death which is reserved for the adulterous Maria, who is left to pass the remainder of her life with Aunt Norris.

The underlying pattern of the novel focusses on the protagonist's attitudes to parent-figures. As is natural in a fairy tale with a female protagonist the mother-figures are all in various degrees detestable and the father-figures more complex. The father-figures are the pivot of the action. As in the strictly defined 'family romance' the heroine's real parents and especially the father are ordinary and deplorable, but there are fantasy-parents available, Sir Thomas and Lady Bertram, of whom the father in particular is admirable and interesting, though as befits a novel, somewhat complex. The father-figure dominates the novel's pattern. Of the real father in the novel little need be said. Like all fathers of adolescent children he is an embarrassment whose only virtue lies in his absence when friends, especially of the opposite sex, call at home. He is coarse, indifferent and unintellectual, swears and drinks, and scarcely ever notices Fanny 'but to make her the object of a coarse joke', presumably about marriage (Chapter XXXIX). Even Jane Austen however attributes to him deficiencies only in manners, severe as they are.

Sir Thomas is more than such a witty, one-sided caricature; he is portrayed in himself ambivalently. An anxious and loving father, he is deeply reserved and represses all the flow of his daughters' spirits before him. He terrifies Fanny, when as a forlorn and uneducated little girl she first comes to the alarming grandeurs and polished manners of Mansfield Park (Chapter II). In the end, the awe with which he strikes her becomes her principle of action. 'She had a rule to apply to, which settled everything. Her awe of her uncle, and her dread of taking a liberty with him, made it instantly plain to her, what she had to do' (Chapter XLV) (the fear of the Lord is the beginning of wisdom!).

Sir Thomas's presence or absence is the mainspring of the plot. His absence in the West Indies allows the play to be rehearsed which brings in the Crawfords, initiates Edmund's infatuation with Mary and Henry's more hesitant love for Fanny, and establishes more firmly than ever Fanny's righteous isolation. She takes up his view of drama as a corruption, and in his absence is its sole exponent. In other words, Fanny is progressively identified with Sir Thomas. But though crucial to the action he is not in the latent sense the activator. That remains the sphere of the apparently passive protagonist. There is considerable reference to education in *Mansfield Park*, mostly about the value of suffering and deprivation when young, and very sensible it is, but the latent progress in education is that of Sir Thomas, who is thus more interesting than Edmund, whom in a sense he subsumes. Sir Thomas is a stiff reserved man, though conversational in his own way, and Fanny is the only one of the young persons who appreciates his talk. He loves his children and is more agitated than his wife when their daughter Maria marries Mr. Rushworth. He is even the only one really to express, or rather to have attributed to him by Edmund, a proper appreciation of Fanny's physical beauty, including her figure (all these comments arising in Chapter XXI). But he is not jealous or possessive and here is an important difference in both Sir Thomas and Fanny's real father, Mr. Price, from fairy-tale fathers. They unequivocally want to get her married off, and the protagonist does not want to be, except to someone almost as fatherly as the father-image. Sir Thomas has to learn this and to endure the reverse kind of opposition of that normally offered in fairy tales to kind fathers. He expresses a 'cold sternness' towards Fanny when she refuses Henry Crawford so positively and she resists him (Chapter XXXII) in the wonderful scene in the East room which is as comic in its way as Elizabeth Bennet's celebrated interview in *Pride and Prejudice* with her father in his study when she too refuses a proposal, though to different effect. It is after this that Sir Thomas sends Fanny to Portsmouth. But events at the literal level, and the protagonist's tenacity at both literal and latent level, show him the error of his ways. He comes to understand Fanny clearly and learns to regret how badly he has brought up his own daughters. He becomes conscious of his own errors as a parent. His anguish in this respect is never 'entirely done away' but he becomes in part reconciled to himself through the recovery and reformation of his eldest son, the marriage of Edmund to Fanny, and Fanny's own ministrations. She is the daughter he wanted, and though he might have made her childhood happier, and is implicitly reproached for this, we know that suffering has been very good for her character. Suffering is never in any way desirable, however, and the symbol of achieved happiness is the sloughing off of Mrs. Norris, of whom it is said, in some remarkable sentences:

> He had felt her as an hourly evil, which was so much the worse, as there seemed no chance of its ceasing but with life; she seemed a part of himself that must be borne for ever. To be relieved from her, therefore, was so great a felicity, that had she not left bitter remembrances behind her, there might have been danger of his learning almost to approve the evil which produced such a good.
>
> (Chapter XLVIII)

That evil may produce good – a version of the *felix culpa* – is a traditional comment several times made in *Mansfield Park*, but what is striking is the metaphorical identification of Mrs. Norris as a part of himself. No doubt I am pressing this further than the literal conscious intention of the artist, but that is always justifiable if the text and the pattern of the work will stand it, and there can be no objection in this novel to asserting the close link between father-figures and mother-figures, of whom Mrs. Norris is clearly one.

The mother-image is multiple, comprised of the three Ward sisters, the eldest, Miss Ward (whose Christian name we never learn), becoming Mrs. Norris, another, Maria, becoming Lady Bertram, and Frances becoming Mrs. Price. They are all in some sort of maternal relationship with Fanny, and present a beautifully satirical analysis, entirely in the spirit of the fairy tale, of the ways mothers can be resented by daughters in the world of imagination. Mrs. Price, Fanny's real mother, though vaguely affectionate, cares little for Fanny while doting on her sons, especially William. Lady Bertram, though good humoured, is entirely selfish, idle and silly. Mrs. Norris is the mean hypocritical selfish tyrant, one of nature's stepmothers if ever there was one. All three are very bad managers and hardly a good word is said for Lady Bertram and Mrs. Price, while Mrs. Norris is presented with a gloriously comic savagery that is utterly remorseless. The novelist's loathing of her is equalled only by Fanny's long-suffering patience. There are some deplorable characters in literature who are presented with such zest that one cannot but like them – the Wife of Bath and Falstaff are the obvious examples. There is as much zest in the presentation of Mrs. Norris, but no one could in the very slightest like her. She is the kind of character who in a fairy tale might well be finished off by making her dance in red-hot iron shoes. If she could poison Fanny she would – no secret is made of her real malice towards her. Thus when she hears that Fanny has refused Henry Crawford:

> Angry she was, bitterly angry; but she was more angry with Fanny for having received such an offer, than for refusing it. It was an injury and an affront to Julia, who ought to have been Mr. Crawford's choice; and, independently of that, she disliked Fanny, because she had neglected her; and she would have grudged such an elevation to one whom she had been always trying to depress.

> (Chapter XXXIII)

No doubt here of the Stepmother-Ugly Sister syndrome nor of the story's sympathy with the protagonist. It might almost be said to be the protagonist speaking at the latent level – not the timid Fanny at the literal level. But timid as Fanny may seem, she is much more powerful than she appears to be in the plausible world.

Odious, idle, incompetent, trivially worldly as the composite mother-image is, with absolutely no compensating 'splits', no Fairy godmothers anywhere (only a Fairy godfather), no one at all, let alone the protagonist, speaks a harsh word to any of them. This is of the essence of the moral quality of the verbal realisation. 'Honour your father and mother' even though they are very inferior people. Duty, principle, suffering are all involved here, with the reward that your days will be long in the land (Mansfield Park) which the Lord God giveth thee. This is far from a utilitarian bargain. It is genuinely selfless and sacrificial, but the tale provides also a genuine reward.

In the fairy tale Cinderella is rescued by Prince Charming. As already suggested, this latent pattern does not work in *Mansfield Park* in the usual way. Fanny marries Edmund, it is true, and removes a short distance to Thornton Lacey, where she sees Sir Thomas every day. Then Dr. Grant by

attending three great institutionary dinners in a week fortunately brings
on apoplexy and death, so that Edmund and Fanny live a short walk from
Mansfield Park in the Parsonage. The psychological detachment from
Mansfield Park is nil: it is already the castle, the court, which Fanny has
mentally made her own and from which she need never remove.
Edmund is not merely the son of the house, though second son; 'Loving,
guiding, protecting her, as he had been doing ever since her being ten
years old, her mind in so great a degree formed by his care, and her
comfort depending on his kindness, an object to him of such close and
peculiar interest . . .' (Chapter XLVIII) – how should he not come to
want her for his wife? The simple answer is that all experience and all
tradition are against it. There is good evidence for the virtuous warmth of
brother-and-sister love in the nineteenth century, as with William and
Dorothy Wordsworth and Jane Austen and her own brothers, the
clergyman James (model in part for Edmund Bertram) and the sailors
Francis and Charles in real life, and attachments in novels like Trollope's
Can You Forgive Her. This is quite a different matter from marriage.
Exogamy is the rule in European story and life alike. But the pattern is
different in Jane Austen's novels.

Whereas in fairy tale and life the natural rule is for the protagonist to
break out of the family circle, for Jane Austen there is no such need or
desire. From this point of view it is not important whether Edmund, the
dullest Prince Charming, is father- or brother-figure. The self-sufficiency
of the family circle is several times insisted upon, even by the young
people when putting on their play (Chapter XVII).

This accounts for the totally unacceptable charm of the other Prince
Charming figure, Henry Crawford. He is all that Prince Charming
naturally would be. He is rich, and if not handsome, not replusive, for his
manners are indeed charming. He is witty, intelligent, well-read, accomplished. But he comes from the wicked outside world, is disrespectful
of parent-figures, and above all is restless. He will not stay at home, and
home is the only acceptable place, the whole of the pattern, for Jane
Austen. There is no place for Henry Crawford. He is brought in and sent
away in the novel in accordance with the narrative needs, literal or latent.
This incidentally is one of the great advantages to Jane Austen of setting
her characters within an environment that allows them complete freedom. No one has a job or regular obligations except the clergy, and they
are either idle or inconspicuous. There is no need to interweave the
emotional pattern within obligations that would make frequent meeting,
or its opposite, unavoidable. It is true that Sir Thomas is forced to go away
to attend to his interests in the West Indies but such an exception proves
the rule. Henry Crawford in particular is brought in, or sent away,
according as the protagonist needs to be tested, and he is only an extreme
example of the absence of ordinary pressures of an 'historical' everyday
kind upon the characters. The field is clear for social, moral and emotional
forces. It is accordingly useless to question the plausibility of presentation
of Henry Crawford's motives, or of the nature of his character, apparently

a practised *roué* yet so deeply attracted by Fanny. The pattern requires that he be attracted and rejected. The ideal man is quiet and domestic, as there is hope of making even Julia's husband Mr. Yates in the end, though this is different again from being indolent and stay-at-home (and greedy) like Dr. Grant (Chapter V).

In *Mansfield Park* Jane Austen accepts and rejects the traditional fairy-tale pattern, developing a powerful somewhat idiosyncratic pattern of her own. It underlies a most brilliant verbal realisation and a subtle and complex web of strong traditional moral values, among which, after chastity and marital faithfulness, can hardly be over-rated those of suffering (especially when young – it was good for Cinderella to be Cinderella!) and self-knowledge. These are connected with the theme of education, and Edmund sums them both up to the unreceptive Mary Crawford and the infinitely understanding Fanny when he refers to 'the most valuable knowledge we could any of us acquire – the knowledge of ourselves and of our duty to the lessons of affliction' (Chapter XLVII). Fanny, Edmund, Sir Thomas, and even the reformed rake, Edmund's elder brother, in his minor significance, all acquire this knowledge; none of the others does; and it sets them apart.

It is tempting to see the underlying pattern as especially the projection of an unmarried woman (certainly in the confident advice on how to bring up children!), who responds with such warmth to the demands, the pains, the rewards and joys of the original family circle that most unusually she feels no need to go beyond it. *Mansfield Park* may never be the most favoured of Jane Austen's novels generally, but to the addict it is the most complete expression within a single volume of her remarkable, independent, religious, solitary, yet family-loving genius.

It is as if Jane Austen worked something of the Cinderella theme out of herself with *Mansfield Park*. It is much less strong in her next novel, *Emma*, begun in January 1814 and published December 1815 (dated 1816). The Cinderella theme is much more subsidiary, mainly realised in a subsidiary heroine, Jane Fairfax, and is even ironically inverted with poor Harriet, for whom Emma is satirised for trying to make grander than she really is. Emma is isolated, and her father is a good silly ineffectual old man. There are other inadequate parents and plenty of family stress. But Emma herself is more criticised and the novel makes a major theme of her own awakening to that most valuable knowledge, the knowledge of herself and of her duty to the lessons of affliction. It is notable that unlike Fanny Price, Emma has to forgive herself. The fatherly superiority of Prince Charming as Mr. Knightley is much emphasised. We now approach a more amiable mother-figure in the person of Mrs. Weston, Emma's former governess and present friend.

Northanger Abbey (1817) forbids any simple chronological treatment of Jane Austen's development of, or from, the family drama, because though published so late it was begun very early, and the theme is only faint. I conclude with a brief note on *Persuasion*, published like *Northanger Abbey* just after Jane Austen's death, in 1817. The family drama is here strong. The heroine, Anne, is again something of a Cinderella, neglected by her foolish father and unkind sister. Her real mother is dead. There is a mother-figure, Lady Russell, who gives Anne typically bad advice, though this advice is against marrying for love when young. But Anne genuinely loves Lady Russell, who genuinely acts for the best. We may say here that in this novel the protagonist learns to forgive the mother, and allows that she may, though always acting wrongly, be trying to act for the best. The hardest thing for children is to forgive their parents. Jane Austen always writes from the point of view of the young person emerging into maturity, as is the case with most fairy tales. It is part of her enduring fascination. But here the protagonist grows up into actual maturity. Anne Elliott is twenty-seven. As usual, the protagonist marries an authoritative father-substitute; less usually, she forgives her erring mother.

III

After so extended a consideration of Jane Austen it is natural to think of other great nineteenth-century novelists, but there is space here for only the briefest notes. Charlotte Bronte offers the most obvious comparable instance. *Jane Eyre* tells the story of the emergence of a female protagonist, expelled from a series of 'homes', confronted by a series of hostile parent- and especially mother-images. The most striking part of the story from this point of view is the heroine's relationship with the Byronic Rochester. When first introduced he is much older, Jane's employer, and married to a mysterious, unseen but evidently controlling and apparently baleful wife. Rochester attempts to seduce Jane. He is obviously a quite archaic father-figure. Who can the father-figure's wife be but a mother-figure? Since the protagonist seems set on marrying Rochester, it will be necessary at the latent level to destroy the defining mother-figure and convert the vertical father-relationship, or at any rate to neutralise the paternity. The mother-figure is destroyed by fire in her own home (this is justified at the literal level and perhaps the latent too by making her mad). The artistic and perhaps psychological disadvantage of this device is that it is not achieved at any cost to the protagonist herself, is not earned by suffering, unless we take into account her long suffering endured from other mother-figures, but even then it still seems somewhat too external. Mr. Rochester loses his sight trying to save his wife. Thus both parent-figures are punished for the suffering of the protagonist as a child repeatedly driven out of home. The father-figure is saved on condition that he be subjugated to the protagonist. In other words, Rochester's blindness makes him as dependent as a helpless child on his much younger female conqueror. More than this: blindness has long been recognised as in its symbolic aspects a punishment or neutralisation of male sexuality. Oedipus and Samson are both blinded because of their relationship with a woman. A man's glance can be taken as a phallic symbol, an expression of masculine sexual aggressiveness, which modest women recognise when they modestly turn down their eyes, and others boldly meet. More simply, the glance of an eye is simply masculine aggressiveness, as town roughs recognise when they make it an excuse for assault. The question in *Jane Eyre* is whether the father-figure is merely safely neutralised so that the protagonist can marry him. To put it another way, has the father-image been sufficiently disentangled from the character of Mr. Rochester to allow him to be presented as a peer? Has the vertical relationship been really changed to a lateral one? Since Rochester sufficiently regains his sight for Jane to have a baby we may perhaps conclude that the switch has been made, but the real imaginative power in the representation of Mr. Rochester lies in his earlier rather than in his final appearance.

In *Villette* the similar father-figure, the fiery M. Paul, is never thus ruthlessly broken down, which is why at the end of the novel, we are left a little in doubt whether he will return from his dangerous voyage; or rather, it is not made absolutely explicit that he is drowned. According to the latent imaginative pattern he must die.

Lucy Snow, symbolical name – brightness and cold, internal flame, external ice – is never able to melt her outward reserve. There is much painful but satisfying truth in the final frustration of the brave and lonely heroine, whose cool lucidity is admirably realised and self-aware. The protagonist, having failed to create the image of a lover from the testy father-image presented in M. Paul, recognises that the marriage cannot take place, and yet that fathers must die. In that the protagonist fails to find her peer this is tragic. Nevertheless success is the dominant note, for the protagonist survives into self-aware maturity. By sheer moral and artistic strength, derived from the passionate Christian conviction that underlies the story, the protagonist, like Sir Gawain, emerges into fully conscious identity, a fully independent, if lonely, grown-up, after the testing time of solitude, fear and suffering endured as she passes from youth to adulthood. By contrast with this ending there is a touch of weakening wish-fulfilment, of not quite adhering to the basic pattern and its inevitable implications, in *Jane Eyre*.

It is clear that the theme could be much further explored in these and other nineteenth-century novels. For the present book one novel of Dickens must stand as exemplar for the rest.

CHAPTER VIII

Great Expectations

The narrator-protagonist of *Great Expectations*, who is called Pip, when well into his apprenticeship as a blacksmith to his brother-in-law Joe Gargery, having some years back been brought to play at the eccentric Miss Havisham's house, calls there again hoping to see Estella, the beautiful remote girl with whom he is in love. Estella has been sent abroad to be educated as a lady and Pip wanders disconsolately down the High Street. There he is pounced upon by the absurd parish clerk, Mr. Wopsle, who insists on reading to him and Mr. Pumblechook the tragedy of George Barnwell, a once famous eighteenth-century melodrama.

> As I never assisted at any other representation of George Barnwell, I don't know how long it may usually take; but I know very well that it took until half-past nine o'clock that night, and that when Mr. Wopsle got into Newgate, I thought he never would go to the scaffold, he became so much slower than at any former period of his disgraceful career. I thought it a little too much that he should complain of being cut short in his flower after all, as if he had not been running to seed, leaf after leaf, ever since his course began. This, however, was a mere question of length and wearisomeness. What stung me, was the identification of the whole affair with my unoffending self. When Barnwell began to go wrong, I declare that I felt positively apologetic, Pumblechook's indignant stare so taxed me with it. Wopsle, too, took pains to present me in the worst light. At once ferocious and maudlin, I was made to murder my uncle with no extenuating circumstances whatever; Millwood put me down in argument, on every occasion; it became sheer monomania in my master's daughter to care a button for me; and all I can say for my gasping and procrastinating conduct on the fatal morning, is, that it was worthy of the general feebleness of my character. Even after I was happily hanged, and Wopsle had closed the book, Pumblechook sat staring at me, and shaking his head, and saying, 'Take warning, boy, take warning!' as if it were a well-known fact that I contemplated murdering a near relation, provided I could only induce one to have the weakness to become my benefactor.

> (Chapter XV)

After this affecting performance Pip and Mr. Wopsle begin to walk home to where Pip lives with Joe and his shrewish wife, who is Pip's sister and more than twenty years older than him. They meet Dolge Orlick, Joe's journeyman, no friend to Pip and a sullen loutish character. The guns are sounding off over the marshes from the prison-hulks on the river, to notify the escape of a prisoner. Then it is discovered that a savage attack has been made on Joe's wife. She has been given a tremendous blow on the back of her head. The next chapter begins immediately:

> With my head full of George Barnwell, I was at first disposed to believe that *I* must have had some hand in the attack upon my sister, or at all events that as her near relation, popularly known to be under obligations to her, I was a more legitimate object of suspicion than any one else. But when, in the clearer light of next morning, I began to reconsider the matter and to hear it discussed around me on all sides, I took another view of the case, which was more reasonable.
>
> (Chapter XVI)

Mrs. Gargery has been hit by a prisoner's leg-iron discarded by the convict Pip had helped some years before, and had always felt guilty about, but Pip believes that Orlick or possibly another strange man must have struck the blow. There is no evidence against Orlick. He and Joe's wife had recently quarrelled but 'my sister had quarrelled with him, and with everybody else about her, ten thousand times'.

> It was horrible to think that I had provided the weapon, however undesignedly, but I could hardly think otherwise. I suffered unspeakable trouble while I considered and reconsidered whether I should at last dissolve that spell of my childhood, and tell Joe all the story. For months afterwards, I every day settled the question finally in the negative, and reopened and reargued it next morning.
>
> (Chapter XVI)

Pip does not tell Joe at this stage about how he had helped the convict, stealing food for him from the larder. Mrs. Joe becomes an almost helpless, speechless invalid, but her temper is greatly improved, and she shows herself particularly anxious to conciliate and be on good terms with Orlick.

The tragedy of George Barnwell is centred on the family drama. An uncle is a displaced father-figure: the hero fails to win the girl outside the family circle and is himself killed by the paternal forces of law and order. The reading is comic in itself but is one of the many variants of the family drama, which though obviously at the heart of so many of Dickens's novels is particularly elaborately worked out in *Great Expectations*. The episode of Mr. Wopsle's reading is also a singularly vivid demonstration of how the hearer or reader of a piece of imaginative literature associates himself with the protagonist, becomes himself the protagonist, sharing his anxieties and joys. So, as we read, we become Pip, just as we centre ourselves on Cinderella, or Jack, or Fanny Price. Unless we place ourselves there, at the centre of the web of relationships, we cannot understand the pattern. Thus it is that we 'are' George Barnwell, not his uncle, we 'are' Hamlet, or Lear, or Gawain, or Gareth. If we identify ourselves with a character other than the protagonist we confuse the perspective.

In *Great Expectations* the dominant emotions felt by the protagonist are guilt and shame.[1] Pip's response to George Barnwell emphasises guilt. Then we meet Orlick, and find the effectively destroyed Mrs. Gargery. Pip himself feels illogically guilty, he feels he must somehow have done it, that it was horrible to have provided the weapon, though undesignedly, and that it is all connected with the earliest episode of all in Chapter I, when Pip helped the convict and thus experienced torments of guilt from when he was six years old (as is made clear at the end of Chapter L). Towards the end of the novel Dickens shows why this should be so. Pip is trying to get his 'uncle Provis', that is, the illegally returned convict Magwitch, whom he had helped and who has become his secret benefactor, out of the country. In response to a mysterious letter connected with this he goes alone to the sluice-house in the marshes on a dark night, telling no one. There he is trapped and bound by Orlick, who proposes to kill him, but who first jeers at him and works out his malice. Orlick wants his revenge on Pip for preventing him, as he claims, from marrying Biddy, or getting a job: but he is fundamentally jealous of Pip and always has been since working for Joe Gargery. He calls himself Old Orlick, though he can be little more than ten years older than Pip. Orlick has been drinking.

> 'Old Orlick's a-going to tell you somethink. It was you as did for your shrew sister.'
>
> Again my mind, with its former inconceivable rapidity, had exhausted the whole subject of the attack upon my sister, her illness, and her death, before his slow and hesitating speech had formed those words.
>
> 'It was you, villain,' said I.
>
> 'I tell you it was your doing – I tell you it was done through you,' he retorted, catching up the gun, and making a blow with the stock at the vacant air between us. 'I come upon her from behind, as I come upon you to-night. *I* giv' it her! I left her for dead, and if there had been a lime-kiln as nigh her as there is now nigh you, she shouldn't have come to life again. But it warn't Old Orlick as did it; it was you. You was favoured, and he was bullied and beat. Old Orlick bullied and beat, eh? Now you pays for it. You done it; now you pays for it.'

> (Chapter LIII)

Melodramatic as this scene is, it derives its justifications partly from superb narrative skill and poetic images of dark and light, of mist from the lime-kiln, and partly from the underlying pattern whereby Dickens here clearly presents Orlick as in the latent sense a 'split' of the protagonist. He is that dark part of the protagonist which wishes to kill the hateful Mrs. Gargery, who brings Pip up cruelly 'by hand', his sister but twenty years older, and clearly a mother-figure. The whole novel is based on a potently multiple protagonist and a whole series of mother- and father-images. Its great power lies not only in the remarkable verbal realisation, Dickens's genius at its highest and least flawed, but in the strange and dark fantasies about parents and associates of the protagonist which are its heart, as Dickens makes all but explicit, as with Pip's guilt when Mrs. Joe is attacked. Like *Mansfield Park*, *Great Expectations* is at both latent and manifest levels about growing up, wrestling with parent-images; and about what is a 'good education', what are the moral standards we must acquire. From this point of view both novels are elaborated and moralised fairy tales. In each case the mother-images are dangerous or at least unpleasant, while the protagonist has to learn to identify with, after rejecting, the father-images. In each case the protagonist's *real* escape from the family circle is dubious.

Pip's friends or associates of his own age may be looked at as extensions of the protagonist, but first something must be said of Pip himself, though the richness of Dickens's representation escapes bare summarising. Quite explicitly Dickens shows through Pip many of the characteristic emotional problems of growing up. Pip's guilt has already been mentioned. The occasion of it has already been mentioned, but it is complex. In itself to feed a starving fellow-creature, even if a convict, would be no sin, as Joe himself makes clear when the convict, on re-capture, exonerates Pip. Pip would not have felt fear because of taking food from Joe's larder. It is because of *Mrs*. Joe that he feels *fear*, as is made clear in the hilariously comic account of his terror at the Christmas dinner, with a whole gaggle of ludicrously disagreeable parent-figures tormenting the child with their conversation. Both protagonist and the novelist who identifies with him (as the reader does) take their revenge in comic satire, but the hatred is real, and the centre of the target is the mother-figure in the very essence of her function as food provider, malevolent (in this case) goddess of the kitchen. The protagonist on the other hand explicitly states that he felt no pangs of conscience about robbing Mrs. Joe once he was safe from being found out. His conscience afflicted him because he kept a secret from Joe and dreaded to lose his trust and confidence. One may wonder here if Dickens does not unduly moralise the issue, but there will be more to say about Joe later. Here it is sufficient to emphasise how important he is as a point of moral reference. Throughout the novel Pip feels guilt and sorrow about breaking away from home and especially from Joe, yet he does break away, and comments:

> it was now too late and too far to go back, and I went on. And the mists had all solemnly risen now, and the world lay spread before me.
> THIS IS THE END OF THE FIRST STAGE OF PIP'S EXPECTATIONS

> (Chapter XIX, end)

Later Pip refers to himself as a 'self-swindler', again taking the point of reference from Joe (Chapter XXVIII). When Pip's benefactor becomes known to him, Pip is again shown, in his agony of mind, to consider his conduct to Joe worthless (Chapter XXXIX).

The guilt is related to the shame. The shame is that most familiar to the emerging adult:

171

> It is a most miserable thing to feel ashamed of home. There may be black
> ingratitude in the thing, and the punishment may be retributive and well
> deserved; but, that it is a miserable thing, I can testify.
>
> Home had never been a very pleasant place to me, because of my sister's
> temper. But Joe had sanctified it, and I had believed in it.

> (Chapter XIV, beginning)

In this instance, as in so much else in the novel, we may associate the
narrator-protagonist with the novelist, the artist, the writing personality
in this case – for short, Dickens: granted that the writing part of a
personality is only a part, though maybe the largest or most representative part, of the whole personality-in-the-world. There is in this book no
sense of distance between the artist and the narrator of a kind to produce
irony. We know there must be *some* distance, since Dickens in actual life
was not Pip in actual life and *Great Expectations* is not a literal autobiography. Great artistic power is at work in shaping this novel, analys-
ing the development of Pip in a detached way, laying down the lines,
some of which are being traced here. But in the sentiments and moral
values expressed, and ultimately, it may be argued, in the general shape
of the whole work, the narrator and the novelist are essentially one. From
this derive much power, some idiosyncrasy of pattern, and the surface
flaws, the occasional sentimentality, lack of taste, that occur here and
elsewhere in the work of Dickens.

Pip's shame is based also on the nature of his work as a blacksmith and
particularly on his love for Estella.

> What I dreaded was, that in some unlucky hour I, being at my grimiest and
> commonest, should lift up my eyes and see Estella looking in at one of the
> wooden windows of the forge. I was haunted by the fear that she would, sooner
> or later, find me out, with a black face and hands, doing the coarsest part of my
> work, and would exult over me and despise me . . . and I would feel more
> ashamed of home than ever, in my own ungracious breast.

> (Chapter XIV, end)

Pip's hopeless love for Estella is precisely and brilliantly conveyed: '. . . it
was impossible for me to separate her, in the past or in the present, from
the innermost life of my life' (Chapter XXIX).

At the beginning of this same chapter Dickens sets out with beautiful
clarity how the young Pip had hoped to shape his life, precisely in the
terms of medieval romance which for so long in our culture offered the
paradigm of the romance and interest of growing up.

> [Miss Havisham] reserved it for me to restore the desolate house, admit the
> sunshine into the dark rooms, set the clocks a-going and the cold hearths
> a-blazing, tear down the cobwebs, destroy the vermin – in short, do all the
> shining deeds of the young Knight of romance, and marry the Princess.

> (Chapter XXIX)

The story Pip tells will make a wry but not satirical variant of the pattern.

Pip's friend Herbert Pocket, the gentleman born, may be seen at the latent level as an *alter ego*, an aspect of the protagonist, who allows for further elaboration of parental relationships. At the literal level he helps work out the plot, since Pip needs an aid and confidant, but he does not affect any of the issues. Their virtual identity as partners in the firm, and the observation that Herbert's 'inaptitude' previously perceived by Pip was in fact Pip's own (Chapter LVIII, end), emphasises their symbolic identity as 'splits' of the protagonist.

The richness of the pattern consists in the parent-images. The multiple mother-figure is predominantly hostile, the multiple father-figure ambivalent. Enough has already been said of Pip's sister who brings him up so painfully. Comic as it is, the picture is savage. No seductive mother here! What is particularly unusual is that the protagonist, through his 'dark' side, Orlick, 'kills' the principal mother-figure. This is rare indeed in our literature, the only comparable but not very similar pattern among major novels to my recollection being D. H. Lawrence's *Sons and Lovers*, where cancer is the agent of the death that frees the protagonist from his mother.

The other outstanding mother-figure in *Great Expectations* is Miss Havisham, the disappointed bride, who 'stops' time at the moment of her betrayal, keeps the house decaying in the state of the aborted marriage-breakfast, continues to wear her bridal gown, brings up Estella to break men's hearts, has Pip in to play as her first humble victim, and allows him to grow up believing that his 'great expectations' come from her. Her house is a desolate image of home, and she is another remorseless indictment of the mother-figure. Grotesque as she is, she derives her great imaginative power from the part she plays as a perverted Fairy godmother. Pip explicitly when still ignorant of her true role calls her his 'Fairy godmother', though the underlying truth is made symbolically plain by setting her in her dismal and sinister surroundings (Chapter XIX). Yet being distanced in literal relationship she is portrayed with some complexity and pity, betrayed as she has been effectively by a minor variant of the father-figure. In the end she repents and therefore attracts forgiveness. She too is killed, though by the more neutral agent of fire. This occurs at the moment when Pip returns after his formal visit to see if she is all right, and even if this is a narrative device at the literal level to give plausibility to the vivid scene of the fire and allow Pip the merit of trying to save her, we may still note the latent ambivalence. She 'runs at' Pip when aflame, and 'we were on the ground struggling like desperate enemies, and . . . the closer I covered her, the more wildly she shrieked and tried to free herself . . .' (Chapter XLIX). This is a subconscious image of rape and animal sexuality.

A minor, amusing, and in her way equally deplorable mother-figure is Herbert Pocket's feckless and prolific mother, who makes poor Mr. Pocket so perplexed. Her home is a disorderly mess of tumbling babies and children.

173

There are two girls in the story, Estella and Biddy, and the underlying pattern is such that neither is fully disengaged from the mother-figure. Estella is always regarded as superior by Pip, and is represented as essentially cold. It is pattern, not any chain of cause and effect, that brings Estella and Pip together by an astounding coincidence that we never question, on the site of where else but Miss Havisham's destroyed house, in the last couple of pages of the novel. She still has her 'indescribable majesty', but has been humbled and made affectionate by suffering. In the last stage of the story I think we can see a division in Dickens the novelist between what he, or his readers, superficially wanted, and what the actual pattern of his imagination actually dictated. In the last line of the novel it is made clear that Pip finally marries Estella; the conventional happy ending, though they are now about forty years old. This delayed success may seem a mere concession to the escapist desire of the public, and of Dickens himself, for a happy ending, but in fact in its muted cautious way it is fully in accord with the whole progress of the story. Both Pip and Estella have been brought to recognise themselves and their true though humble origins, of which the significance is discussed below. They have cleared away, or have had torn away from them by suffering, illusions of grandeur, and the truth can make them one. Their successful passage to maturity is not achieved without suffering, and it takes time, but the success is genuine.

The portrayal at the literal level of the other girl, Biddy, is consistent with the latent pattern. She is introduced while still very young as the only useful helper at the inefficient Dame School which the even younger Pip attends as a child, and her role is throughout one of doting but clear-minded helpfulness to Pip, first in continuing to teach him, though she knows little herself, and then in advising and supporting him. She eventually moves into Joe's house, where with the utmost respectability and kindness she looks after the crippled Mrs. Gargery and minds the house for her. Pip tells her he loves Estella, and we realise she loves Pip (Chapter XVII). She is a wonderful domestic manager. Though Pip is not ashamed of her, he patronises and disregards her as part of the home background. She is clearly a youthful and kindly 'split' of the mother-figure, occupying in this respect the same place as the lady in *Sir Gawain and the Green Knight*, though in social and moral portrayal at the literal level worlds apart! It is characteristic of the presentation of such characters, as so often noted, that we never see them (from this point of view projections of the mind of the protagonist) in relation to each other. It is therefore natural from the point of view of the pattern, and given plausibility at the literal level by the autobiographical mode of presentation of the novel, that we never see any inter-action as autonomous characters between Biddy and others, and especially Joe. It is equally natural that at the manifest level just when the protagonist, who has always treated Biddy as inferior (though dependent on her) and therefore has never loved her with love *paramours*, at last, in a temporarily regressive emotional movement towards the end of the novel, comes to the decision to marry Biddy, he finds that she has just married Joe. Then later when he returns from the East Pip finds that she has a couple of children and the little boy is presented almost another incarnation of the protagonist, with the same name, and at the latent level with the same relationship to Biddy. This is indeed how things should be for a protagonist who is represented at the end as above all wishing to return to the home which he had despised and left for the sake of the giant's treasure.

Though the mother-images are essential to the pattern, it is the protagonist's relationship to the father-images which provides the deep motive force of the story. This may be summed up in the brilliant essential surprise of the general pattern of the story. Pip thinks that his 'great expectations' come from the apparent, though false, Fairy godmother of the story, Miss Havisham. In fact they derive from the convict, Magwitch, who is the major father-figure of the story, the other father-figure, Joe, being a rather special case.

The major process of the story is to be seen, at the latent level, as the progressive identification *of* the 'true' father-figure, the benefactor, then progressive identification *with* the father-figure, and then his progressive partial *destruction*. This is so to speak the 'wrong' order: destruction should precede identification with the father, as in medieval romance. Then the son can grow up. In *Great Expectations* the processes are linked with the guilt and shame which the protagonist feels for both his literal and his latent origins, and he conquers those emotions as he conquers the dominating father-figure. In destroying them he comes appropriately to value 'home', but he thereby goes back home. He destroys the father, but in so doing limits his own hope of mature masculinity. The convict is dead; the giant, with his untrustworthy bags of gold, is destroyed. When Pip goes back to Joe's home, after eleven years of absence, *nothing is changed*. We have a striking symbol of regression.

> I laid my hand softly on the latch of the old kitchen door. I touched it so softly that I was not heard, and looked in unseen. There, smoking his pipe in the old place by the kitchen firelight, as hale and as strong as ever, though a little grey, sat Joe; and there, fenced into the corner with Joe's leg, and sitting on my own little stool looking at the fire, was – I again!

(Chapter LIX)

It is a wonderful genre picture, though one may wonder how a healthy six-year-old boy is constrained to sit night after night by the fire with nothing to do. In order to underline the quality of fantasy, not adversely to criticise it, we may focus it within the literal chronological sequence called for by the novel. At this stage Pip must be thirty-nine, like Estella, as can be worked out from references in the last few chapters. Biddy is older by at least three or four years. Joe's age we must deduce by reference to that of his first wife, Pip's sister. Pip's sister was over twenty years older than Pip, so that at the beginning of the novel when Pip is certainly six, she must be at least twenty-six. Joe can hardly be younger, since he has built up his trade from nothing and apparently owns house and forge; he may well be older. So Joe is also at least twenty years older than Pip. Thus when we see him with a six-year-old elder child, some twelve or more years after marriage, in this charming scene at the beginning of the last chapter of the book, he is at least sixty, though as strong and healthy as ever. There is nothing implausible in all this, but to evoke such considerations goes significantly against the grain of the scene, whose purpose is to establish a timeless, or at least, a recurrent, time-evading, constant of childish security which is the bedrock of the novel, the centre, as it were, of the pattern. The centre of the centre is Joe, the achieved father-figure. In this scene Biddy does not appear.

In order to understand this resting place we must now examine the rise and fall of the more dynamic father-figure, whose identity it is the novel's purpose to establish. An important basis here is the 'taint of prisons' which Pip, as he becomes accustomed to his wealth, feels has encompassed him ever since his childhood (Chapter XXXII). This is a dark image of 'home', as firmly attached to the alternative father-figure as the bright static image of home is attached to Joe.

When Pip is twenty-three an elderly man visits him while he is alone reading in his London room. The man is pleased and incomprehensibly affectionate in greeting. He is strong on his legs, muscular, with iron-grey hair, and about sixty. In short he is physically an ideal father-figure for a young man. Pip finds him repulsive even when he recognises in him the convict he had helped as a child. Offered money, the man burns it: he both frowns and smiles. Soon the appalling disclosure is made. This coarse vulgar man is Pip's benefactor, has made a 'gentleman' of him.

> The abhorrence in which I held the man, the dread I had of him, the repugnance with which I shrank from him, could not have been exceeded if he had been some terrible beast.
>
> 'Look'ee here, Pip. I'm your second father. You're my son – more to me nor any son.'

> (Chapter XXXIX)

The tension between father and son, especially when the father is so inexorably loving a benefactor, could not be better conveyed than in this scene. We need no sexual jealousy, no rivalry for the mother, no Oedipus complex, to create this familiar (in all senses) aspect of the drama of growing up.

Dickens enriches this theme with other elements – the concepts of the 'gentleman' (with satirical implications for that and for society at large), of education, of criminality and punishment, etc. But at the heart of all this is the drama of conflict between father and grown-up son. The father offers the son all a person could want, but the son cannot accept gifts or advancement. 'O, that he had never come! That he had left me at the forge . . .' (Chapter XXXIX). Oh, that I had never been torn from home, never been educated, never left a humble labouring job!

A further horror emerges. The convict, having been transported for life to Australia, will, if caught in London, be executed. Of course all fathers are under sentence of death by the Almighty – as Magwitch later says to the Judge (and all sons, too, but they/we are less conscious of it). The son's consciousness of the sentence of death on the father is the crucial element here. It brings an intolerable sense of responsibility:

> . . . the wretched man, after loading wretched me with his gold and silver chains for years, had risked his life to come to me, and I held it there in my keeping!

> (Chapter XXXIX)

The sharpest of all Pip's pains is that he has 'deserted' Joe for this convict. Joe and the convict are rival figures. Guilt and shame at origins are given a further turn of the screw. Pip now feels them in relation to his 'second father'. 'In every rage of wind and rush of rain I heard pursuers.' He feels terror also of his benefactor and locks him in his room when he is asleep. In order to account for his unwelcome visitor's presence to servants and others he resolves to describe him as his 'uncle', but while still groping about in the dark stumbles over a man on the stairs who runs away and escapes. This later turns out to have been Orlick on the track of the convict; it is another implausible co-incidence in itself, but we do not question it. At first mysterious, it is finally accounted for as another element in the patterns of hostility and ambivalence of the family drama, for Orlick in a latent sense represents Pip's own determination, on his 'dark' side, to get rid of the father-figure, just as he represents, more obviously, Pip's hostility to the mother-figure, his sister.

We now learn the convict's true name, Abel Magwitch – grotesque enough, though he is to be called Provis – and his uncouth table-manners and language afflict Pip, whom he continually calls 'dear boy'. It is even worse – as well as comic – when he apologises to the dear boy, whom he has educated and enriched so far beyond his own station by his own self-sacrificing efforts, for being 'low'.

> The imaginary student pursued by the misshapen creature he had impiously made, was not more wretched than I, pursued by the creature who had made me, and recoiling from him with a stronger repulsion, the more he admired me and the fonder he was of me.

> (Chapter XL)

Here, apart from the literal meaning, we may detect the latent sense that the protagonist has himself 'made a misshapen creature', that is, has projected a father-figure repellent to himself. This is borne out by the way change is developed in Provis as Pip himself is shown to develop a more charitable attitude. Pip is deeply ambivalent. He loathes Magwitch, yet dreads his being captured – an ambivalence clearly recognised at the literal level in the text, when Pip explains to Herbert how he both cannot bear Magwitch and yet would be wretched if he were caught.

I was so struck by the horror of this idea, which had weighed upon me from the first, and the working out of which would make me regard myself, in some sort, as his murderer, that I could not rest in my chair . . .

(Chapter XLI)

But of course Magwitch *is* eventually caught. The net begins to close in on him because his former evil genius Compeyson is seeking him in order to betray his presence to the police. Pip and Herbert endeavour to get him out of the country. The sequence of concealment, anxiety and excitement is superbly conveyed with great variety and plausibility. Dickens always excels at themes of flight and pursuit. During the period of hiding Magwitch is 'indefinably' – the words are Dickens's – 'softened' (Chapter XLVI). There is no cause and effect at work here. Nothing accounts for the change in the events or experiences that Magwitch undergoes. Under such circumstances he might just as well have become hardened, enraged or bitter. Simply, a softening is vital to the development of the latent pattern. It corresponds with Pip's increasingly loving efforts to help him escape; in another sense, with the protagonist's efforts to get rid of him.

The story of the abortive escape is a superb verbal realisation of an imagined event, full of uncertainty and suspense and vivid detail, superficially a product of inevitable cause and effect, where the event is uncertain until the last moment, but all in actual fact is the clothing of a pre-determined pattern, which requires that Magwitch should not escape. He has to die.

For now my repugnance to him had all melted away, and in the hunted, wounded, shackled creature who held my hand in his, I only saw a man who had meant to be my benefactor, and who had felt affectionately, gratefully, and generously towards me with great constancy through a series of years. I only saw in him a much better man than I had been to Joe.

(Chapter LIV)

The fatherly superiority and terror has been removed, in effect by the protagonist's own efforts. All Magwitch's wealth is forfeit to the Crown. Magwitch has been injured in the capture and is dying in prison. The protagonist can now be reconciled to him. Pip most faithfully attends him.

'Thank'ee, dear boy, thank'ee. God bless you! You've never deserted me, dear boy.'

I pressed his hand in silence, for I could not forget that I had once meant to desert him.

(Chapter LVI)

As he dies, Pip tells him that his daughter, thought to be lost, lives, is beautiful and rich, and beloved by Pip. She is indeed Estella.

The dynamic father-figure is thus removed, but it is not within the pattern of this story that he provided the opposition, like some possessive king, to the hero's marriage with his daughter. The daughter has never been attached to a father-figure, but to a mother-figure, whose characteristics of pride and hardness she has inherited. Nor has the son inherited a father's sword, a father's strength. When Magwitch dies Pip falls into a calamitous illness. He is also to be arrested for debt. What is most implausible is that he is not in any way accused of helping a convicted felon to escape. Although he has broken the law, the law pays no attention. In other words, the drama is essentially internal, not social or externally objective, wonderfully well realised as the attempted escape is.

The protagonist is now reduced to his former childish state – poor, helpless, unknown. He has not taken over any of the father's strength. The father-figure is indeed pleased to see how the son has outdone him, has become a 'gentleman', but the son rejects this because when all is said the father has done it for his own gratification, not the son's real good, or he would not have kept him in the dark about the source of his good fortune. The rejection of the father-figure is a kind of mythic indictment of him, but it leaves the son as weak as a child. His growth and development have been based on a double falsehood, Miss Havisham's and Magwitch's, and he cannot, must not, accept it. And we may say that this is surely a true insight.

But it leaves him childish. Herein comes the other father-figure, Joe, who comes to nurse him.

> Joe stayed with me, and I fancied I was little Pip again.
>
> For the tenderness of Joe was so beautifully proportioned to my need, that I was like a child in his hands. He would sit and talk to me in the old confidence, and with the old simplicity, and in the old unassertive protecting way, so that I would half believe that all my life since the days of the old kitchen was one of the mental troubles of the fever that was gone. He did everything for me except the household work . . .
>
> We looked forward to the day when I should go out for a ride, as we had once looked forward to the day of my apprenticeship. And when the day came, and an open carriage was got into the Lane, Joe wrapped me up, took me in his arms, carried me down to it, and put me in, as if I were still the small helpless creature to whom he had so abundantly given of the wealth of his great nature.
>
> (Chapter LVII)

It is (of course!) a Sunday. A few lines later Pip lays his head on Joe's shoulder and either faints or weeps – it is not clear which. The text re-iterates that 'There was no change whatever in Joe.'

Yet Joe has practically no superiority over Pip, as is emphasised in early chapters even when Pip is a child. In that Joe lives under the tyranny of his wife, Pip's sister, and is unable to protect Pip from her ill-treatment, he has the characteristic weakness of the good fairy-tale father, even though the protagonist is male. He is the faintest of father-figures, and though such virtue as Pip shows as an apprentice is due to his imitation of Joe (end of Chapter XIV), the general drift of the story is to show the shame and guilt that Pip feels as he repudiates or abandons these virtues and Joe himself.

It is plain that in truth Joe is not so much a father-figure as a displaced mother-figure. True, we see him knock Orlick down in a quarrel, but this is exceptional. Every emphasis is laid on his gentleness, infinite patience and forgiveness, and, it must be said, his ignorance. Typical projected mother-figure! It reminds one of the song-parody, 'Thy mother's a lady more gentle than bright'. His chief association is with the kitchen and the fire in the hearth, though he does go to the local pub of an evening for a quiet drink and a smoke. Never for a moment out of temper or unduly demanding, he is even well-to-do, for he pays Pip's debts of over a hundred pounds, which could well represent a year's earnings or more for him. But as with all such characters it is as useless to enquire into his autonomous circumstances as into his motives. His character is the product of the protagonist's need for an uncritical mother-figure. Since no female figure of an appropriate age can supply it, the father-figure, its menace destroyed in the person of Magwitch, is deflected into supplying the lack. And the protagonist effectively, like Jack of Beanstalk fame, goes back to Mummy. Here, however, the exigencies of the novel as 'true history' and 'autobiography', imitating life as it seems actually to be lived on the surface, to some extent force the pattern into a sequence of cause and effect. The hero, telling his story, has to be still alive. It would be excessively improbable for him to go back to blacksmithing, which might seem to be what the pattern of the story demands. He could hardly write his autobiography in the evenings by the light of the kitchen fire, after a day's hammering. In a most interesting way the need for plausibility forces an apparently regressive element in the story to bend to a reality which in itself is represented by the more traditional pattern of success in fairy tale. Since he cannot plausibly go back to blacksmithing, but nevertheless in order to be writing his memoirs must survive and earn a living, the hero is sent abroad to become a moderately successful businessman in the East. The reason for this is that, unlike Jack with his Beanstalk, Pip with his middle-class morality has refused not merely to steal the giant's wealth but to accept it as a gift. He has been forced to leave home and work for his living, to achieve independence and maturity without the Princess. Work as substitution for religion! *Laborare est orare.*

The almost fatally regressive pull of home is well but surely unintentionally imaged by Dickens in the sentimental portrayal of Joe's domestic felicity at the beginning of the last chapter. It is not quite fatal because it is a genuine image of unaspiring unaffected goodness in personal relationships, of reconciliation within the family circle, and because the protagonist is excluded from full participation in it. But the account of Joe is so heavily laden with moral approbation at the literal level that one must say that Dickens was not really aware of the underlying regressive and slightly contradictory pattern he had created here. The presentation of Joe is therefore powerful but not quite at the highest reach of art, not fully self-aware.

Dickens is more effective at demolishing father-figures. There are a number of aspects of the book which fit into the overall pattern of sons establishing superiority over fathers, which are not called for by sequential logic – Wemmick and the Aged P. for example – but minute exposition would be excessive and tiresome. I cannot refrain from noting, however, the pleasure with which Uncle Pumblechook, that glorious parody of benefactor and protector, is taken down by being robbed and having his nose pulled etc. This is pure pattern, delightful variation on a repeated theme. And who does it? Obviously Pip cannot do so. It has to be done by Pip's dark *alter ego*, Orlick.

The destruction of father-figures and mother-figures is an intrinsic element in fairy tales, and in many traditional stories and even novels. One further aspect of Dickens's treatment of the theme here has yet to be noticed. It powerfully compensates for the touch of sentimentality shown in the presentation of Joe, and incidentally offers an interesting contrast to Jane Austen and Shakespeare. The course of the story of Pip's great expectations is a variant of the theme of the specific 'family romance'. Pip's great unknown benefactor, who he believes is Miss Havisham and is really Magwitch, is a version of the unknown 'royal parent', who is greatly superior to the known parent. In *Cymbeline* the fantasy is shown to be truth for the King's two abducted sons. In *Mansfield Park* it is made to come emotionally and financially true. The point of the story of *Great Expectations* is to *reject* the 'family romance', to attempt to come to terms with the real humbleness and real goodness of our own true origins, which are what Joe represents. There is a true nobility and realism in this, and one may well admire the morality of Dickens's attempt, as well as the great if not quite flawless achievement of his art. The attempt is difficult, for it tries to steer an unusual course between both traditional romance and traditional tragedy. In this Dickens no doubt draws on nineteenth-century radicalism as well as on Christian inspiration (for example Christ being born to the wife of a humble carpenter, in a shed). To assert the 'ordinariness' of Everyman is complementary to asserting the 'royalty' of Everyman. Each is an aspect of the truth, and for some writers, and some periods, it is important to emphasise one rather than the other.

The great desire, in *Great Expectations*, is in fact an ironic reversal of the title; it is to discover true, and implicitly *not* great, origins. This becomes even clearer in Pip's obsessive desire to discover Estella's origins which he himself comments on, but which is never accounted for at the literal level. We discover that Estella, so hard and proud, is the illegitimate offspring of no one else but Magwitch and the tragic 'tamed' housekeeper of Mr. Jaggers (who himself is yet another version of the dangerous, frightening, gift-bringing, father-figure). Estella's own origin is thus also surrounded with mystery, guilt and shame. Since Pip for most of the novel regards his own origins with guilt and shame one may well wonder if, in this apparently sexless novel, there is not a deep trauma of sexual anxiety at its very root. There is a significant set of links between Magwitch and Compeyson, and between Compeyson and Miss Havisham who was betrayed by Compeyson on the very day of their wedding. The abandoned marriage, image of breakdown in basic sexual and personal relationships, of refusal to begin to construct another family in an open legitimate way, is protrayed, at the latent as well as the literal level, as the origin of the evil in the story. From this act of betrayal arise all the faults and misdirections, the sorrow and misery, the partial failure to grow up, the muted tragedy of the book.

Yet as always the truth, if recognised and accepted, brings its own healing. That is certainly what Dickens intends to convey in the portrayal of Pip's recognition of what he owes to Joe, and the portrayal of Joe's merits and his deserved happiness in marriage and in having children. A similar recognition, by both Pip and Estella, of the truth of her own origins, is what presumably, in the emotional pattern, allows her to accept Pip, and permits their belated marriage. The immense power of the story culminates in acceptance of things as they are, and in a faith in the basic strength of goodness, which is in itself an artistic act of great moral courage and insight, even if not untouched by some few regressive elements.

The story of *Great Expectations* is as wildly implausible as that of any medieval romance. Its contemporary audience could accept it as 'real' just as the contemporary audiences of medieval tales, give or take a few dragons etc., could accept them as 'real', that is, as dealing with the real issues of the psychic life of recognisable characters in familiar environments, whether forest or decaying Inns of Court, described in somewhat heightened terms. The deep concern, and many of the basic modes of conveying meaning through actions and characters, are much the same.

There is no space here to trace in detail the various treatments of the family drama found in the rest of Dickens's novels, though such a task would be worth undertaking. Dickens returns insistently and passionately to it. Almost all his characters can be recognised as aspects, 'splits', projections, often deeply ambivalent, of the personages of the family drama. Everywhere we find variants of dynamic oppressive father-figures, often only very lightly disguised, like Mr. Murdstone (significant name) in *David Copperfield*, where he is balanced by the genial but ineffective father-figure, Mr. Micawber. The wicked Ralph Nickleby is balanced by the Cheeryble Brothers, not ineffectual in this case, but not very convincing either. Fagin and Bill Sykes in *Oliver Twist* are much more powerful than their good counterpart, Mr. Brownlow, though they are of course killed. Mother-figures are ludicrously ineffectual and normally at least tiresome, like Mrs. Nickleby in *Nickolas Nickleby*, or alternatively are witch-like figures, like 'Good Mrs. Brown' in *Dombey and Son*, or dragonish ladies like Mrs. Wilfer in *Our Mutual Friend* (with her genial but ineffectual husband). There are also a few good mother-figures, like Betsy Trotwood in *David Copperfield*, genuine Fairy godmothers, so to speak.

The protagonist is invariably a child or youth at the beginning, and the general process of most of the novels is quite explicitly the problem of growing up, doing something about the parent-figures, and finding a mate. This is not a reductive 'formula'; it is the basis of many rich variations.

Dickens understood the situation quite clearly. He knew and understood very well the nature of fairy tales, and was well versed in the popular literature of his time – street-ballads, chapbooks, etc. – whose characteristics, at their low artistic level, are the same as those of traditional literature. His creative insight as expressed in the structure of stories is truly amazing.

Epilogue

The nexus of tensions, constraints, problems and oppositions that constitutes the family drama has so far continued vigorously in the stories, mostly novels, of the twentieth century. D. H. Lawrence, E. M. Forster, James Joyce, are obvious examples. So are the less portentous names of P. G. Wodehouse (Jeeves a displaced mother-figure) and J. R. R. Tolkien (*The Lord of the Rings* is a romance of adolescence[1]). But the range is world-wide and from all ages.

Many further questions arise about the nature of the family drama. What recurrent patterns are most favoured? Are there cultural differences? What influence has social custom? To what extent do similar narrative procedures hold good in different periods or cultures? How far is there continuity, and what is the nature of change in the series of these tales? Most interesting of all, perhaps, what will happen to the family drama in those societies where, after many centuries, the institution of marriage seems to be losing its stability, and parent-images rapidly change or disappear, the roles of the sexes have changed, and sex itself has for many become commonplace, no longer connected with integrity, maturity and procreation? Will these stories become incomprehensible? If the case of Jane Austen, who parents were so unlike those in her books, is anything to go by, the stories may have little to do with the actual behaviour of actual parents. We all, as children, impose our fantasies upon the world with only an approximate reference to actual behaviour, or at least to actual behaviour as it may be observed in the everyday world by other adults. But the world of stories is a different world, fictional but not less real for that, nor necessarily less true. Since the human race always needs to tell itself stories it seems likely that we shall continue to find fictions that present the problems of growing up, and that growing up will itself continue to present quite familiar problems.

References

Introduction

1 A. Aarne and S. Thompson, *The Types of the Folktale*, 2nd ed., Helsinki, 1973. Cf. *The Study of Folklore*, ed. A. Dundes, Englewood Cliffs, New Jersey, 1965; *Analytic Essays in Folklore*, The Hague and Paris, 1975; Anne Wilson, *Traditional Romance and Tale*, Cambridge and Ipswich, 1975; M. Lüthi, *Once upon a Time: On the Nature of Fairy Tales*, Bloomington, 1977; Derek Brewer, 'The Gospels and the Laws of Folktale', *Folklore* 90 (1979), 37–52. Frank Kermode, *The Genesis of Secrecy*, Cambridge, Mass., 1979, was published too late to be used, but makes a valuable contribution to the general subject.

2 See Brewer, note 1 above.

3 *The Literary Context of Chaucer's Fabliaux*, ed. L. D. Benson and T. M. Andersson, Indianapolis and New York, 1971.

4 See Brewer, note 1 above.

5 V. Propp, *Morphology of Folktale*, 2nd edn, Austin and London, 1968.

6 See Lüthi, note 1 above. The latest survey is M. Lüthi, *Märchen*, Sechste Auflage, Stuttgart 1976.

7 The concept of the three characters was first elaborated in the context of myth by O. Rank, *Der Mythus der Geburt des Helden*, Leipzig and Vienna, 1909, repr. *Gesammelte Werke*, London, 1941, vol. VII, p. 224; transl. by F. Robbins and S. A. Jelliffe, Robert Brunner, New York, 1957. Cf. Bruno Bettelheim, *The Uses of Enchantment*, London and New York, 1976, Penguin Books, 1978. The concept of the 'canonical folktale' is that of V. Propp, *Le radice storiche dei racconti di fate*, Turin, 1972.

8 See Derek Brewer, 'Some Observations on the Development of Literalism and Verbal Criticism', *Poetica* (Tokyo) 2 (1974); 'Towards a Chaucerian Poetic', *Proceedings of the British Academy* 60 (1974), 219–52; *The Critical Heritage: Chaucer*, London and Boston, Mass., 1977.

9 J. S. Mill, 'What is Poetry?', in *Early Essays*, selected by J. W. M. Gibbs, 1897, pp. 201–229.

10 See above, note 8.

11 For further detail see Derek Brewer, 'The Interpretation of Dream, Folktale and Romance with special reference to *Sir Gawain and the Green Knight*', *Neuphilologische Mitteilungen* 77 (1976), 569–81; Calvin S. Hall, 'A cognitive Theory of Dreams', *Journal of General Psychology* 49 (1953), 273–82, repr. in *Dreams and Dreaming*, ed. S. G. M. Lee and A. R. Mayes, Penguin Books, London, 1973. The collection of articles is a very useful general survey. See also E. Fromm, *The Forgotten Language*, London, 1952. An excellent critical account of the various terms used and the concepts involved is in Charles Rycroft, *A Critical Dictionary of Psychoanalysis*, London, 1968.

187

Chapter I

1 See Introduction, notes 1 and 6.

2 R. Kirk, *The Secret Commonwealth*, ed. S. Sanderson, Cambridge and Ipswich, 1976, but written in 1691 or 1692.

3 M. R. Cox, *Cinderella: Three Hundred and Forty-Five Variants of Cinderella, Catskin and Cap o' Rushes, abstracted and tabulated, with a Discussion of Medieval Analogues*, and *Notes*, The Folklore Society, London, 1893.

4 Wilson, *Traditional Romance* (Introduction, note 1).

5 Cf. Stith Thompson, *The Folktale*, 1951, p. 58.

6 Cf. H. Humphreys in *The Study of Folklore* (Introduction, note 1), pp. 103–9, and M. Wolfenstein, ibid. pp. 110–13; Bettelheim, *The Uses of Enchantment* (Introduction, note 7), pp. 183–94.

Chapter II

1 Cf. Introduction, note 7.

2 Cf. Derek Brewer, 'The Nature of Romance', *Poetica* 9 (1978), 9–48.

3 P. F. Baum, 'The Medieval Legend of Judas Iscariot', *PMLA* 31 (1916), 481–630. V. J. Propp, *Edipo alla luce del folclore*, Turin, 1975.

4 *Eger and Grime*, ed. J. R. Caldwell, Harvard Studies in Comparative Literature 9, Cambridge, Mass., 1933. *Sire Degarre*, ed. G. Schleich, Heidelberg, 1929, and *Middle English Metrical Romances*, ed. W. H. French and C. B. Hale, New York, 1930. *King Horn*, ed. J. Hall, Oxford, 1901, and French and Hale. For a general account see D. Mehl, *The Middle English Romances of the Thirteenth and Fourteenth Centuries*, London, 1968.

5 Wilson, *Traditional Romance* (Introduction, note 1).

Chapter III

1 For an earlier statement of the argument in the present chapter see my article referred to in note in 10 of the Introduction. *Sir Gawain and the Green Knight*, ed. J. R. R. Tolkien and E. V. Gordon (2nd edn rev. N. Davis), Oxford, 1967.

2 L. D. Benson, *Malory's Morte Darthur*, Cambridge, Mass., and London, 1976.

3 A. C. Spearing, *Criticism and Medieval Poetry*, London, 1964, p. 40, and *The Gawain Poet*, Cambridge, 1970.

4 See Derek Brewer, 'The Arming of the Hero', *Tradition and Innovation in Chaucer*, London, 1982, pp. 142–60.

5 M. Mauss, *The Gift: Forms and Functions of Exchange in Archaic Societies*, transl. by I. Cunnison, Introduction by E. E. Evans-Pritchard, London, 1954, repr. 1974.

6 Derek Brewer, 'Courtesy and the *Gawain*-poet', *Patterns of Love and Courtesy*, ed. J. Lawlor, 1966, pp. 54–85.

7 J. A. Burrow, *A Reading of Sir Gawain and the Green Knight*, London, 1965.

8 Brewer, 'Romance' (chapter II, note 2).

9 Helen Cooper, 'Magic that Does Not Work', *Medievalia et Humanistica*, n.s. 7 (1976), 131–45.

10 Derek Brewer, 'The *Gawain*-Poet', *Essays in Criticism* 17 (1967), 130–42. Other examples of the perception of such self-contradiction as inherent in the very nature of existence are to be found in Chrétien's use in *Erec* of the work by Alanus de Insulis, *Anticlaudianus*, as noted by C. Luttrell, *The Creation of the First Arthurian Romance*, London, 1974, p. 77.